A Theory of
Linguistic Signs

A Theory of Linguistic Signs

RUDI KELLER

Translated by
Kimberley Duenwald

OXFORD UNIVERSITY PRESS
1998

Oxford University Press, Great Clarendon Street, Oxford OX2 6DP

Oxford New York

Athens Auckland Bangkok Bogota Bombay Buenos Aires
Calcutta Cape Town Dar es Salaam Delhi Florence Hong Kong Istanbul
Karachi Kuala Lumpur Madras Madrid Melbourne Mexico City
Nairobi Paris Singapore Taipei Tokyo Toronto Warsaw
and associated companies in
Berlin Ibadan

Oxford is a trade mark of Oxford University Press

Published in the United States
by Oxford University Press Inc., New York

© Rudi Keller 1995
Translation © Oxford University Press 1998
Die Herausgabe dieses Werks wurde aus Mitteln von INTER NATIONES, Bonn, gefördert
The moral rights of the author have been asserted

British Library Cataloguing in Publication Data
Data available

Library of Congress Cataloging in Publication Data
Data available

ISBN 0–19–823733–2
ISBN 0–19–823795–2 Pbk

1 3 5 7 9 10 8 6 4 2

Typeset by Peter Kahrel, Lancaster
Printed in Great Britain on acid-free paper by
Biddles Ltd., Guildford and King's Lynn

"Was Ihr denkt, das weiß ich nicht,"
antwortete der Schalk, "wie kann einer
des anderen Gedanken erraten! Aber
was Ihr mir gesagt habt, das weiß ich."
Till Eulenspiegel (Münchgesang 1948: 82)

PREFACE

This book is about linguistic signs and their dynamics. Its aim is to show how signs emerge, function and change in the process of human communication. Linguistic signs are not a prerequisite for our communicative attempts; they are their (usually unintended) result. My addition to the already innumerable publications dealing with this topic calls for explanation. Derek Bickerton wrote in 1990 that "most of what we know about language has been learned in the last three decades" (1990: 5). If this claim is meant to be more than an autobiographical legacy, it is most likely incorrect. In any case, it does not apply to the study of linguistic signs. Everything that can be said about the signs of language has probably been said between Plato's time and our own. In the field of language philosophy, with a history of more than two thousand years, it is hardly possible to say anything new. In other words, none of the true statements in this book claims to be original. (The false ones might be more so.) Nevertheless, I believe that the rash charge "But so-and-so said that already" should not be given too much weight. On closer examination, it usually becomes evident that at least the connections made in earlier studies are different ones. First and foremost, I see the usefulness of this volume in its recombination of thoughts and ideas, gleaned from a variety of traditions, and in its perspective regarding their choice.

At first glance, the considerations of linguistic sign theory may seem to be empirically irrelevant and useless philosophizing. Martti Nyman clearly states what's wrong with this view: "A theory of language change depends on the underlying theory of language. Therefore . . . it is not at all idle ivory-towering to dwell upon ontological questions about language. For example, if we look upon language as an abstract Platonic object . . . we get virtually no theory of language change at all" (Nyman 1994: 157). Every psycholinguistic interpretation that situates language's existence in the human mind is unable to envisage language change as an inherent phenomenon. "Language, after all, has no existence apart from its mental representation," writes Noam Chomsky (1972: 95), thus depriving himself of the possibility of grasping the state of a language (also) in its historical contingency. The understanding of the change and genesis of language is a constitutive moment in the understanding of its essence, and vice versa. Every theory of language is based upon a certain concept of linguistic signs. Signs don't just fall from the sky. Nyman's observation about language in general is particularly true of signs: if we see them as part of a Platonic sky, or believe them to exist exclusively in the human mind, we will never find out where they come from. According to psycholinguistic theories, our use of signs to reach communicative goals is contingent. Such theories obscure the fact that signs emerge in the process of our attempts to reach communicative goals. The following considerations of linguistic sign theory assume that the language we speak today, along with the signs we use, is just one episode in the permanent process of language change (cf. Keller 1994).

In the Platonic dialogue *Cratylus*, Socrates poses the following question, among others: "When I utter *this* sound" and "have *that* thing in mind," how is it possible that "you know that I have it in mind"? (1953: 434e).[1] With this question, Plato formulated a basic problem in the theory of signs, one that has been discussed in various versions right up to the present day. Till Eulenspiegel, a medieval German jester who exasperated his contemporaries by interpreting everything literally, put it like this: "What you think, this I do not know . . . how can one guess the thoughts of another! But that which you tell me, I know" (Münchgesang 1948: 821).[2] Another version of this question can be found in Ludwig Wittgenstein's *Philosophical Investigations*[3] (PI § 504): "But if you say: 'How am I to know what he means, when I see nothing but the signs he gives?' then I say: 'How is *he* to know what he means, when he has nothing but the signs either?'" The question posed, albeit with differing emphasis, by Plato, Till Eulenspiegel and Wittgenstein, is the following: by virtue of what qualities are linguistic signs able to make known the com-

[1] Throughout I quote Plato's *Cratylus* from the revised 4th edition of B. Jowett's translation (1953), and cite passages using the traditional Stephanus system.

[2] Trans. K.D.

[3] I cite this work in the accepted manner, i.e., the title's abbreviation followed by the paragraph number.

municative intent the speaker intends to realize with their use? This is the central question of this book. The leitmotif with which it was written has been formulated by Raimo Anttila and Sheila Embleton: "Change is the essence of meaning" (Anttila and Embleton 1989: 157). Elsewhere Anttila writes that "only a full understanding of the notion 'linguistic sign' makes both change and reconstruction comprehensible and theoretically possible" (Anttila 1989: 13). It is my intention to propose a coherent outline of a theory of signs, one that makes a contribution to understanding the dynamics and the evolution of natural languages. However, I am aware that the chances of hitting this mark are fewer than those of missing it.

With a conspicuous lack of self-critique, Dan Sperber and Deirdre Wilson write that "the recent history of semiotics has been one of simultaneous institutional success and intellectual bankruptcy" (1986a: 7). But even if one views such "bankruptcy" less dramatically, it nevertheless must be admitted that most theories of linguistic signs have remained largely without consequences for linguistics.[4] "After the publication in 1957 of Noam Chomsky's *Syntactic Structures*," as Sperber and Wilson continue, "linguistics took a new turn and did undergo remarkable developments; but these owed nothing to semiotics" (1986a: 8). It might be argued that this has less to do with the semiotic theories in question than with the Chomskyan paradigm. However, no matter what judgment is made, it seems to me that the lack of consequence of semiotics, or sign theory, applies in the case of every other linguistic paradigm as well. I believe that there are two reasons for this.

First, the ruling metaphor for communication, the metaphor in light of which it is commonly perceived, is inadequate. The problem of communication is conceptualized as a problem of transport. According to the view expressed in this book, communication has nothing to do with the operations of packing, sending and unpacking. Rather, communication is an inferential process. It is the attempt to bring the addressee to certain conclusions. Linguistic signs thus have less the character of packing cartons than that of premises for drawing interpretive conclusions.

Second, linguistic signs generally are seen as basically stable entities, entities that sometimes are met by the cruel winds of change. Sign theory is usually concerned with questions of sign architecture: How are signs

---

[4] Gricean theory is a notable exception.

built? How many sides do they have? What are their parts? How can signs be classified according to their architecture? This kind of semiotic question is analogous to pre-Chomskyan syntax theory, which was mostly concerned with the architecture of sentences. The theory of signs presented here takes a different course. Its primary goal is not to answer questions about the architecture of signs, but to discuss the principles of their formation. This way, answers to questions about their architecture result automatically. Humans are capable of interpreting things (in the widest sense of the word) *as* signs. From "things" they have perceived by means of their senses, they are able to draw interpretive inferences. It is exactly this ability that they exploit in order to communicate. Communication consists in doing something or producing something sensibly perceptible, with the intention of bringing another being to interpretive inferences. Communication is an intelligent guessing game.[5] The ability to provide the addressee with interpretive models for guessing the communicative goal I will call *semiotic competence*. The knowledge that underlies this ability I will call *semiotic knowledge*. The theory of signs presented here is designed to be a theory of semiotic knowledge. Semiotic competence and semiotic knowledge are logical prerequisites of language competence: thanks to our ability to use perceptions interpretively, and thanks to the ability to use this ability for the purposes of communication, linguistic signs emerge as instances of spontaneous order. To shorten this statement somewhat, one might say that languages are the result of using semiotic knowledge for the purpose of influencing others.

This book has five central parts, divided into seventeen chapters.[6] In Part I, two prototypical notions of signs are contrasted. Examples of one classic and one modern philosopher of language are used to introduce both the instrumental and the representational notions of linguistic signs. The first will be documented with the writings of Plato and Wittgenstein, the second with those of Frege and Aristotle. Part II addresses the relation between semantics and cognition. I will attempt to show that the identification of linguistic signs' meaning with their (possible) corresponding cognitive units is inadequate for the explanatory objectives of this book. Simply put, concepts are not good candidates for meanings.

---

[5] Erica García writes of "intelligent guesswork" (1994: 15).

[6] Please note that chapter divisions in the current volume differ from those of the original German text.

Preface

Part III is concerned with the three processes of sign development that make up the core of our semiotic competence: the symptomic, iconic and symbolic processes. In Part IV, I attempt to demonstrate that these three basic processes of sign development have a sort of inner dynamic. One process may be replaced by another without the involvement of plan or intent. Symptoms and icons can become symbols, and they do so exclusively by means of the way they are used for the purpose of communication. The three basic processes of sign formation can be newly applied on a higher level. We use them in creating metonymy and metaphor, and in using language to talk about language. Finally, in Part V, I show by means of several examples the relevance of the observations of the sign theory presented here to explanatory theories of language change.

Writings about sign theory are often difficult to understand. It is my hope that this not be true of the following pages. I have made considerable effort to write as clearly, unpretentiously and understandably as I can. In order to make this book user-friendly for individual readers, and, just as important, for the purposes of the academic classroom, I have tried to compose each chapter to be as autonomous as possible. Ideally, each one should be complete in itself and suitable for separate reading. I hope to have been somewhat successful in reaching this goal, though I realize that unacceptable redundancy would have been the price for its really consistent execution. In particular, Chapter 8 is a necessary preliminary for all those that follow it.

Provisional versions of the theories presented here were read in part or in their entirety and subjected to constructive criticism by Raimo Anttila, Axel Bühler, Sheila Embleton, Fritz Hermanns, Jochen Lechner and Frank Liedtke. To all of these I wish to express my heartfelt thanks. Petra Radtke served as a loyal discussion partner for every phase of this book's development. Her influence on the content and language of the final version is so extensive that it would be impossible to localize its every instance. She herself is best able to judge the extent to which I am indebted to her. I am grateful also to all the students, colleagues and discussion partners who became familiar with parts of this book in the classroom or in lectures, and whose reception and comments have added much to its final form. Finally, kind thanks to my publishers at Oxford University Press, particularly the ever-helpful Frances Morphy, John Davey, Leonie Hayler and Susan Faircloth, for their conscientious and always cooperative support.

CONTENTS

Introduction: Signs in Everyday Life   I

PART I: TWO NOTIONS OF SIGNS

1. Plato's Instrumental Notion of Signs   I I
2. Aristotle's Representational Notion of Signs   24
3. Frege's Representational Notion of Signs   3I
4. Wittgenstein's Instrumental Notion of Signs   44

PART II: SEMANTICS AND COGNITION

5. Conceptual Realism versus Conceptual Relativism   59
6. Types of Concepts versus Types of Rules   73
7. Expression and Meaning   87

PART III: SIGN EMERGENCE

8. Basic Techniques of Interpretation   99
9. Inferential Procedures   I16
10. Arbitrariness versus Motivatedness   I30

PART IV: SIGN METAMORPHOSIS

I I. Iconification and Symbolification   143
12. Metaphorization, Metonymization and Lexicalization   156
13. Literal and Metaphorical Sense   168
14. Rationality and Implicatures   182

PART V: THE DIACHRONIC DIMENSION

15. Costs and Benefits of the Metaphorical Technique   201
16. The Metaphorical Use of Modal Verbs   2II
17. The Epistemic *Weil*   22I

Contents

Summary   238

Bibliography   243
Name Index   255
Subject Index   257

INTRODUCTION

Signs in Everyday Life

Signs shape our lives. This is true not only of the signs of language: we are surrounded by signs, we surround ourselves with signs, and usually we are completely unaware of them. Frequently, we become aware of the complete semiotic saturation of our lives only when the signs we use, and with which we surround ourselves, lead to unexpected interpretations. My car is a sign, and so is my bicycle. Even if I have no car, this too is a sign. Eating oysters is just as much a sign as gobbling hamburgers. It's a sign when I wear a tie, and just as much so when I refrain from wearing one. The same is true of jeans, suits and corduroy pants. Some people might protest, "Does everything I do have to *mean* something? I refuse to play along!" But there are styles of dress even for those of this opinion—individualists can be identified by means of their clothing just as easily as the followers of fashion. There's no getting away from interpretability. One is reminded of Watzlawick, Beavin, and Jackson's famous assertion, *"one cannot* not *communicate"* (1967: 51; emphasis in original). This view, however, will not be endorsed here. It assumes a judgment whose inaccuracy will become evident, namely, that everything interpretable must have been communicated. This is not the case.

Important for our lives is not only *how* something is interpreted, but also *what* is interpreted. Cultures and subcultures can be distinguished according to those areas of life that they subject to interpretation as signs, and the degree to which they do so. The amount of symbolic character accorded by a group to certain aspects of life is used as a virtual measure of the level of civilization that group is believed to have attained. The more life in a group has been "semiotized," the more cultured we perceive that group to be. Culture consists of, among other things, the ascription of symbolic meaning to things in daily life. "Culture depends on symbolic structure," writes Raimo Anttila, continuing that "culture is learned sign behavior" (1989: 19). Consistency of practice in use is what makes something into a sign, a fact that will be discussed extensively in the following pages. When we speak of "primitive cultures," we mean those whose way of life has more sign-free spaces than our own culture does, or whose signs we fail to recognize as such. When we discover in a foreign culture a part of life that is free of symbolism, one which in our own culture is laden with meaning, we tend to find the foreign culture "uncivilized" in that particular regard. One simple example of this is bodily sounds such as smacking one's lips, burping, and even more offensive noises, which in many cultures are strictly regulated. With no small amount of zeal, children are taught exactly where and when certain actions are appropriate and acceptable, and where they are not; smacking one's lips while eating at the table is seen as uncouth, for instance. However, there is one bodily sound—not only is it unpleasant, it also includes an unappetizing excretion—that goes almost completely unchecked in European and Anglo-American culture: blowing one's nose. In most Western cultures, you can blow your nose at just about any time and in any place: in the bus, in class, sometimes even at the table. In Korea and other East Asian countries, this action is seen in a somewhat different light. There it is nothing less than the epitome of barbarism to remove slime from one's nostrils and deposit it in a cloth while sitting at the table. Largely unnoticed in Western culture, it is there an object of interpretation, perceived as improper, uncivilized and disgusting. Failure to regulate certain actions results in the creation of semiotic gaps. The ones who notice these gaps are usually only the people in whose cultures they are closed.

It seems that one of the identifying characteristics of so-called "advanced civilizations" is that they approach wishes and needs not (only) concretely, but also, and primarily, symbolically. When Germans are gripped by *Abenteuerlust*, they don't travel to the wilderness; they smoke Marlboros or Camels, and drive to work in four-wheel-drive trucks. Important men, and the ones who think they are, have big offices, big desks, big chairs, and smoke fat cigars. This is the symbolization of a claim to social territory. Of course, such an observation is an oversimplification. But the truth of the matter is that if we want to understand our way of life, we must attempt to interpret it in its semioticity. The home,

for example, is a part of life that is thoroughly semiotized. This is particularly true of the German living room, which Alphons Silbermann calls
a "Symbolmilieu" (1966: 29). Germans live in a culture in which it is
common to receive guests in the home, a fact that has direct influence on
the structure of their living spaces (Kanacher 1987: 95). This is surely
true of other cultures as well. One result of this custom are those "public" places in the house which serve the purpose of self-presentation.
The house's "public" part usually consists of the hallways and living
room, while the kitchen and bathroom are both semi-public and semi-
private. Visitors are meant to form their impression of the rest of the
house, and ultimately of their hosts' personalities, from what they see in
those parts of the house to which they are admitted. Studies have indicated that German homeowners invest more care and expense in these
areas of the house than others (Tränkle 1972: 113). This, too, serves the
purpose of claiming social territory. As an example of everyday
semioticity, consider the middle-class German living room (and analogously, the living rooms of other Western nations) in light of its semiotic
role.

(1) In a comparison of the floor plans of commonly available pre-
fabricated houses in Germany, it can be seen that, while the
child's bedroom usually occupies about 8 per cent of the house's
total area, the living room takes up 30 per cent. Generally, the
larger the total area of the house, the smaller the percentage of the
total area taken up by the child's room. Additional space is inevitably dedicated to the expansion of the living room (Tränkle 1972:
59 ff.). The living room might be seen as a republican development of the salons of eighteenth- and nineteenth-century Europe.[1]
As Mitscherlich has noted, it is reminiscent of "a prince's room
without the adjoining palace" (1969: 138).[2]

(2) Until approximately the first half of the twentieth century, many
middle-class homes featured a parlor (in German, *die gute Stube*).
This room existed solely for purposes of representation. It was
used only to receive guests and for the family's other special occasions. Due to the fact that the parlor was used exclusively on
such occasions, it was ironically called *die kalte Pracht* ("cold

---

[1] For a history of house and apartment floor plans, see Kanacher 1987 and Elias 1969.
[2] Trans. K.D.

splendor"; Kanacher 1987: 112ff.; Tränkle 1972: 111). The bus-
tle of everyday life could be found in the kitchen. The modern
living room, however, is expected to assume both functions; it is
both the room that serves as a representation of the family and the
center of family activity. For the first role, it must always be "pre-
sentable," that is, clean and tidy—a state that, as the family's activity center, it seldom enjoys. This has three consequences with
which, if hearsay means anything, most people are familiar. First,
there is constant conflict with the children, who want to play in
the room where the adults are, but who may do so only to a limited extent because the living room must always be "present-
able." Second, to avoid an "unnecessary mess," the so-called
dining area of the living room is never used by the family, but
only when guests are present at mealtime. The rest of the time
the family is forced to eat at a small table in a cramped kitchen.
Finally, larger celebrations are confined to another area of the
house, such as the basement, for fear that the guests may cause
damage in the living room and destroy its presentability.

(3) Living room furnishings exhibit (and studies confirm) an unusu-
ally high degree of conformity, a phenomenon whose occurrence
increases steadily as the social class of the owners of the furnishings declines. The living rooms of the lower middle class exhibit
a higher degree of conformity than those of the upper middle
class, while the living rooms of the upper middle class are less
individual than the living rooms of the upper classes. This, too, is
partially an effect of the room's symbolic character, as we will
see.

  The living rooms of lower-middle-class American families are
usually furnished, for example, with heavy, overstuffed sofa sets,
consisting of a three-section sofa and two deep armchairs in a
muted, multi-color upholstery pattern (plaid, striped, checked or
floral) or in a rustic combination of leather and wood. Glancing
through the sales brochures of furniture stores in the United
States, one notes that descriptions such as "sturdy" and "warm
and inviting," along with "enduring style" or a "contemporary
look," appear frequently and describe what are evidently desir-
able qualities. The recliner, a version of the armchair, is a popular

4

fixture in the middle-class living room. Other obligatory additions to the sofa set are a knee-high coffee table, and perhaps a china cabinet for the display of family treasures. Of course, the dominant element in the room is the television.

While furniture symbolic of traditional values dominates in lower-middle-class living rooms, those of the upper middle class feature symbols of education. Here, one finds bookshelves, art prints, antiques and musical instruments as elements of the decor. In general, the furniture of the upper middle class is less ponderous (Tränkle 1972: 115).

Returning to the question of the high degree of living room conformity, evident in spite of data which would suggest otherwise—such as questionnaires demonstrating homeowners' high esteem for individuality and originality (Tränkle 1972: 115)—we see that the answer lies in the representational character of the living room. Representation (in the sense relevant to this context) is the presentation, through symbols, of the values one has or claims to have. Hence a room that is meant to represent the family must express the values that count; these are, generally stated, prosperity, social prestige and education. The success of living room representation is dependent upon the correct interpretation of its symbols, that is, that they are appreciated as they are meant to be. Hence those who want to display their values in a symbolically understandable way must accommodate themselves to their addressees' interpretive abilities and values. The desire to be understood in this sense leads to the homogeneity of the means of self-representation of the respective social class.

Generally, the higher the social class, the more subtle and hidden the symbols of self-representation. This is due, first, to the wider range of values to be represented; second, to the broader interpretive abilities of the addressees; and third, to Western cultures' ethical dictum of modesty.[3] Educated people like to be rich, but they disdain those who show it openly. In such circles, a gold front tooth wins the respect of no one. The dictum of modesty leads to a paradox of self-representation: "I am wealthy and educated, and I want everybody to know it, but I can't be obvious

---

[3] Cf. "luxury as a negative category" in Tränkle 1972: 118ff.

about it." This situation necessarily results in the kind of self-representation demanded by the maxim, "Make sure the others know how much you have and who you are, but in such a way that they do not recognize your intent to do so." The perfect job of self-representation, according to this maxim, is to impress upon others that you are so rich and educated that you have no need to impress upon others that you are rich and educated. This is the goal of the strategy of understatement. The best way to produce this effect is to use symbols whose interpretation is possible only for those "in the know": art, exotic objects, rare antiques, designer furniture and carpets, and so on. Such possessions have exact targets: only those who are meant to understand the message of this kind of representation have the inside knowledge necessary to understand their significance. However, since understatement is also dependent upon being understood, conventions of even this kind of symbolism arise, reducing the range of theoretically possible signs to a manageable repertoire of those that are actually used.

(4) To conclude my excursus, I would like to point out one more of the aspects of the living room, one that is probably a result of its symbolic role: the hostility of its atmosphere to communication. Everyone has experienced the following scenario at least once: after the meal, the host or hostess rises and graciously suggests that the group make themselves comfortable in the living room. However, the move from the table to the living room is certain to put an end to the conversation, and to any ambience that might have arisen up to that point. Either the guests sit far apart, lost in the cushions of their own deep armchairs, or they line up uncomfortably on a three-section sofa like a trio of laying hens. At this point, they have the choice of two options: they can assume the position that is expected and encouraged by "warm and inviting" furniture, and lean back comfortably. This, however, is exactly the opposite of a posture that indicates an interest in others and the willingness to participate in conversation. From such a comfortable, laid-back position, lively conversation is all but impossible. In spite of this, the desire to communicate sometimes emerges victorious over the temptation to succumb to the furniture. In that

case, the occupants of the armchairs balance on the edges of their seats, on cushions too soft for the purpose; for more stability, they rest their elbows on their knees. The people sitting on the sofa have the worst lot: the one in the middle leans back so that the two on the ends are able see each other and talk. But if this is actually attempted, the conversationalists find themselves slowly falling into the middle of the sofa and the lap of the middle occupant. Nevertheless, for all its disadvantages, the second option—waging a persistent battle against the furniture—does allow the guests to sustain a certain kind and level of conversation.

The point of this description has been to show that our living rooms exist to symbolize our wealth, social prestige and level of education. Their size, the amount of time and money invested in their furnishings and decor, and their high degree of conformity are results of their symbolic character. Sofas and armchairs, for example, are symbols of leisure, and are quite clearly not made for stimulating conversation. Thus viewed, it is clear why most guests eventually end up in the kitchen, having sensed its advantages for personal interaction.

What does living room furniture have in common with linguistic signs? Both are means of influence. We use both with the intention of bringing our addressees to recognize something. This is the most essential characteristic of communicatively employed signs. From this point on, we will concern ourselves primarily with linguistic signs and the forms of their genesis, beginning with the first known theory of signs. In contrast to myths of the origin of language, Plato's *Cratylus* may claim scholarly rank.

PART I

Two Notions of Signs

1

Plato's Instrumental Notion of Signs

Symbols do not occur in nature. They are made; or, to express it less misleadingly, they emerge. As the American philosopher and sign theorist Charles Sanders Peirce wrote, "Symbols grow" (CP 2.302).[1] In the social and cultural sciences of the nineteenth century, as well as in linguistics, the word *growth* had a particular meaning—the sense in which we use the word today when we say that a city "grew naturally" in order to convey that it was not "artificially" plotted out on a drawing board. This is one of the organismic metaphors so popular in the nineteenth century, and as long as it is allowed to stand unexplained, it explains little itself. One of the goals of this study is to decipher it. The metaphor of growth correctly suggests, at any rate, that symbols generally are not created by people according to plan or intent, and that their development is a process. This is just as true for the so-called status symbols examined in the Introduction as it is for linguistic symbols. Of course, there are also artificially and intentionally generated symbols, such as company logos or the terms of scientific definition. But it is exactly their artificial generation that makes such symbols relatively uninteresting for sign theory. One of the feeble myths of the linguistic disciplines is the belief that language's history began with a phase of *Urschöpfung*, typically followed by one of decay (cf. Ehrismann 1986). The residue of this linguistic creation myth is still around today. Johannes Erben, for example, writes that "for a developed language of culture and literature, such as German or English, the beginning

---

[1] I employ the common method of citing Peirce's *Collected Papers*, i.e., "CP" followed by volume number (here, 2) and paragraph (302).

phase of *word creation*—the first assignment of completely new sounds to certain contents, and their conventionalization as understandable and reproducible linguistic signs—is long past" (1993: 18).[2] Are we meant to conclude from this statement that in less developed languages, the phase of word creation is still in full steam? In order to understand the nature of our linguistic signs and (a closely related aspect) the principles of their use, we must attempt to explain how symbols develop and how signs "grow." The question of how the signs of a language come to be, or how they came to be, has clearly always preoccupied humanity. Hardly a single creation myth exists in which there is no reference to how human beings came into the possession of language (cf. Peters 1985). The earliest scholarly text available to us which considers this question is the Platonic dialogue *Cratylus*, believed to have been conceived in approximately 388 BC. I would like to examine this text in detail, but not because of its unique historical and philosophical rank or eminent influence on theories of language even up to our own time. These aspects have been sufficiently discussed in a number of other studies.[3] Rather, my reason for a closer look at Plato's *Cratylus* is its contemporary relevance. Most of the questions currently under discussion in studies of sign theory are broached in Plato's text. Therefore, my intent is less to situate Plato's dialogue historically than to read it with today's eyes, so to speak, locating its central arguments and evaluating it on the basis of present-day scholarship.

In the dialogue, Hermogenes, Cratylus and Socrates discuss whether the meaning of a sign is determined by the nature of the thing it denotes or if meaning is based on convention. In modern terms, one might say that the the question around which the dialogue revolves is whether a language's signs are arbitrary (*nomo*)[4] or if they should naturally suit the things they name (*physei*). Cratylus supports the idea that "they are natural and not conventional . . . that there is a truth or correctness in them, which is the same by nature for all, both Hellenes and barbarians" (383b). Hermogenes plays the role of Cratylus' opponent. His job is to present a case for the theory of arbitrariness: "I have often talked over this matter, both with Cratylus and others, and cannot convince myself

---

[2] Trans. K.D.

[3] See, for example, Steinthal 1971, Gadamer 1975: 367 ff., Derbolav 1972, Coseriu 1975, and particularly Itkonen 1991.

[4] For an explanation of the concept of arbitrariness, see Chapter 10.

that there is any principle of correctness in names other than convention and agreement" (384d). Finally, Socrates is the quick-witted dialogist who tries, mostly in his exchanges with Hermogenes, to get the best of the others, thereby testing the soundness of their arguments. It should be noted that the subject of this dialogue is not whether language is natural to humans, or if signs have natural meanings rather than meanings given them by people. That the names for things are made by people, or more exactly, by the maker of words (*nomothetes*) is uncontested. Rather, the dialogue's central question is whether it makes sense to distinguish between correctness and incorrectness in naming. Cratylus pleads the case "Yes, it makes sense," while Hermogenes advocates the position "No, it does not." The exchange consists of two argumentative sequences, one destructive and one constructive part. In the first part, Socrates attempts to dismantle the argument for the arbitrariness of linguistic signs; in the second part, he tries to explain wherein a word's "correctness" may be sought. The dialogue ends amenably. The first part of the sparring can be broken down into three rounds. Let us examine its arguments in detail.

PART ONE, ROUND ONE

The examples listed for Cratylus' thesis provide an initial reference to how the theory of correctness in naming might be meant. "I ask him whether his own name is truly Cratylus or not, and he answers, 'Yes'," Hermogenes says to Socrates, continuing, " 'And Socrates—is that a true name?' 'Yes.' Then every man's name, as I tell him, is that which he is called. To this he replies—'If all the world were to call you Hermogenes, that would not be your name' " (383b). What makes Cratylus think that *Hermogenes* is not really Hermogenes' name, in spite of the fact that this is the name that everyone calls him? (Socrates suggests to Hermogenes that "he is only making fun of you" (348c).) Cratylus' argument is based on etymological analysis: Hermo-genes is not a descendant of Hermes!

Hermogenes now adds an explanation to his theory of conventionality and arbitrariness that will prove disastrous: "any name which you give, in my opinion, is the right one, and if you change that and give another, the new name is as correct as the old—we frequently change the names of our slaves" (384d). With this assumption of radical arbitrariness, Hermogenes overshoots by far the goal of his argument. His basic theory, that "there is no name given to anything by nature; all is convention and habit of the users" (384d), does not, of course, imply the assumption that individuals may re-name things according to whim, a practice which at that time and place apparently was common in regard to slaves' names. Socrates doesn't fail to see the chance to counter this point, and does so immediately: "Well, now, let me take an instance; suppose that I call a man a horse or a horse a man, you mean to say that a man will be rightly called a horse by me individually, and rightly called a man by the rest of the world; and a horse again would be rightly called a man by me and a horse by the world—that is your meaning?" (385a). And Hermogenes takes the bait: "He would, according to my view" (385b).

The first round ends with a clear loss for Hermogenes. Nevertheless, his theory, that a thing's name is determined solely by the convention of use and that the question of correctness in naming is therefore irrelevant, is correct if charitably interpreted. A charitable interpretation is necessary, though, because language may not be viewed as simply a system of names for given, extralinguistic entities. Many categories are actually created by way of the respective language in which they occur, and are not just named; furthermore, naming is not the only action that we perform with words. However, we can hardly fault Hermogenes for this mistake, as the assumption of such an objectivist view of language remains unquestioned by all three of the participants in the dialogue. Hermogenes' assumption is misleading, that words are to their objects of reference as proper names are to their bearers—as if proper names were a prototypical case, so to speak, of referential expressions.[5] This exaggerated generalization of proper name relationships is most likely due to the fact that the proper name is one of the few cases in which humans can deliberately and consciously carry out an act of reference affixation—as in the ceremony of baptism, for example. In fact, proper names are an exception to the rule and cannot be used as analogous arguments for the norm. Hermogenes fails to recognize this, allowing himself erroneously to infer the possibility of idiosyncratic and random proper names from the arbitrariness of convention. His conclusion is invalid. This will become clear in Chapter 10, where the concept of arbitrariness is explained in its relation to the concepts of conventionality and rule. Two

[5] For a description of the relationship of name and word in Plato, see Gadamer 1975: 367 ff.

thousand years after Plato, Ferdinand de Saussure found it necessary to issue a warning against the false assumption of radically idiosyncratic arbitrariness: "The word *arbitrary* also calls for comment. The term should not imply that the choice of the signifier is left entirely to the speaker" (Saussure 1960: 68–9).

PART ONE, ROUND TWO

The second argument with which Socrates attempts to fool Hermogenes has the following structure: Socrates suggests to Hermogenes four premises, and Hermogenes agrees with all of them. From these premises, Socrates comes to the valid conclusion that there is correctness in naming, based on a natural correspondence to the things named. The four premises are (385b–c):

(1) A proposition can be true or false.

(2) Every proposition consists of parts.

(3) If a proposition is to be understood as true, all of its parts must be true.

(4) The name is the smallest part of a proposition.

Therefore, it follows that

(5) A name in a true proposition is a true name.

From this, it also follows that incorrect names are possible. Thus challenged, Hermogenes initially admits defeat. "So we must infer" (385d), he concedes in regard to Socrates' conclusion, but remains unconvinced. He tries to counter Socrates' theory with evidence: "in different cities and countries there are different names for the same things; Hellenes differ from barbarians in their use of names, and the several Hellenic tribes from one another" (385e). Saussure, too, uses this argument to support his theory of the arbitrariness of signs: it "is proved by differences among languages and by the very existence of different languages: the signified 'ox' has as its signifier *b-ö-f* on one side of the border and *o-k-s* (*Ochs*) on the other" (Saussure 1960: 68). Of course, linguistic variation due to linguistic arbitrariness does not follow from an exact understanding of this argument (for it is not inconceivable that Hellenes and barbarians could have exactly the same linguistic conventions); nor does linguistic arbitrariness follow from linguistic variation (for there could be other reasons for linguistic variation). However, variation does suggest the assumption of linguistic conventionality and thus that of arbitrariness.

Socrates' argument contains two crucial mistakes. First, it is an equivocation to proceed silently from the question of the correctness or incorrectness of a name to the question of the truth or falsity of a proposition. Correctness is not the same thing as truth. The labels "correct" and "incorrect" do not describe a proposition's truth value, but serve to judge actions in regard to their correctness. The question of the arbitrariness of a sign is independent of the question of whether statements are are truth-definite. Second, Socrates' third premise is incorrect: it is a fallacy to go from the (correct) theory that statements can be true or false to the (incorrect) theory that all of their parts must also be truth-definite. Obviously, Socrates assumes a linguistic homomorphism that reaches right down to the level of words. The principle of the homomorphism of depiction, first formulated by the physicist Heinrich Hertz (1956: 2; Beeh 1993), says that a part of a reproduction is always a reproduction of a part. This is true of every reproduction, and for some cases of linguistic reproduction. A part of a photo of a house, for example, is always a photo of a part of a house, and a part of a description of a meal is always a description of a part of the meal. However, this principle reaches the limit of its validity as one proceeds downward. The exact location of the limit of its validity in regard to language is still an object of debate among philosophers of language (Beeh 1993). A part of a true description is the true description of a part; but only down to the level of truth-definite units—that is, the level of statements or propositions. "Hertz's principle is not only invalid for language as one proceeds downward; it is also not true of photographs. Words are like the grains of a photograph. Grains are not pictures. Their relation to the original is achieved only in context to the picture. They, too, are arbitrary" (Beeh 1993: 36).[6] Socrates attempts to apply the principle of homomorphism in language right down to the level of words (and even, as we will see, to the level of sound). In fact, this error was discovered as early as by Plato's pupil Aristotle, who discreetly mentions it (with no direct reference to Plato) in his *De Interpretatione*:

[6] Trans. K.D.

Just as some thoughts in the soul are neither true nor false while some are necessarily one or the other, so also with spoken sounds. For falsity and truth have to
do with combination and separation. Thus names and verbs by themselves—for
instance "man" or "white" when nothing further is added—are like the
thoughts that are without combination and separation; for so far they are neither
true nor false. A sign of this is that "goat-stag" signifies something but not, as
yet, anything true or false—unless "is" or "is not" is added (either simply or
with reference to time). (Aristotle 1984: 25)

Thus Hermogenes loses the second round of the argument, too. Even
though he supports an obviously more plausible theory, namely the
theory of arbitrariness, he's not up to Socrates' crafty arguments.
Hermogenes' agreement with Socrates' third premise, which assumes
the homomorphism of a statement and its parts, proves particularly
fatal. Socrates now begins a series of arguments that build on the
thought of the instrumental properties of words.

PART ONE, ROUND THREE

Just as things "have their own proper and permanent essence" (386e),
and are not relative to how they are seen by one person or the other,
Socrates argues that actions, too, have their own proper nature (387a).
This means that actions can be performed correctly or incorrectly. Now,
speaking is an action, and naming is a part of the action of speaking. So,
"is not naming also a sort of action?" (387c). From this it follows that
we cannot just name things as we see fit and "at our pleasure" (387d);
there is a correctness in naming "according to a natural process, and
with a proper instrument" (387d). Hermogenes concurs: "I agree."

Based on the correct thesis that naming is an action which can be
performed correctly or incorrectly, Socrates continues to construct his
counter-arguments. In order to perform the actions of a craft correctly,
one needs the appropriate instruments: a shuttle for weaving, an awl for
piercing. And what do we use in naming? Hermogenes: "A name."
"Very good," says Socrates, "then a name is an instrument?" (388a),
immediately specifying the action in which words serve as instruments:
when we "give information to one another, and distinguish things
according to their natures" (388b). Thus words are used to teach, to

distinguish things from one another and, of course, for naming. With this, Socrates has concisely summarized language's three essential functions: **communication**, **classification** and **representation**. In fact, these are exactly the three aspects of language that we must keep in mind if we are to understand how our language and its signs function. However, and as will be demonstrated shortly, Socrates exaggerates the idea of words as instruments. He understands the metaphor absolutely literally, and does so in the course of three closely interdependent argumentative steps which lead to fallacious conclusions. These three steps are as follows:

(1) Not just anyone, says Socrates, is capable of making a shuttle or an awl. A specialist is required for the job, a person familiar with the art of producing such instruments. Since this is true of all kinds of instruments, it must also be true of words. "Then, Hermogenes, not every man is able to give a name but only a maker of names; and this seems to be the legislator, who of all skilled artisans in the world is the rarest" (389a).

(2) Every instrument has a certain purpose. Therefore, it must be made in a way that enables it to fulfill that purpose. Different fabrics require different shuttles, for example. The maker of names therefore must know how to "put the true natural name of each thing into sounds and syllables" (389d). Of course, even Plato's Socrates did not overlook the fact that there are many different languages. He has a theory that accounts for this, which is also his reply to Hermogenes' evidence mentioned above: just as not every smith makes all instruments of the same iron, though he may be making the same instrument for the same purpose, neither do all "legislators" use the same syllables. "Provided he expresses the form of the name proper to each subject in whatever syllables" (390a), a barbarian legislator is not deemed a worse legislator than a Hellenic one.

(3) Who, then, is in the best position to judge whether an instrument is well made? asks Socrates. Naturally, the one who has to use it. The weaver is best able to determine the quality of a shuttle. The work of the word-makers and legislators can best be evaluated by the dialectician, he "who knows how to ask and answer" (390c).

The upshot of Socrates' arguments is that "Cratylus is right in saying that things have names by nature, and that not every man is an artificer of names, but he only who looks to the name which each thing by nature has, and is able to express this name in letters and syllables" (390e).

Where is the mistake? Socrates asserts two fallacies. I will call the first of the two the **instrumentalist** fallacy, the second the **rationalist** one. Socrates' instrumentalist fallacy is more important for the context of our argument; historically, though, his rationalist fallacy proved to be the more fatal of the two.[7] We will take a brief look at both in turn.

The instrumentalist fallacy runs like this: all instruments, thanks to their specific makeup, are suitable for their own particular purposes. According to this, their makeup is dictated by the purpose they are expected to fulfill. (Thus only specialists can produce good instruments or judge their quality.) Names are instruments. Therefore, the above is true for all names.

As this conclusion is formally sound, the error must lie in the premises. There are two ways to sidestep the conclusion. We might say "Words are not instruments." Or "Not all instruments have a form which is dictated by their purpose." The meaning of the word *instrument* appears to me indefinite enough that we are not obligated to choose one of these two options over the other. Both ways of circumventing the conclusion seem tenable. The first way out consists in the assumption that "Words are only instruments in a metaphorical sense, and the metaphor does not cover the aspect of whether their makeup determines their adequacy in regard to a certain purpose." (Although, as we will see, a defining characteristic of metaphor is that it *not* cover every aspect.) The second means of getting around Socrates' conclusion is to say that "Some instruments are able to fulfill their respective purposes solely due to conventional use; words are such instruments, as are playing cards and money." There doesn't have to be anything bovine about a hundred-dollar bill to make it good for the purchase of a cow. Words, then, are not prototypical instruments, but instruments that exist to call forth certain effects in their addressees. In Chapter 10 I will discuss in more detail the correlation between the instrumentality, arbitrariness and conventionality of words.

Socrates' rationalistic fallacy consists in the assumption that all of humanity's beneficial institutions which are not natural are the result of wise planning and judicious execution. Sensible institutions must have

---

[7] For an excellent description of this, see Hayek 1988.

been invented by sensible people—where else would they come from? The spontaneous emergence of "intelligent" and highly useful socio-cultural institutions is not taken into consideration. "Man imagines himself to be much cleverer than he is" (Hayek 1983: 234).[8] This is one of the leitmotifs of Friedrich August von Hayek's sociophilosophical thought. Socrates' clever legislator, "of all skilled artisans . . . the rarest" (389a)—for it seems that he has never been sighted by anyone—is a fatal conceit of rationality (cf. Hayek 1983). In reality, words (with few exceptions) are not the creation of some talented artisan, but the unintended side effects of the everyday communication of everyday people. They are the result of processes of cultural evolution, whose path we will attempt to trace in the next chapter. So much for the two fallacies; let's return to the dialogue.

Socrates' arguments have succeeded in making Hermogenes unsure of his own, but they still haven't won him over. "I cannot see how to answer your arguments, Socrates; but I find a difficulty in changing my opinion all in a moment" (391a), he says, challenging Socrates not only to argue that names have a natural correctness, but to show him exactly wherein this correctness lies. So begins the second and constructive argumentative sequence of the dialogue.

PART TWO

Socrates makes considerable effort to deliver positive arguments for the theory of a natural correctness in naming. However, he is fully aware of their weakness. As this segment of the dialogue is less productive for sign theory, I will be brief.

Socrates distinguishes between root words and their derivations. His first move is to demonstrate, with countless examples, that many word derivations (including many of Greek mythology's proper names) have been "correctly" formed. As we saw with the example of the name *Hermo-genes*, this is the method of etymological analysis. (*Hermogenes* is not the "right" name for Hermogenes, since he is not really a descendant of Hermes.) Transferring the argument to English, Socrates might argue as follows: "Winter's name is correct, because the word *winter* is

---

[8] Trans. K.D.

related to Old Gallic *vindo* or 'white', and denotes the time of year in which the earth is covered with snow" (cf. Klein 1971: 829). Or "The expression *wisdom tooth* is correctly formulated, because people get this kind of tooth at an age by which they have acquired some wisdom." Those who find this way of arguing naive should keep in mind that it is still widely practiced today, especially by language critics. Some argue, for instance, that in the sentence "Hopefully he'll come to my party," the word *hopefully* is incorrectly used—unless *he* is the hopeful person. *Hopefully* underwent a semantic change in the course of the twentieth century, taking on an epistemological meaning. Those who argue in this vein employ the same method as Socrates, including the assumption that words have a "natural correctness." This kind of "correctness," consisting of the systematically or logically correct derivation or formation of words, is sometimes called the "secondary motivatedness of signs." To etymologize is to trace linguistic signs back to their motivated state (cf. Levin 1994: 6).

Of course, this argument reaches its limit with names that cannot be etymologically traced from basic words, from "primary elements" or "primary names," as Socrates calls them (422b). The correctness of "secondary names" (422d) consists in their ability to show "what each thing is like" (422d). They do this by means of the fact that they "derive their significance from the primary [names]" (422d). For the original or primary names, Socrates develops a kind of onomatopoeic picture theory. "For the name, like the picture, is an imitation" (431a). The letter *r* is "the general instrument expressing all motion" (426c): *d*, *t*, *b* and *p* are "expressive of binding and rest in place," and since, in the pronunciation of *l* "the tongue slips," it is particularly suited to "the expression of smoothness, as in λεῖος (level), and in the word ὀλισθάνειν (to slip) itself, λιπαρόν (sleek), and in the word κολλῶδες (gluey), and the like" (427b). This is nonsense, of course, and Socrates knows it. "My first notions of original names are truly wild and ridiculous" (426b), he concedes. However, he sees no other solution: "but it cannot be avoided —there is no better principle to which we can look for the truth of first names" (425d). Socrates has not only observed that his theory of onomatopoeic representation is wild and ridiculous; he is forced in the end to recognize that a countless number of counter-examples exist (432d–e). This finally compels his retreat, in the course of which he approaches Hermogenes' theory of conventionality after all.

21

First, Socrates checks with Hermogenes to find out what exactly he means by 'custom': "And what is custom but convention? When I utter *this* sound, I have *that* thing in mind; and you know that I have it in mind; is this not what you mean by 'custom'?" (434e). Since we are obviously capable of letting the other person know what we have in mind by means of words that have no resemblance whatsoever to the things they denote, it must be true that custom is able to indicate things, and "by the unlike as well as by the like" (435b). This is, I think, an important insight. It means that the alternatives for representing something are not either only custom or only similarity. Even when a word does have a certain similarity to its referent, custom is still required to indicate that the referent is indicated by means of similarity. The aspect of similarity alone is "a kind of hunger" (435c); "custom and convention must be supposed to contribute to the indication of our thoughts" (435b). Custom is "mechanical" (435c). In other words, onomatopoeia alone is far from sufficient for making a sound into a linguistic sign; the addition of convention is indispensable in using an onomatopoeic expression as an "indication of thoughts." It is one of our conventions, for example, that we use the onomatopoeic word *cuckoo* to denote the cuckoo.

To close, let's once more briefly summarize the course and results of the discussion. At first, Socrates introduces basically three arguments against the theory of arbitrariness:

(1) Radical arbitrariness is not possible.

(2) If there are true and false propositions, there must also be true and false names.

(3) If names are instruments, they must be suitably formed for their specific purpose.

The first argument is valid, but it tackles a problem that does not follow from the thesis of arbitrariness. The two arguments that follow it are invalid, as I have attempted to demonstrate.

Socrates tries to support the thesis of non-arbitrariness by relying on etymological reconstruction and a theory of onomatopoeic representation. The recognition of the weakness of this "picture theory" finally forces him to concede that "the signification of words is given by custom and not by likeness, for custom may indicate by the unlike as well as by the like" (435b).

The outcome of the discussion between Socrates and Hermogenes can be summed up as follows: by means of conventions, we are able to indicate things, a process by which we bring others to recognize what we are thinking—whether or not the signs we use are similar to the things we denote. However, as Socrates adds, language is in "the most perfect state" (435c) if similarity between word and thing exists. These thoughts are absolutely correct, and we will return to them later.

The dialogue provides us with four thoughts which are still true today:

(a) the relative arbitrariness of signs;

(b) speech characterized as an action;

(c) the instrumental character of linguistic signs; and

(d) the determination of the functions of language as communication, classification and representation.

They will concern us further.

2

Aristotle's Representational Notion of Signs

In considering signs, their relationship to the cognitive world and to the world of things, it is important to distinguish clearly between three separate levels of observation:

- (a) the **linguistic** level of signs (words, sentences);
- (b) the **epistemological** level of cognitive correlates (concepts, propositions, etc.); and
- (c) the **ontological** level of things, truth values,[1] and facts.

To keep these levels distinct, it will be necessary to adopt a convention for writing about them. One may speak of an elephant, of 'elephant' and of *elephant*. In the first case, we are talking about a certain animal, in the second, about a concept, and in the third, about an English noun. Please note that this distinction binds us neither to the assumption that every linguistic sign corresponds to a conceptual correlate, nor to the assumption that the meaning of a sign is to be situated on the epistemological level. Both of these assumptions will be discussed in detail later.

In Plato's *Cratylus*, three levels of observation are distinguished: the levels of words, of thoughts and of things.[2] However, this distinction is made in a less than obvious manner. Convention, Socrates states, serves the purpose of letting you know what I have in mind (434e). Therefore, words serve the speaker in getting across his thoughts to the addressee.

---

[1] That is, the True and the False in Frege's sense; cf. Chap. 3, p. 38.
[2] This version is somewhat abridged, as Plato believes that every thing is accorded an *eidos* or Idea of the thing.

It is thus logical to ask what properties of words enable the addressee to recognize what the speaker has in mind. Plato's answer: words' similarity to things and/or their conventionality. However, a word is not a representation of a thought, but a representation of the thing that the speaker has in mind. Simply put, the model of similarity is as follows: the word I use resembles the essence of the thing I have in mind, and this enables you to pick up on what I am thinking. As we will see, this is a model of the kind of communication that uses iconic signs. Anyone who recognizes that a crossed-out picture of a pig (a sign that can be found on some "no pork" flights, for example) means that the flight menu conforms to the Koran's laws, can be said to recognize "what the speaker has in mind" by means of the "similarity" of the sign employed to the food in question.

The distinction of the three levels of observation named above was clearly made for the first time by Aristotle, specifically in his previously mentioned *De Interpretatione*. Aristotle was primarily interested in the theory of syllogism and logic. His comments in regard to sign theory, to be found in the first three pages of this work, have more the character of preliminary observations in service of a theory of the sentence, itself conceived with a theory of syllogism in mind.[3] Nevertheless, as sketchy as Aristotle's comments on signs are, they have exerted considerable influence on European philosophies of language.[4]

Aristotle's central statements on sign theory are as follows:

Now spoken sounds [*phonai*] are symbols [*symbola*] of affections in the soul [*pathemata*], and written marks symbols of spoken sounds. And just as written marks are not the same for all men, neither are spoken sounds. But what these are in the first place signs of—affections of the soul—are the same for all; and what these affections are likenesses of—actual things [*pragmata*]—are also the same. . . . A *name* is a spoken sound significant by convention, without time, none of whose parts is significant in separation. For in "Whitfield" the "field" does not signify anything in its own right, as it does in the phrase "white field." . . . I say "by convention" because no name is a name naturally but only when it has become a symbol. Even inarticulate noises (of beasts, for instance) do indeed reveal something, yet none of them is a name. (Aristotle 1984: 25)[5]

---

[3] See Itkonen 1991: 174 ff., as well as Coseriu 1975: 70.

[4] Cf. Arens 1984: chap. 1. Chapter 3 of Arens' book provides a detailed discussion of Aristotle.

[5] Addition of Greek terms (in brackets) mine, R.K.

To clarify Aristotle's position, I will attempt to list his statements in new formulation (leaving aside those having to do with writing):

(1) Sounds are conventional symbols of "affections" or "thoughts in the soul."

(2) Sounds are language-specific.

(3) The soul's affections are likenesses of actual things.

(4) The soul's affections and actual things are universal.

(5) The meaning of a name is not compositional.

(6) A natural sign cannot be a name.

This model of signs thus contains three elements and four relationships:

sound ———————— affections of the soul ——————— actual thing
       symbolizes   resembles
     (conventionally)   (naturally)

Norman Kretzmann summarizes this model of signs as follows: "It seems that, according to this account, words signify things in virtue of serving as symbols of mental modifications resembling those things" (Kretzmann 1967: 362).[6] Compared to the theory of signs that unfolds in the course of Plato's *Cratylus*, the Aristotelian theory is a great stride forward. Its advance consists in the following four points.

(1) Truth and falsity are no longer applied to words, but only to sentences, whereby Aristotle takes into account even cases of non-assertive speech acts: "a prayer is a sentence but is neither true nor false" (17a).

(2) The meanings of words and names are not viewed as pieced together from the meanings of the parts of words or sounds.

(3) The meanings of proper names are not etymologically understood (cf. Aristotle's example *Whitfield* with Plato's *Hermogenes*).

(4) Symbolic character is ascribed only to conventionally symbolizing sounds. With this, symbols and symptoms (such as animal sounds) are distinguished for the first time.

[6] Coseriu 1975: 80 ff. offers an alternative explanation; cf. also Itkonen 1991: 175.

26

However, Aristotle's thesis also contains—from today's perspective—three distinct misinterpretations or flaws, and—from the perspective of the theory of signs promoted in the following pages—a disadvantage in comparison to Plato's notion of signs:

(1) The world of things, as well as the world of the soul's affections, is objectivistically conceived. Language is for Aristotle a conventional system of nomenclature for cognitive likenesses or ideas of objectively pre-given things.

(2) Convention is equated with agreement.

(3) The relation of symbolization is not explicated.

Aristotle appears to have proceeded from this *Weltbild*: the world of things exists objectively, exactly as we perceive it. By means of perception, inner likenesses or ideas of things arise. Such likenesses are symbolized by means of agreed-upon sounds. From this, it follows that (a) the inner likenesses, or, ideas, must have a "natural correctness" in Plato's sense—that is, they are *physei*; and (b) since language only *symbolizes* the ideas of things, the classifications that we create with language are already extant in, and can stem only from, the natures of things. Hence only the expression of the idea is arbitrary, not the idea itself, nor the conceptual categories that we create with language. Following this theory, however, it is hardly possible to comprehend why English speakers need two concepts, 'meat' and 'flesh', whereas German speakers need only 'Fleisch' for both, or why German speakers' single concept 'Salat' covers two concepts, both 'lettuce' and 'salad', in English. As far as I know, there exists no satisfactory theory regarding the relationships between the ontological, epistemological and linguistic levels of signs. In any case, Aristotle's objectivist notion is certainly wrong. A better theory is one such as Derek Bickerton's, when he writes that "the categories into which we divide nature are not in nature, they emerge solely through interaction between nature and ourselves" (1990: 53). Our system of concepts is not a mirror of the world, but a mirror of our interaction with the world. We may assume that a continuum might be observed between different languages in regard to concepts that are of a more or less universal nature, such as 'tree', 'red', 'water' and 'five', and those that are extremely culture- and/or language-specific, like

'Tex-Mex', 'homeboy', 'snafu' and 'corny'. We will return to this topic in Chapter 5.

The weaknesses of Aristotle's theory named in (2) and (3) are still prevalent today. For now, I will discuss them only briefly, saving a thorough discussion for a later chapter. First, a word on the concept 'convention': conventions and agreements are different things. Not all agreements are conventions, and not all conventions arise through agreement. Linguistic symbols usually are not founded on agreement. As David Lewis has demonstrated, conventions are a population's regularities in behavior and come into existence through complex mutual expectations (Lewis 1969). For the sake of simplicity, we will assume for a moment that Aristotle's presumption is correct, that sounds symbolize ideas on the basis of agreement. We will agree that the sound [kulp] should symbolize the idea of a round, knee-high table with three legs. How can we get [kulp] actually to symbolize this idea? If we agree that [x] should symbolize y, how does [x] do this? Does [x] symbolize y if we agree that it does? Every theory that postulates the relation of the sign to a correlate as essential to its nature must be able to answer this question. One might hypothesize that [x] symbolizes y if and only if [x] stands for y or iff [x] represents y. With this argument, the conundrum simply has been doubled or tripled. "Stand for" and "represent" require no less explanation than "symbolize."[7] In other words, it must be made perfectly clear just what it means to say that something symbolizes something else. Even if we assume that a sound has meaning if and only if it stands for or represents something else, whether this be an idea or a thing (assumptions I would not endorse), we still must answer the question of just how the speaker and the addressee know, or can learn, for which thing or idea the sound stands. Presuming that the meaning of a sound or a sign consists in its correspondence to a correlate, whatever kind of correlate it is, does not free us from the obligation of specifying how the connection to the correlate is produced and maintained.

Returning for a moment to Plato's concept of language and signs and comparing it with Aristotle's, we note that for Plato, words exist for the purpose of giving the addressee to understand what the speaker is thinking, by means of either similarity or conventionality. Evidently, to

---

[7] A thorough discussion of this point can be found in Tugendhat 1982, Lecture 20.

communicate means for Plato to provide the addressee with a means of guessing what the speaker is thinking. For Aristotle, words exist to signify things by symbolizing thoughts that are likenesses of those things. To the question with which Plato struggled—"How do words manage to tell us something about thoughts?"—Aristotle gives only an apparent answer: they do it by means of symbolization! "The famous question of . . . the rightness of names, which was the subject of *Cratylus*, can no longer arise," writes Hans Arens, adding enthusiastically that "[t]his is a remarkable progress" (Arens 1984: 28). I find it difficult to share Arens' enthusiasm in regard to this "progress." Plato's inadequate answer says nothing against the adequacy of the question—a question that is still open. Aristotle sees language as a phonetic system of representation for a cognitive system of representation. Thus language is a secondary system of representation, an idea also struck upon, though independently of Aristotle, by Derek Bickerton (1990: chapter 4). While Plato supports an instrumental notion of signs, Aristotle's is representational. He does not even pose the question that Plato (to a certain extent) insufficiently answered.

Does Aristotle introduce a psychologistic theory of meaning? Usually this question is answered in the affirmative.[8] "There can be no doubt that Aristotle has generally been understood as representing the psychologistic theory of meaning: meanings are just those mental concepts and judgments which are expressed by words and sentences (more precisely: by strings of sounds identifiable as word-forms and sentence-forms)" (Itkonen 1991: 176). But this belief has two conditions: first, that the thing which a sound symbolizes be regarded as its meaning, and second, that the "soul's affections" (*pathemata*), that is, ideas, are psychological entities. The first assumption might seem so natural that alternatives do not even come to mind. In the following discussion of this topic, I will advance the opinion that it makes little sense to regard meaning as that which sounds "stand for"; rather, meaning should be seen as that which makes a sound into a sign. Assessing the second assumption is more difficult. Psychology as it is understood today surely did not exist in Aristotle's time. At least, a purely psychologistic interpretation would not be appropriate from today's perspective. The *pathemata* of which Aristotle speaks are, first of all, superindividual ("the same for all");

---

[8] For discussion of this point, see Ax 1992: 252 ff.

furthermore, they are timeless. Neither is true of ideas in the psychological sense. Aristotle's *pathemata* are objective likenesses of things, while ideas in the psychological sense are always, to a certain degree, individual.[9] *Pathemata* are the result of the knowledge of things, but the study of this kind of knowledge is not psychology. Hans Arens is quite clear on this point: "He [Aristotle] does not say: 'all human beings form the same notions in their minds' " (Arens 1984: 28). Nevertheless, Arens finds himself compelled to introduce lavish arguments in the attempt to rescue the viability of Aristotle's theory, that *pathemata* are the same for all people. I will leave the question of whether Aristotle introduced a psychologistic theory of meaning to the experts, noting only that, without additional justification, this conclusion cannot be drawn on the simple fact that he uses the word *pathemata*. The two notions of signs described in the previous pages, the instrumental and the representational, remain in opposition in modern linguistics and philosophies of language. In the next chapter I will discuss, as the most prototypical and probably most influential theorist of representational concepts of language, Gottlob Frege and his theories of *Sinn* and *Bedeutung*. The most prominent representative of the instrumental concept of language is Ludwig Wittgenstein, with the theory of his later work, meaning as use. Together, these theories will form the basis of the remainder of my considerations.

[9] On the concept of ideas in general, see Frege 1977: 13 ff.

3

Frege's Representational Notion of Signs

Frege presented his theory of signs in a series of essays,[1] the most important of which is entitled "Über Sinn und Bedeutung." Its English title is "On Sense and Reference." I will introduce the basic thoughts of Fregean sign theory by means of this essay, referring to his other writings at points where further explanation seems necessary.

Frege was primarily a mathematician and logician, and only secondarily a philosopher of language. His thoughts on language were motivated essentially by his aspiration to formulate the fundamentals of mathematics and logic clearly and rigorously. Evidently it was not common among the mathematicians of his time to differentiate clearly between "form" and "content," for example (Frege 1966a: 21), specifying whether a number sign meant the numeral (that is, the written character) or what the numeral stands for (the number). As Frege writes, this can lead to "numerals being taken to be numbers, the proper objects of our discussion; and then, I admit, 7 and 2+5 would indeed be different. But such a conception is untenable, for we cannot speak of any arithmetical properties of numbers whatsoever without going back to what the signs stand for" (Frege 1966a: 21). In other words, it is absolutely necessary to distinguish between "form and content, sign and thing signified" (Frege 1966a: 21). Yet the distinction of form and content frequently does not suffice for the adequate interpretation of a sentence. Frege makes this clear with the example of statements of equality of the form $a=b$: "Is it [equality] a relation? A relation between objects, or between

---

[1] Their English titles are "Function and Concept" (Frege 1966a), "On Sense and Reference" (Frege 1966b), "On Concept and Object" (Frege 1966c) and "Thoughts" (Frege 1977). A good introduction to Frege's philosophy can be found in Fabian 1975.

names or signs of objects?" (1966*b*: 56). If one differentiates duly between form and content, the following dilemma results: assuming that the equation *a=b* is meant to convey information about the signs, it is clearly false. The sign *a* is not the same as the sign *b*. However, if we assume that the equation is meant in regard to designated objects, *a=b* asserts, per definition, the same thing as the statement *a=a*. Because, if *b* is identical with *a*, *b* should be replaceable with *a*. Now, *a=a* and *a=b* "are obviously statements of differing cognitive value" (Frege 1966*b*: 56). A statement in the form *a=b*, such as the assertion *The morning star is the evening star*, can contribute to a useful expansion of knowledge, while the statement *a=a*, that is, *The morning star is the morning star*, tells us something we knew all along, namely that a thing is identical to itself. What exactly does one assert, then, with a statement of the form *a=b*? This is the problem that Frege set out to solve. How does his solution look?

We recall, as noted in the previous chapter, the importance of distinguishing between three levels of observation—linguistic, epistemological and ontological—in any consideration of signs; to put it differently, these are the levels of language, of knowledge and of things. The Fregean dilemma demonstrates that differentiating between the linguistic and ontological levels is not sufficient for comprehending the point of statements of the form *a=b*. Statements like *a=b* are neither statements about language nor statements about the world; rather, they are statements about the relation of language to the world. This statement asserts neither that "the sign *a* is identical to the sign *b*" nor that "the thing is identical to itself," but rather that "the thing that is designated with *a* is identical to the thing designated with *b*." Frege calls the way in which a thing is represented in language "die Art des Gegebenseins" or "mode of presentation" (1966*b*: 57). A difference in cognitive value between *a=a* and *a=b* "can arise only if the difference between the signs corresponds to a difference in the mode of presentation of that which is designated" (Frege 1966*b*: 57). That is, with a statement of the form *a=b*, we say that the signs *a* and *b* are different "modes" of "presenting" one and the same thing. At this point, Frege introduces a terminology that takes some getting used to,[2] saying that "it is natural, now, to think of there being

---

[2] Frege's *Bedeutung* has most commonly been rendered in English as "reference." In concurrence with Long and White's translation of Frege's posthumous writings (Frege 1979), I will depart from this tradition, choosing instead "meaning," the natural

connected with a sign (name, combination of words, letter), besides that to which the signs refers, which may be called the reference [meaning$_F$] of the sign, also what I should like to call the sense of the sign, wherein the mode of presentation is contained" (1966*b*: 57). Frege thus differentiates between the linguistic level of signs (essentially names, predicates, and sentences), the conceptual level of sense (*Sinn*) and the ontological level of meaning$_F$ (*Bedeutung*). Two theses concerning Frege's distinction are in wide circulation. The first is that "sense and meaning$_F$" are what are usually called "intension and extension." The second is that Frege's "sense" is that which is usually called "meaning" (see Lyons 1977: 199, for example). Both theses are incorrect. Let's examine these categories and distinctions more closely.

Before we begin, a few remarks are necessary for the understanding of Frege's use of the expressions *name, predicate* and *sentence*. According to him, a name is a designation which "has as its reference [meaning$_F$] a definite object (this word taken in the widest range)" (Frege 1966*b*: 57)—that is, actual proper names such as *Aristotle*, as well as other referential expressions and definite descriptions such as *the current US president*. Predicates are all expressions which are incomplete or "unsaturated," such as *( ) is sleeping* or *( ) conquered Gaul*. (For purposes of intelligibility, their incompleteness is indicated with empty parentheses.) If a predicate is completed with a name, a sentence results, such as *Aristotle is sleeping* or *Caesar conquered Gaul*.

Now for an explication of what Frege understands as the sense and the meaning$_F$ of names, predicates and sentences. I have already alluded to the answer concerning names: Frege understands the meaning$_F$ of names as being the object to which the name refers. In respect to natural language, this is a rather unusual use of the word *meaning* (and the reason that *Bedeutung* is usually translated into English as *reference*). One is consequently able to say unusual things about meanings—that

---

English equivalent of *Bedeutung*. As Long and White point out, "renderings such as 'reference' and 'denotation' are strictly incorrect and have only been adopted by other translators for exegetical reasons ... if his [Frege's] later use of *'bedeuten'* and *'Bedeutung'* reads oddly in German, this oddness should be reflected in translation and not ironed out by mistranslation" (Translators' Preface, pp. vi–vii). Meaning in the Fregean sense will henceforth be designated as meaning$_F$. In translated quotations that contain "Bedeutung" in this sense in the German original, I have placed "meaning$_F$" after their translation of the word as "reference."—K.D.

33

they are made of wood, or are dead, or 25 years old, and suchlike. The meaning$_F$ of the name *Tokyo*, for example, has a population of 26.5 million, and the meaning$_F$ of the name *Gottlob Frege* is dead. This terminology may seem peculiar at first, but as we will see, it lends itself to the creation of a rigorous edifice. For the field of mathematics, which was, after all, Frege's area of interest, it sounds much less strange to say that the meaning$_F$ of the number sign *4*, as well as of the number sign *−2²* or *16÷4*, is the number 4. Number signs can be erased, for example; the meaning$_F$ of number signs can be divided. The meaning$_F$ of a name is thus its actual referent. Consequently, not every name has a meaning$_F$. The names *Snow White, the highest possible number* or *4÷0*, for example, have no meaning$_F$. However, each of these names does have a sense. "The sense of a proper name is grasped by everybody who is sufficiently familiar with the language . . . to which it belongs" (Frege 1966*b*: 57–8). Therefore, we may say that the sense of a name is its intension, and the meaning$_F$ of a name is its extension.[3] In regard to actual proper names, this results in a curiosity that is not as unproblematic as Frege seems to suppose. "It [the sense of the proper name *Aristotle*] might, for instance, be taken to be the following: the pupil of Plato and teacher of Alexander the Great. Anybody who does this will attach another sense to the sentence 'Aristotle was born in Stagira' than will a man who takes as the sense of the name: the teacher of Alexander the Great who was born in Stagira" (Frege 1966*b*: 58n.). In other words, in using an actual proper name, we never know whether the person with whom we are conversing attaches the same sense to the name that we do. Usually, however, we're none the worse off for it. "So long as the reference [meaning$_F$] remains the same, such variations of sense may be tolerated," Frege believes (1966*b*: 58n.); for in the use of proper names, the important thing is the fixation of reference.[4]

As a first provisional summary, we will note that "every grammatically well-formed expression representing a proper name" (Frege 1966*b*:

---

[3] For names, the equation of sense and meaning$_F$ with intension and extension, respectively, is correct; this is not true for predicates, as will be demonstrated shortly.

[4] Still, the notion that actual proper names have a sense has the uncomfortable consequence that, for some people, the sentence *Aristotle was Alexander the Great's teacher* is analytical, while for others it is not. With this, the question of analyticity is immediately personalized. The resulting detrimental consequences cannot be further pursued here.

58) has a sense, but not necessarily a meaning$_F$. The meaning$_F$ of a name is its referent, while its sense is that which one knows when one "is sufficiently familiar . . . with the language" (Frege 1966b: 57). Frege calls this the "mode of presentation." The meaning$_F$ of a name is thus independent of language, while the sense of a name is apprehensible only through language.

Now we will consider the sense and meaning$_F$ of predicates. The understanding of Frege's entire theoretical construct rests on the understanding of predicate relations. Therefore, a detailed description is in order. We recall that predicates are incomplete or unsaturated linguistic signs. Sentences result when predicates are completed with proper names. If we complete the predicate ( ) *conquered Gaul* with *Caesar*, we get the sentence *Caesar conquered Gaul*. Frege sees predicates as analogous to expressions of mathematical function. Mathematical functions "must be called incomplete, in need of supplementation, or 'unsaturated'. And in this respect functions differ fundamentally from numbers" (Frege 1966b: 24). Hence names are to predicates as number signs are to expressions of function. If completed with 1, the function $8 \div x^2$ yields the value $8 \div 1^2$ or 8; if completed with 2, it yields the value 2; completed with 4, it yields the value 0.5, and so on. We call numbers with which the function is completed "arguments," and "give the name 'the value of a function for an argument' to the result of completing the function with the argument" (Frege 1966b: 25). The value of the function $8 \div x^2$ for the argument 4 is thus 0.5. Functions are mappings; the function $8 \div x^2$ maps 4 into the value 0.5, and -2 into the value 2. The expression $8 \div 2^2$ is a "mode" of "presenting" the function $8 \div 2^2$; the expression $(4+4) \div x^2$ is another "mode of presentation" of this function. This means that expressions $8 \div 2^2$ and $(4+4) \div x^2$ have different senses, but the same meaning$_F$, namely the function $8 \div 2^2$. There are innumerable modes of presentation for one and the same meaning$_F$. But let's get back to natural languages.

Predicates designate functions just as mathematical expressions do. Frege calls functions that are designated by the predicates of a natural language "concepts." The meaning$_F$ of a predicate like ( ) *conquered Gaul* is consequently a concept. If the concept is a function, the question comes up as to what exactly the concept's arguments are, and what its values. Frege's answer: concepts are functions that map objects into truth values. If a concept is completed or saturated by means of an object (= an argument), the result is a truth value (= a value). To know the meaning$_F$

of the concept 'conquered Gaul' is therefore to know which "saturation" yields which truth value; it is to know, for example, that the truth value "true" results when this concept's argument is Caesar. If the concept 'conquered Gaul' is completed with Aristotle, however, the result is the truth value "false." Of course, this means nothing other than that the assertion of the sentence *Caesar conquered Gaul* asserts a truth, and the assertion of the sentence *Aristotle conquered Gaul* a falsity. Thus, as a second provisional summary, we will bear in mind that predicates designate concepts; that is, the meaning$_F$ of a predicate is a concept.[5] A concept is a function which, when completed with an object, yields a truth value. The sense of a predicate is the mode of presentation of its concept.

I have already indicated that sense and meaning$_F$ may not be generally equated with intension and extension. This becomes clear in the case of predicates. The meaning$_F$ of a predicate is the concept—not the extension of the concept, which Frege terms the *Begriffsumfang* (1971: 26). The extension of a concept is the class of objects that fall under the concept. Frege calls the relation of a concept to its extension "subsumption" (1979: 193, 213).

We have seen that every linguistically well-formed name has a sense, but not necessarily a meaning$_F$. Names to which no objects correspond —such as *Odysseus*, *Snow White* or *the current emperor of China*—have no meaning$_F$. If we ask the analogous question of predicates, are there some which have a sense, but not a meaning$_F$? The answer should be "Yes, there are": specifically, those predicates which designate no concept. Now, what kind of predicates are they? Not, for example, those that denote an empty concept, like *( ) is a round square*! A concept under which no object falls, whose extension is 0, is indeed empty, but still nevertheless a concept. After all, it has to be a concept in order to be empty! According to what has been said so far, a predicate which designates no concept should be one whose completion with a name results in a sentence without a truth value. For concepts map objects into truth values. Just as there are names that only "act as if" they designate objects, there are also predicates that "act as if" they designate concepts. Actually, they designate pseudoconcepts. A genuine concept must yield the value "true" or "false" for any random object; if it does not, it is

---

[5] Searle (1969: 97 ff.) points out that Frege uses the expression *Begriff* ambiguously and undertakes a detailed examination of its double meaning. This problem will not be discussed here.

not a concept. Empty concepts like 'is a round square' do yield a truth value for any particular object, namely "false." They thus satisfy this condition for concepts.

In his posthumous writings, Frege states that a predicate "must have the property of yielding a genuine sentence when saturated by any meaningful proper name; this means that it must yield the proper name of a truth value. This is the requirement that a concept have sharp boundaries. For a given concept, every object must either fall under it or not, *tertium non datur*" (1979: 195). That is, the concept must be so clear that a decision can be reached regarding any random object as to whether that object falls under it or not. With this, Frege undoubtedly imposes a standard that is seldom or never fulfilled by the concepts of natural language. Consider the predicate *( ) is water*. If 'water' is supposed to be a concept in Frege's sense, it should be clear what falls under this concept and what does not. In other words, there must be a sharp boundary between water and non-water. Let's assume that pure H_2O is water, and everything that is not pure H_2O is non-water. Following this assumption, I have never drunk water in my life; nor have I ever swum in water. Let's assume that the concept 'water' will be defined to allow certain concentrations of certain additional substances. Which substances, and how many of them? We would call $H_2O+0.005\%$ acetic acid *water*, but $H_2O+5\%$ acetic acid is vinegar. Somewhere between the two lies the boundary between water and vinegar. "Can you give the boundary?" asks Wittgenstein, only to answer, "No. You can draw one; for none has so far been drawn" (PI § 68). For our everyday communication, it would be extremely inconvenient if all the predicates of our colloquial speech designated concepts in the Fregean sense (cf. Pinkal 1985: 55). The fuzziness of our everyday concepts is not a deficiency of natural languages; rather, as we will see in Chapter 6, it is an advantage.

Now for the question of what Frege regards to be the sense and meaning$_F$ of sentences. The answers practically supply themselves from what has been said thus far: if predicates are completed by proper names, sentences result. From this, it follows that if the meaning$_F$ of a predicate is completed by the meaning$_F$ of a proper name, the meaning$_F$ of the sentence results. The meaning$_F$ of a predicate is a concept; the meaning$_F$ of a proper name is an object. The concept is a function which maps objects in truth values. Therefore, if a concept is completed by an object, a truth value results. It is baffling, but consistent, when Frege writes that "we are therefore driven into accepting the *truth value* of a sentence as constituting its reference [meaning$_F$]" (1966*b*: 63). Considering it from another angle, we reach the same conclusion: in a sentence, if we replace one proper name with another proper name that has the same meaning$_F$, the meaning$_F$ of the sentence cannot change. The truth value, too, remains constant if we replace one name with another that refers to the same object (cf. Frege 1966*b*: 63). Consequently, sentences have exactly two possible meanings$_F$. "By the truth value of a sentence I understand the circumstance that it is true or false. There are no further truth values. For brevity I call the one the True, the other the False" (Frege 1966*b*: 63).

We recall that a name is a linguistic expression that designates an object and "an object is anything that is not a function, so that an expression for it does not contain any empty place" (Frege 1966*a*: 32). A sentence is such an expression, one which contains no empty place, for a sentence results when a predicate is completed. So a sentence is a name! A sentence "is therefore to be regarded as a proper name, and its reference [meaning$_F$], if it has one, is either the True or the False" (Frege 1966*b*: 63). The True and the False are thus not qualities, but objects designated by sentences. An assertoric sentence is a name for the True or the False. (Interestingly, this notion is supported by our colloquial use of language: we say *She speaks the truth* when someone says something true, but not *She speaks the beautiful* when a person says something beautiful.) The sense of a sentence, that is, the mode of presentation of the True or the False, is called by Frege the "thought" (*Gedanke*). Hence a sentence expresses a thought and designates a truth value. Here, too, it is true that a sentence expresses a thought in so far as the sentence is correctly formed in accordance with the rules of language. But not every sentence necessarily designates a truth value; that is, not every sentence has a meaning$_F$. This goes, first, for all non-assertoric sentences, but also for some assertoric sentences, namely, for exactly those assertoric sentences whose predicate designates no concept and/or whose predicate is completed with a name that designates no object. The assertoric sentence *Snow White weighed 160 pounds* has no meaning$_F$ because the name *Snow White* has no meaning$_F$. It's about as easy to judge the truth value of the thought expressed in this sentence as it is to take a picture of Snow White.

Frege differentiates rigorously between (a) the grasp of a thought,

(b) the act of judgment, that is, the acknowledgment of the truth of a thought and (c) the assertion, or manifestation, of this judgment (1977: 7). "*When we inwardly recognize that a thought is true, we are making a judgement: when we communicate this recognition, we are making an assertion*" (1979: 139; Frege's italics). It follows from this that the sentence *Snow White weighed 160 pounds* cannot be asserted. No judgment can be made regarding the thought that this sentence expresses, since the name *Snow White* designates no object, and the concept expressed by the predicate *( ) weighed 160 pounds* is incomplete. When a judgment is not possible, it cannot be communicated. Whoever asserts that Snow White weighed 160 pounds is making a pseudo-assertion!

In regard to Aristotle's theory, we asked whether we must assume that it is a psychologistic theory of meaning. The answer: we don't know, but much speaks against it. Aristotle's "affections of the soul" obviously are not conceived as individually psychological inner events. Even if Aristotle's theory of meaning is a psychologistic one, it has in any case been de-individualized. We might ask the analogous question of Frege's theory. If we proceed from the assumption that Fregean sense approximates what is usually called meaning, we may ask whether Frege, with his concept of sense, introduced a psychologistic theory of meaning. An affirmative answer might be supported thus: Frege calls the sense of a sentence a "thought." A thought is a product of thinking. Thinking is an individual psychological event. Therefore, Frege's theory of sense is a psychologistic theory. Such an argument would have made absolutely no sense to Frege. But unlike Aristotle, Frege makes it easy to answer this question in regard to his theory, having commented explicitly on the subject in his essay "Thoughts."

The thought is for Frege a category of logic, not of psychology. Furthermore, as we will see, the sense of a sentence, the thought expressed by that sentence, is not a category of linguistic semantics. Sense is not to be equated with that which is usually called sentence meaning or sentence content. Let's examine Frege's explanations in more detail.

"All sciences have truth as their goal; it falls to logic to discern the laws of truth" (Frege 1977: 1). Psychology, on the other hand, concerns itself with psychological laws, such as taking something as true (as in superstitious beliefs). One "might come to believe," writes Frege, "that logic deals with the mental processes of thinking and with the psychological laws in accordance with which this takes place. That would be misunderstanding the task of logic, for truth has not here been given its proper place" (1977: 1). We observe that Frege uses the word *thought* in a unique way. The Fregean "thought" is precisely *not* a product of thinking. A thought is something that can be true or false, independent of whether it has ever been thought, not to mention asserted. "That someone thinks it has nothing to do with the truth of a thought" (Frege 1977: 25). How do thoughts come into existence, if not by means of the process of thinking, and where can they be found? They do not come into existence; they are simply there, from eternity to eternity. They are timeless, and their position is neither in the mind nor in the world. "Thoughts are neither things in the world nor ideas. . . . A third realm must be recognized" (Frege 1977: 17). Frege characterizes the thought largely by means of negative features. Its only nameable positive characteristic has already been stated: a thought is what one judges as being true or false when one makes a judgment. "A fact is a thought that is true" (Frege 1977: 25). Facts can be neither seen nor heard! "That the sun has risen is not an object emitting rays that reach my eyes; it is not a visible thing like the sun itself. That the sun has risen is recognized to be true on the basis of sense-impressions" (Frege 1977: 5). One reaches the True, and thus facts, by making judgments about thoughts. What is the thinking of a thought, then, if "thinking" is not to be understood as an act of mental production? To this question, Frege is able to provide only a metaphorical answer: "We are not owners of thoughts as we are owners of our ideas. We do not have a thought as we have, say, a sense-impression, but we also do not see a thought as we see, say, a star. So it is advisable to choose a special expression; the word 'grasp' suggests itself for the purpose. . . . In thinking we do not produce thoughts, we grasp them" (Frege 1977: 24–5). Thoughts are therefore neither in the world nor in our minds. They comprise a world of their own, and when we think, we grasp them. We do not generate thoughts with the sentences of our language; our sentences express them. A thought which has been grasped must not be expressed; nor must it be an object of judgment. In the assertoric sentence *When I am hungry, I eat liverwurst,* neither the antecedent nor the final clause is assigned a truth value. If someone expresses this sentence with assertoric force, he asserts neither that he is hungry nor that he eats liverwurst! Both thoughts are expressed without the "recognition" of a truth value. All that is asserted is their if–then relation.

Why can't the sense of an assertoric sentence be regarded as its content? The problem is the close connection that Frege forges between thoughts and truth values: everything that does not relate to the truth value is not part of the thought. "Words like 'regrettably' and 'fortunately' belong here" (1977: 8). Only the truth-functional part of the sentence content is the thought. The sentence *Alfred has still not come* therefore expresses the same thought as *Alfred has not come*. With the *still*, one "hints—but only hints—that Alfred's arrival is expected" (Frege 1977: 9). The implied expectation of the speaker contributes nothing to the truth value of the sentence. The same goes for the word *but*. It differs from *and* in that "we use it to intimate that what follows it contrasts with what was to be expected from what preceded it. Such conversational suggestions make no difference to the thought" (Frege 1977: 9). However, these "conversational suggestions" are undoubtedly a part of what in non-Fregean terms is called sentence meaning. When Frege writes that "it makes no difference to the thought whether I use the word 'horse' or 'steed' or 'nag' or 'prad' " (1977: 9), it is unmistakably clear that with his category "sense," Frege has only the extensional aspect of word meaning, and thus sentence meaning, in mind.

It is not Frege's intent to do justice to the semantics of natural language, which he calls the content of language. He says little more about content than that it is not identical with sense. "Thus the content of a sentence often goes beyond the thought expressed by it" (Frege 1977: 10). What Frege calls *content* is not the object of his investigations. Nevertheless, his explanations result in the following scenario: we grasp thoughts by means of sentences that express those thoughts, thereby designating—if the sentence is expressed with assertoric force —the True or the False. By virtue of which features does the sentence owe its ability to express the grasped thought? Or, to put the question differently, what are the speaker's criteria for choosing one element from exactly that class of sentences which express the thought he has grasped? Frege neither poses nor answers this question, but there is only one possible answer: the criterion for judging is the content of the sentence. It must be such that it is capable of expressing the thought. The content "is the thought or at least contains the thought" (Frege 1977: 7). The speaker must make a choice of sentence in which sentence content "at least" contains the thought. The thought is superindividual and timeless; the content is language-specific and therefore temporally contingent.

With this, I will end my description of Frege's theory of sense and meaning_F. It is not complete; most obviously lacking is Frege's consideration of different types of subordinate clause. However, the above will do to make Frege's system of categories comprehensible. For clarity's sake, I will attempt a schematic overview of this system, first from the angle of the linguistic signs, and then from the angle of the speaker.

	Linguistic Level	Epistemological Level	Ontological Level
	Sign	Sense	Meaning_F
(1)	Predicate	Mode of presentation	Concept
(2)	Proper name	Mode of presentation	Object
(3)	Sentence	Thought	Truth value

A sign expresses its sense and designates its meaning_F. If an element from Row (1) is completed with an element from the same column of Row (2), the element in the respective column of Row (3) results. This means that

- The completion of a predicate with a proper name yields a sentence.

- The completion of the sense of a predicate with the sense of a proper name yields a thought.

- The completion of a concept with an object yields a truth value.

From the perspective of the asserting speaker, the following pattern results:

- The speaker grasps a thought.

- He (may) recognize the truth of the thought, that is, he makes a judgment.

- He (may) communicate his judgment, that is, he makes an assertion by expressing a sentence with a truth claim—a sentence whose content expresses the thought or at least contains the thought.

With this model, Frege created a consistent conceptual *instrumentarium* whose central idea is that of representation. Linguistic signs are a means of representing concepts and objects. However, in adapting, rejecting or even judging Frege's theory from a linguistic perspective, one must always keep in mind that it was not created for the purpose of describing natural languages, and it is certainly not meant to do justice to the process of communication. It restricts itself to the aspects of language relevant to truth-function. "To a mind concerned with the beauties of language, what is trivial to the logician may seem to be just what is important" (Frege 1977: 10). I do not mean to criticize the restriction to the representational view, but to complement it. To stress my earlier point once more, language fulfills for us the purposes of categorization, representation and communication. All three of these aspects must be kept in mind.

"The sense of a proper name is grasped by everybody who is sufficiently familiar with the language . . . to which it belongs," writes Frege (1966*b*: 57). We may assume that it would be in Frege's spirit to generalize this statement in regard to the sense of linguistic signs altogether; that is, regarding the sense of predicates and sentences. In order to grasp the sense of a linguistic sign, it is necessary to know its content and to know which of its parts is relevant to truth-function. What do people know who are sufficiently familiar with their language? When people know the content of a sign, what linguistic knowledge do they command? Frege gives no answer to this. Content interests him only in so far as it comprises sense. In fact, he does not even succeed in explaining what it means to *grasp* a thought. "This process," he admits, "is perhaps the most mysterious of all" (Frege 1979: 145). Frege does not pretend to want to describe how we understand sentences.[6] Indeed, purely representational theories should not make pretenses of this sort. For in order to do so, they still would have to work out how the relation of representation is engendered! They would have to solve the puzzle that Plato took upon himself in the *Cratylus*. It seems to me that Wittgenstein's heuristic maxim facilitates a solution: " 'The meaning of a word is what is explained by the explanation of the meaning.' i.e.: if you want to understand the use of the word 'meaning', look for what are called 'explanations of meaning' " (Wittgenstein PI § 560; see also BB: 1).[7] Into this maxim, Wittgenstein smuggled the solution to the puzzle: meaning is use. It is to this thesis that I turn my attention in the next chapter.

---

[6] See also Tugendhat 1982: 118. However, Tugendhat is incorrect in writing here that "there seems to be no comprehensive term in Frege for what we understand when we understand a linguistic expression." For this Frege uses the term *Inhalt* ("content"), albeit seldom.

[7] The title of Wittgenstein's *Blue Book* is here abbreviated in the accepted manner.

4

Wittgenstein's Instrumental Notion of Signs

To say of a linguistic sign that it has meaning is to say that it is connected to an idea. The speaker's idea gets packed up for shipping (encoded) in the linguistic sign and unpacked (decoded) by the addressee after the sign is received. This is how addressees come into possession of the ideas that correspond to the linguistic signs they receive. The meaning of a sign is thus the idea with which it is connected.

So runs, approximately, the common-sense theory of meaning. "The characteristic traditional theory of signs was a theory of representation (*Stellvertretertheorie*): the sign represents (*vertritt*) something that could also be given independently of the use of this or some other sign, namely in representation (*Vorstellung*)" (Tugendhat 1982: 376). Generally speaking, such a view might be called an "ideational" theory of meaning. With the help of a few leading questions and comments, I would like to point out the problems involved with such theories. A detailed description and critique of such theories is provided by Tugendhat (1982).

(1) Even if we accept as plausible the assumption that we connect ideas with the words *cow, house, drink*, etc., it remains to be demonstrated what ideas we connect with *nothing, whether, Tuesday, good, cousin, similar* or *unimaginable*.

(2) If we assume the thesis is correct that "the meaning of an expression is the idea connected with it," what meaning, according to this theory, would the expression *idea* have? What meaning would the expression *the idea connected with the expression 'idea'*

44

have? The answer is "The idea of the idea that is connected to the expression *idea*." What does this answer mean for the ideational theory?

(3) How can others (such as children) be taught to have certain ideas, and how does one monitor whether they are the right ideas? How can I compare my ideas with those of another?

(4) Assuming someone claims that the words *almost* and *nearly* have the same meaning, how might one check whether this is true? The ideational theory would recommend the following method as promising: close your eyes, recalling first the idea of *almost* and then the idea of *nearly*. Compare the two ideas and see if they're the same.

(5) Let's assume that, when I say "I've bought myself a cow," my addressee imagines a cow. Her imagining the correct thing obviously requires (among other things) that she has correctly understood the word *cow*. Therefore, understanding the word *cow* cannot be identified with having the corresponding idea. Having an idea can only be an effect of having understood.

(6) Let's assume that, after I've told my conversation partner "To-morrow I'm going on vacation," he imagines sun, sand and sea. My intent, though, is to get three weeks of rest and relaxation in Birmingham. Under these conditions, would we say that he has misunderstood me? Hardly; he simply has the wrong idea about my destination.

(7) In order to count as a theory, the concept of the idea would have to be analytically clarified and explicated. I know of no such attempt, but let's assume that ideas are something like mental pictures. (When I imagine Hawaii, I generate for myself a kind of mental picture.) If something like this is what is meant by the concept of the idea, who helps me, then, to understand my mental pictures? And who guarantees that I interpret them correctly?

These seven leading questions or comments are meant to suggest the following:

(1) The ideational theory becomes completely implausible when it is applied to conjunctions like *whether*, relational expressions like

cousin, purely evaluative expressions like *good,* or expressions that are only structurally definable, such as *Tuesday.*

(2) Applying the ideational theory to the word *idea* leads to iterative regression.

(3) If the communicative use of language is supposed to consist of the exchange of ideas, the teaching of language would require that ideas also be exchangeable by non-linguistic means.

(4) Anyone confronted with the question of synonymy intuitively tests interchangeability, and it would never occur to anyone, as ideational theories would have it, to undertake an introspective comparison of ideas.

(5) Ideas are, at best, secondary side effects of communication, not a substantial part of it.

(6) Reaching the correct understanding of a statement, and having an idea that corresponds adequately to the speaker's intent in making the statement, are independent of each other. The statement "I understand you completely, but I can't imagine what you've said" is not self-contradictory.

(7) If ideas have anything of the character of pictures, these pictures, in order to be understood, would have to be further subjected to interpretation. This assumption also leads to iterative regression.

The point is that, even if we admit to having ideas while communicating (sometimes, always or only with certain sentences or words), they still do not play the role in communication that the ideational theory accords them. Whether or not we have ideas is irrelevant to the question of what the speaker means by what she says, and what the addressee understands. Even if there are systematic ideas that accompany our communication, they have no more meaning in the game of communication than the systematically occurring mirth or irritation that might accompany taking a trick in cards. Neither of them is part of the game.

Every theory that claims that signs stand for something, whether it be ideas, things or anything else, must answer the question of how this relationship of representation is produced and sustained. How do you get a sign to stand for something, to symbolize something, or to represent an idea? Should that for which the sign stands be called its meaning? This is exactly the position I will not espouse. Not that which is communicated, but that which makes communication possible, should be called meaning. We recall that anyone who wants to say something about signs, their relation to the cognitive world and to the world of things, must distinguish—common practice since the time of Aristotle, at the latest—between three levels: the linguistic level of signs, the epistemological level of concepts and the ontological level of things and circumstances. Then it can be asked on which level should be placed what is supposed to be *meaning*. To some extent, this is a terminological question. We have seen that Frege situated what he called *Bedeutung* on the ontological level. Ideational theorists obviously situate meaning on the epistemological level. I will argue, in accordance with Wittgenstein's later writings, for the situation of meaning on the linguistic level. If the decision of level is not to be dismissed as a purely terminological one, there is another question which first must be clarified: what should the notion of meaning accomplish? What should it explain? Without such clarification, the question "What comprises the meaning of a sign?" cannot be meaningfully answered. I opt for saying that *the concept of meaning should explain the interpretability of signs*. Even if we concede that signs stand for something, represent something, denote something, etc.—whether that something is an object, an idea, a concept, a truth value or whatever—we cannot avoid asking ourselves by virtue of which property a sign enables the addressee to ascertain what it stands for. When we communicate with the help of a language, we perform utterances with the intention of bringing the addressee to a certain interpretation. To perform utterances with such an intention is to mean something with them. Thus we might also say that the concept of meaning should serve to explain how it is possible for speakers to bring their addressees to recognize what they (the speakers) mean. It should contribute to the solution of Plato's puzzle (434e): how is it possible, "when I utter *this* sound, [and] I have *that* thing in mind . . . [that] you know that I have it in mind"? The explanation of this mystery requires considerable conceptual effort. In his later work, Ludwig Wittgenstein made decisive headway towards its solution, the fundamentals of which I will now describe by means of a brief explanatory introduction.

Wittgenstein's notion of the meaning of linguistic signs is often called the "theory of meaning as use." To those readers unfamiliar with

Wittgenstein's writings, this manner of speaking suggests a theoretical exposition in which he presents a theory of meaning. No such work exists. Rather, in a series of diverse remarks, mostly in the major work of his later philosophy, entitled *Philosophical Investigations*, Wittgenstein approaches, touches upon and sometimes just grazes the notion of meaning. Therefore, it is not surprising that divergent interpretations of his thought exist. "The philosophical remarks in this book," he remarks in the preface to *Philosophical Investigations*, "are, as it were, a number of sketches of landscapes which were made in the course of long and involved journeyings" (PI ix^e). A theory of meaning as use can result only through interpretive and supplementary efforts, which we will undertake in the following pages.

Paragraph 43 of the *Philosophical Investigations* is generally regarded as a case in point, and runs, in its entirety, as follows:

For a *large* class of cases—though not for all—in which we employ the word "meaning" it can be defined thus: the meaning of a word is its use in the language.
And the *meaning* of a name is sometimes explained by pointing to its *bearer*.

This paragraph contains two traps and a tip. We'll start with the tip. The meaning of a name, writes Wittgenstein, can sometimes be explained by pointing. Since the problem of ostensive explanation is only of marginal interest for our purposes, a brief clarification will do. One might assume —as Frege did, for whom Wittgenstein, in his early writings, expresses great admiration—that the meaning of a name is its bearer. In the *Philosophical Investigations*, however, Wittgenstein distances himself from this assumption. Nevertheless, he concedes that the meaning of a name, or more generally of a word, sometimes can be explained by means of ostensive definition. Why only sometimes? The answer makes sense: imagine that I want to explain to someone what the word *two* means, which I do by pointing to two nuts and saying, "That is called 'two' " (PI § 28). How should the learner know what I am referring to? He might think that I want to teach him the meaning of *nuts*. Let's say I point to a red sweater and say, "That is called *red*." How is the addressee supposed to know that I don't want to explain the meaning of *sweater* or *fleecy* or *wool*? In other words, in order to understand an ostensive explanation, a considerable amount of prior knowledge is necessary.

So one might say: the ostensive definition explains the use—the meaning—of the word when the overall role of the word in [the] language is clear. Thus if I know that someone means to explain a colour-word to me the ostensive definition "That is called 'sepia' " will help me to understand the word. (PI § 30)

The ostensive definition cannot be the starting point, and it is not always successful. For "the ostensive definition can be variously interpreted in *every* case" (PI §28).

What are the two traps? First, the restrictive preliminary remark of the first sentence Paragraph 43, and the key word *use* itself are ambiguous. To start with the restriction: Wittgenstein's explication of the meaning of *meaning* is supposed to be true "for a *large* class of cases [in which we employ the word meaning]—though not for all." The predictable misinterpretation of this statement is formulated with wonderful clarity by George Pitcher: "This is exactly what one would expect from Wittgenstein: just as there are many different kinds of games, so there are many different kinds of meanings, and not all can be identified with the use of the word which is said to have a meaning. Typically, Wittgenstein does not tell us which kinds of cases he would exclude from his general maxim" (Pitcher 1964: 249). This misinterpretation claims that, with his restriction, Wittgenstein wants to get across that there is *a small class* of words whose meaning is *not* their use in the language. If this had been what he wanted to say, his capacity to express himself would surely have been sufficient to do so clearly. "For a large class of word meanings—though not for all cases of word meanings—the word *meaning* can be explained thus." This is not what Wittgenstein says. He is not talking about a large class of word meanings, or a large class of words, but about a large class of the uses of the word *meaning*! In other words, he's talking about the rich variation of the meaning of the word *meaning*. He's telling us what the word *meaning* means. We use the word *meaning* in diverse ways: "John F. Kennedy's meaning for the US," "the meaning of the word *Nature* for the Romantics," "the meaning of the word *polliastre* in English" and so on. In these and other similar uses of the word *meaning*, meaning cannot be equated with "use in the language." Such identification is valid only when the word *meaning* is used in cases relevant to meaning theory: the use of the word *meaning* on the level of *la langue*. In this case, it is unconditionally true that the meaning of a word is its use in the language.

With this, we have reached a transition to the second trap. Where does it say that Wittgenstein here refers to meaning on the level of *la langue*? Doesn't he simply want to make the concept of meaning more flexible and say that, depending on how the word is used, depending on the context, situation or circumstances, a word can have different meanings? Gisela Harras promotes this theory: "This means that *the* meaning of a word does not exist, but that there are different meanings depending on the situation and the speakers' objectives. Behind this is the concept that the use of linguistic expressions—and thus their respective meanings—are dependent on the speakers' respective intentions" (1983: 97).[1] Supporters as well as opponents of Wittgenstein's approach make use of this misinterpretation. Thus Derek Bickerton cautions: "But we must be careful here, or we shall fall into the trap of Wittgenstein's . . . theory of 'meaning as use.' This approach holds that things mean what we choose them to mean—and it is a useful gambit against naive realists who believe that language merely labels what is already there" (Bickerton 1990: 48). This 'theory of meaning' is frequently lauded as the great achievement of pragmatically oriented linguistics, and is used by its opponents as an argument for its inadequacy.[2] What's wrong with an interpretation that states that *the* meaning of a word does not exist, but that a word has differing meanings, dependent on the context and on speakers' intentions? Following Paragraph 43, nothing is wrong with such an interpretation, except that it offends the "principle of charity," which states: "Assume of your conversation partner that he does not want to talk nonsense." If the concept of meaning should serve to explain how it is possible for the speaker to mean something in and by a language, meaning cannot be equated with what the speaker means in one case and then in another. If meaning is supposed to help the understanding of what a person intends by an utterance in any given situation, it cannot be conceptualized as dependent on the situation or the speaker's intentions. If I must have understood the speaker in order to know the meaning of her words, meaning cannot be something that aids in understanding. That which Wittgenstein understands to be *meaning* is meant to be the basis of understanding, not its result. Therefore, the expression *use* cannot refer to individual instances of use, but to the form of use in the

---

[1] Trans. K.D.
[2] Cf. Bierwisch 1979: 120, where this interpretation is used as an opposing argument.

language, the *rule* of use. However, if I am correct, Wittgenstein did in fact neglect to introduce a terminological difference for clearly distinguishing what a word means from that which a speaker means by a particular utterance of that word. I will return to the matter of this distinction in Chapter 8 and recommend an appropriate terminology.

What Wittgenstein means to say in the quoted paragraph is that *the meaning of a word in a language, L, consists of the rule of its use in L.* This is true for all the words in a language. If you know how a word is used—if you know the rule of its use in the language L—you know everything there is to know. If you want to teach people the meaning of a word, teach them how the word is used in the language. (In doing this, you don't need to teach them anything about your ideas or other aspects of your mental life!) Sometimes, if numerous preliminary explanations have been made, an ostensive definition can replace an explanation of use.

It is not only the principle of charity that leads to this interpretation. It results primarily from its connection with other key concepts of Wittgenstein's late philosophy, such as the language game, the form of life, rules, and private language. I will not go into the details of their interrelatedness here. Second, this interpretation is the result of a series of further assorted explanations, illustrations, and synonymous expressions:

Let us say that the meaning of a piece is its role in the game. (PI § 563)

Think of the tools in a tool-box: there is a hammer, pliers, a saw, a screwdriver, a rule, a glue-pot, nails and screws.—The functions of words are as diverse as the functions of these objects. (And in both cases there are similarities.) (PI § 11)

It is not possible that there should have been only one occasion on which someone obeyed a rule. It is not possible that there should have been only one occasion on which a report was made, an order given or understood; and so on.— To obey a rule, to make a report, to give an order, to play a game of chess, are *customs* (uses, institutions).

To understand a sentence means to understand a language. To understand a language means to be a master of a technique. (PI § 199)

The expressions *role, function, custom* and *technique* make it sufficiently clear that Wittgenstein wants to have understood as meaning not only that which is sometimes called "contextual meaning." In § 559 he states this explicitly:

One would like to speak of the function of a word in *this* sentence. As if the sentence were a mechanism in which the word had a particular function. But what does this function consist in? How does it come to light? For there isn't anything hidden—don't we see the whole sentence? The function must come out in operating with the word. (PI § 559)

When Wittgenstein talks about function, role or use, he means it in reference to the operation of the entire language. To know the meaning of the rook in chess is to know how one may, and may not, move it. There is nothing more to know about the rook (or about any other piece). Knowing the meaning of the rook is different from knowing the meaning of a certain move. The former is a prerequisite of the latter. Meaning is nothing secret, mental, or otherwise internal. Meaning is a technique, and this is exactly why we can teach and learn and modify it. Wittgenstein's theory does not say that you have to know the meaning of a word in order to be able to use it correctly. (You have to know the meaning of the rook to move it correctly.) To use a word correctly means to know its meaning. There is nothing "behind" the rule of use that guarantees the correctness of the use, as it were. Use does not "flow" from meaning; it is not a result of meaning; it *is* meaning.

One must be careful, with the category of use or of the rule of use, not to quietly smuggle in a new relationship of representation: the word does not represent its rule of use; rather, the rule of use makes the word meaningful (Kutschera 1975: 234). Words do not relate to their meanings as money relates to the cow you can buy with it, but as money relates to its use. To know the meaning of the word *no* means to know what you can do with it in English, such as agreeing with negatively posed questions like *Aren't there any universities in Andorra?—No.* Of course, the knowledge of the rule of use includes the knowledge of truth conditions, but it does not exclude non-truth-functional conditions of use. Truth conditions are a special case of the parameters of use. *Horse* and *nag*, to return to Frege's example as quoted in the previous chapter, might have the same truth conditions: both expressions can be used (for example) to refer to hoofed animals of a certain genus. But their other rules of use are different: *nag* is used (for example) to express a certain deprecation; this is not true of *horse*. Knowing the meaning of a word is (sometimes) not only knowing which requirements an object must fulfill in order for the word to be truthfully applicable to it; it also is knowing what kind of "conversational suggestions," as Frege aptly called them, can be made with that word. When Frege writes that "the way that 'but' differs from 'and' is that we use it to intimate that what follows it contrasts with what was to be expected from what preceded it" (1977: 9), he formulates (part of) the meaning of *but*. For with this, he says that the word *but* is used in English to suggest such-and-such. To know this is to know its meaning.

This notion of meaning has decided advantages over all others:

(1) Meaning is nothing secret. Just as I can learn the use of an electric shaver or of the rook in chess, and learn it partially or completely, I can learn the use of a word.

(2) Just as it can be verified whether people know the use of the rook or not, it can be verified, without peering into their minds or souls, whether they have command of the meaning of a word.

(3) Meaning is not a "part" of words, just as the use of my electric shaver is not one of its "parts." Meaning is an aspect of words, or more generally, of signs.

(4) Meanings can be formulated without the creation of strange entities: semantic features, semes, and suchlike.

(5) Meanings can be compared, analyzed and tested without looking into the mind or the soul. Looking at language use with purely linguistic methods is sufficient: frequency counts, commutation procedures, implication and presupposition tests, and so on.

In sum: meanings, according to this view, are something very handy. They are neither in the mind nor in the soul, and that makes them so much easier to examine! "Cut the pie any way you like, 'meanings' just ain't in the head!" (Putnam 1978: 65).

Nevertheless, some still have difficulties in accepting that the meaningfulness of a linguistic sign should be nothing more than its rule of use. The reason for this, it seems to me, is that representational theories live in the comforting fiction that there is an extralinguistic guarantee for the correct use of signs, whether it be an inner event or a thing in the outside world. "We all use the word *frustration* in the same way because we all connect it with the same idea," a hard-core ideationalist would object—failing to notice that the *only* criterion for the hypothesis of the sameness of everyone's idea is the sameness of everyone's use of the word. The development of meaningfulness through the development of a rule of use can be clearly illustrated with an instance of color symbolism. As a first example, let's take black ties. Wearing a black tie is a symbol of grief. If we ask a child, "Why is black the color for mourning?" we get the answer, "Because black is such a sad color." As long as we're unaware of the fact that in other countries, white is the color for mourning, or that the Catholic Church uses purple before Easter as the color of suffering and red as the color for martyrs, such an answer has something spontaneously convincing about it. But this is the same kind of logic behind the idea that pigs are called *pigs* because they're so dirty. (In a personal communication to the author, Raimo Anttila appropriately calls the fact that we tend to look for some sort of motivatedness in our symbols the "voodoo effect" of language.) The only thing that makes black the color of mourning is the fact that wearing this color in Western countries is regulated and that there is mutual knowledge concerning it.

To demonstrate this, we will consider a fictitious example of the genesis of a color's meaningfulness in four phases, assuming that:

(1) I have a quirk. Whenever I have a cold, I wear a yellow tie. (This is not yet an example of a rule, but one of regular behavior. A rule includes the possibility of violations against it. If one day, however, in spite of having a cold, I fail to wear a yellow tie, I could not be accused of incorrect behavior—at most, I could be accused of inconsistency. A rule of behavior is always a matter of the actions of many, of a population.)

(2) The people around me see through my quirk. (Thus my yellow tie has become *for others* a sign, in a certain sense, that I have a cold. But it is not a sign in the way a linguistic sign is. I will return to the difference in Chapter 11. The basis of significance is, in this case, the knowledge of a regular behavior, just as my full mailbox can be for me a sign that it's ten o'clock, if I know that the mail always arrives at about that time.)

(3) Other men find my quirk amusing and start to imitate it. (This is still not a situation in which a rule for yellow ties exists, but simply one in which there are a number of instances of behavioral regularity.)

(4) Through observation, conversation, sanctioning behavior ("What?! Even though you have a nasty cold, you're wearing a green tie?"), and suchlike, collective knowledge about this behavioral regularity arises in the population: everyone knows that all men wear yellow ties when they have colds; and everyone knows that everyone knows this of everyone else. With this, a certain expectation in regard to others' behavior comes about, and as a result, a certain obligation in regard to one's own behavior. When you (as a man) have a cold, *you* wear a yellow tie. (Thus is a rule born from an individual quirk. A yellow tie has become a sign for a cold. Not only can others now see that I have a cold; from now on, the tie is used to indicate to others that the wearer of the tie has a cold. Also, from this point on, the tie can be used to lie.)

What does this example show us? It doesn't take much for something to become meaningful. It is probably approximately how light purple bib overalls became a symbol of women's emancipation in Germany, and purple cloth became a symbol of the Easter Passion in the Catholic Church. When a process like this is completed, and following the rule has become a part of everyday life, children answer the question "Why do men wear a yellow tie when they have colds?" with "Because yellow is such a sickly color." Now the ideational theorists can say that "Because people associate the thought of sniffles and colds with yellow, men wear yellow ties to let the others know that they have colds. The person wearing the tie encodes his idea of a cold in the yellow tie, and the observer decodes it, thereby coming to the recognition of the idea of the person wearing the tie." And for theorists of componential analysis, *yellow* has, from this point on, the semantic features [+HUMAN, +MASCULINE, +ADULT, +HAS A COLD].

PART II

Semantics and Cognition

5

Conceptual Realism versus Conceptual Relativism

It's time for a provisional summary. Two fundamental notions of signs have been contrasted, the representational and the instrumental. Aristotle and Frege were introduced as exemplary of representational notions, Plato and Wittgenstein as exemplary of instrumental notions of signs.

These are the central questions that representational notions of signs try to answer: What does a sign stand for? What are the extra-linguistic correspondents of signs? Of course, behind such questions is a certain notion of what communication is. According to this notion, communication is the transferal to the addressee(s) of ideas, concepts, and so on, by the provision of substitutes for those ideas, concepts, etc.: you don't have direct access to my thoughts, so I give you access by means of signs that stand for my ideas. In such a scenario, the people involved in communicating can safely be left out of the picture. They have no significant role in the conception of such notions of signs. However, representational theories have to live with one big mystery: by virtue of which characteristic do signs manage to stand for ideas? The answer "By symbolizing those ideas" is not a real answer; it only shifts the problem, for we find ourselves faced with another, analogous question.

The question that representational notions of signs leave open is exactly the question that instrumental sign theories attempt to answer: words must somehow show you what I am thinking. I *tell* you what I am thinking by using means that *show* you. This seems to have been Plato's basic idea. However, onomatopoeic imitation was the only way he could conceive of the ability of words to show what the speaker is thinking.

The words I use are imitations of the things of which I am thinking. This thought, too, is obviously tied to a certain idea of what it means to communicate. While the basic problem of representationally based notions of communication is one of transportation—how do signs manage to transport ideas from A to B?—the basic problem of instrumentally based theories of communication is one of influence: how do I get you to recognize what I am thinking, what I want from you, or what you should do or believe? Signs are conceived as a means of influence. Means of influence are a certain kind of instrument. However, as we have seen, the analogy with instruments can't be pushed too far, or the notion of arbitrariness suddenly becomes nonsensical. Representational notions of signs generally see the meaning of a sign in the thing that the sign stands for. Instrumental theories of signs see the meaning of the sign in that which makes it a sign. These two questions, what a sign stands for and what makes it a sign, are not equivalent. What makes a linguistic sign a sign is the fact that consistency of practice in use lends it a communicative function. It plays a part in the game of communication. Briefly stated, this is Wittgenstein's notion of signs: "if we had to name anything which is the life of a sign, we should have to say that it was its *use*" (BB: 4). Imagine that we want to create a board game that is played with differently colored buttons. If we forget to include the red buttons in the rules of the game, they remain nothing but buttons. Only the rules of the game, and exclusively those rules, make of them pieces which have a function in the game. Signs are pieces in the game of communication.

Recalling the end of Chapter 3, we remember that in order to understand Frege's "sense," we have to understand what Frege means by "content," and know what about it is relevant to truth-value functions. Frege did not comment on what it means to know the content of a linguistic expression. In fact, he probably would have made no answer to such a question: knowing the content of a linguistic expression means knowing how that expression is used in the language. But regardless of whether Frege would have made this reply or not, it is the appropriate one, and as far as I can see, it contradicts nothing that Frege wrote. To know the Fregean sense of an expression means to know the rule of use of that expression and to know which conditions of use are relevant to truth-value functions. In reading studies that provide an overview of various theories of meaning, one constantly gets the impression that representational theories and theories of meaning as use are mutually exclusive alternatives (see, for example, Alston 1964). But this is not the case! They are different answers to different questions, which, independently of each other, can be valid or invalid. Both approaches have their justifications, and they are reciprocally compatible. The question of the relation of signs to the world, be it the world of things or the world of cognitive entities, is just as legitimate as the question of how this relation, if it exists, comes to be.

Plato's Socrates says that language serves to give information, to distinguish things from one another, and to name. Broadly interpreted, we might say that this translates into communication, classification, and representation. We have discussed the communicative and the representative aspects of language. What, then, is the classificatory aspect of language? Roughly speaking, we may distinguish two theses, both of which throw out the baby with the bathwater. The theory of naive realism states that things are as they are, "the same for all," as Aristotle put it, and that language serves only the purpose of representation. According to this theory, language really has no classificatory function. The world comes with its own classifications. Plato seems to prefer a partial solution: things are as they are, but if the wise maker of words had not fitted words with a natural correctness that correctly reproduces natural categories, we would probably get the wrong impressions about the makeup of the things of this world.

The complementary view is just as naive. It might be called naive relativism, and can be formulated approximately thus: we see the world exclusively through the window of our language. Reality is "always already" linguistically mediated. Whether the categories that we perceive through language really exist is an inappropriate question, for any answer that we might give can only be provided in a language in which the categories are already given.

Who's right? Of course, supporters of the second kind of theory would reject this question as naive: since our world is "always already" linguistically mediated, this is also true of the categories used to discuss the question. Thus, if naive relativism is true, it is also incontestable. However, this fact does not make it a better theory. Fundamentalistically presented, both views are untenable, but both also contain a grain of truth. Finding it is an empirical task that one may approach by means of psychological perception tests and comparative and historical linguistics.

In recent years, such studies have been undertaken in increasing number.[1] Perhaps the best known of them is the color-category research of Berlin and Kay (1969), as well as that of Kay and McDaniel (1978). These studies demonstrate that, in spite of considerable variation in kind and number among color categories pre-given in the basic color words of various languages, the categories still exhibit similarities. Native speakers of different languages, regardless of the color categories that are pre-given in their own languages, make surprisingly concurring judgments in regard to typical representatives of certain color categories. These concurrences are evidently determined by the physiology of human color perception. There are colors that "jump out at us."

The study of so-called basic-level categories[2] also makes clear that, in spite of all the language-specific differences in the formation of categories, universal tendencies still exist. When we examine category hierarchies, such as 'cocker spaniel', 'spaniel', 'dog', 'pet', 'mammal', 'creature'; or 'elm', 'deciduous tree', 'tree', 'plant', 'living thing'; or 'carpenter's hammer', 'hammer', 'tool', comparative studies of language and culture show that in every case, the mid-level category is seen as central: in our examples, 'dog', 'tree', and 'hammer'. Children learn these words earlier than the other ones, and even if a language does not contain linguistic signs for all levels of the category, it inevitably has, if any, the one for the basic category.

Both examples, that of color categories and that of basic-level categories, demonstrate that although categorization can vary considerably in kind and number from one language to another, it nevertheless appears to be not entirely arbitrary. There are different possible reasons for this. For one, human biology could play a direct role, such as in the neurophysiology of human color perception; for another, similarities in humans' way of approaching the world might be a determining factor. In spite of all their cultural differences, people have similar wishes, similar needs and similar problems to solve. This fact finds expression in language and its categories, just as it does in culture-specific uniqueness. The categories 'tree', 'dog', and 'hammer' concern our lives more directly than, say, 'plant', 'mammal', and 'tool'. If we were playing a game in which the idea is to pantomime certain categories, coming up

---

[1] See the thorough description in Lakoff 1987: chap. 2.
[2] See Brown 1958, as well as the description in Lakoff 1987.

with gestures for 'hammer', 'dog', and 'tree' would be considerably easier than for 'carpenter's hammer', 'cocker spaniel', and 'oak', or for 'tool', 'animal', and 'plant'. The mid-level category is the mid-level of relevance, as it were, between the microscopic and the macroscopic levels. Our categories are of an interactive nature. The development of language is both a part and a special case of that nature. As Derek Bickerton writes, "the categories into which we divide nature are not in nature, they emerge solely through the interaction between nature and ourselves" (1990: 53). One of the constitutive features of evolutionary processes (though not a necessary one) is adaptability. This is also true of linguistic evolution. Linguistic expressions—along with the conceptual categories they engender—which prove themselves to be more suitable than potential alternatives, in the course of our practical, mental and communicative attempts to come to terms with the world, are more likely to be retained, that is, to be further used, taught and learned, than expressions which are less suitable. Information about reality is thus built into the language, so to speak, by generations of language users.

Since cultural knowledge about reality is stored in language, language can trivially be said to stand in a certain relationship of "imitation" or "representation" to "its" reality. This can be demonstrated with the following examples of non-linguistic, evolutionary adaptation. A fish's shape is the product of the genetic storage of the experience of millions of its ancestors with hydrodynamics. In this sense, the fish's shape is a representation of the structure of water. The shape of a mason's trowel is a product of the cultural storage of experience gleaned by thousands of generations of masons in the practice of their craft. "And, once a more efficient tool is available, it will be used without our knowing why it is better, or even what the alternatives are" (Hayek 1960: 27). In this sense, the masons' trowels of today are representations of the activity of masonry. It is in exactly this sense that the categories of our language, as engendered through its rules of use, are also a representation of reality. Adaptation is the storage of successful experiential knowledge about reality. "Cultural evolution can be regarded as a process of 'collective learning' in the sense that it consists in the transmission and accumulation, from generation to generation, of knowledge and experience" (Vanberg 1994: 175).

The thought of adaptation assumes the acceptance of a reality that is independent of language and perception. If our form of perception is the result of evolutionary adaptation, there must be something to which it adapted. And if our language, along with its classifications, is the result of evolutionary adaptation, it, too, must have adapted to something. Konrad Lorenz called this epistemological position *hypothetical realism* (Lorenz 1977: 6).[3] However, language does not simply adapt itself to the world of things as the horse's hoof adapts to the steppe; it also adapts to social realities, where values play an important role. The change of the medieval German system of form of address *ir–du*, which served to mark social hierarchy (high–low), to the system *Sie–du*, which—roughly stated—serves to mark distance and intimacy (far–near), is a process of adaptation: not to the world of things, but to the world of values. That we distinguish between 'red' and 'green' seems to be an adaptation to our perceptual mechanism; that we distinguish between 'murder' and 'manslaughter' an adaptation to our legal values; that we distinguish between 'chair' and 'stool', an adaptation to our daily form of life.

"Concepts are linguistic tools of thought" (Feilke 1996: 40).[4] They are the mental correlates of our rules of use and are usually produced by them. In the following pages, I would like to attempt an explication of the connection between types of rules of use and types of categories.

The rules of use of our language and the categories that are produced by them are the contemporary results of the potentially endless process of cultural learning. The system of categories that we acquire through the use of our language endows us with problem-solving strategies, for problems with which the individual must never have dealt. As we acquire our language, "we learn to classify things in a certain manner without acquiring the actual experiences which have led successive generations to evolve this system of classification" (Hayek 1952: 150). "Learning without insight" is Viktor Vanberg's apt term for this form of knowledge growth (1994: 187). Societies practice not only the division of labor, they also practice the division of knowledge and of experience, so to speak. With my language, I acquire the knowledge of experience gathered by the generations that preceded me. In his essay "Über den 'Sinn' sozialer Institutionen" ("On the 'Sense' of Social Institutions"), von Hayek discusses in detail the implicit experiential knowledge contained and handed down in those "unintentionally arisen

---

[3] Lorenz here refers to Campbell, but does not quote directly.

[4] Trans. K.D.

developments such as morals, customs, language, and . . . the market"
(1956: 512):

> The important thing here is not only that we learn to use language without really knowing what complicated rules we constantly employ . . . but that along with language, we gain much knowledge about the world, knowledge that is contained in the language, as it were, and which, although we would not be able to formulate it, continually guides us when we think or speak in that language. Naturally, that language often leads us astray has been repeatedly emphasized. But much more often, the acquired use of language helps us to orient ourselves in the world in which we live and to solve many problems automatically, so to speak, without our really being able to explain how we reach our solutions . . . It is anything but self-evident that things and events are grouped together in the same way as they are with the names that we impose upon them; much experience is latent in the inclusion of essentially different things under the same name. (Hayek 1956: 517)[5]

The categories formed through our communicative practice survive according to the degree of their functional suitability within the respective culture. Logically, nothing would stop us from creating a category that includes all living things that lay edible eggs: chickens and other birds, sea urchins, ants, sturgeon and other fish. We could also create a category of all the things that can be transported by bicycle. In our language, there are no words that generate these classifications. This is not because of the "ridiculousness" of such categories, but solely because there is evidently no recurring need for them in our form of life. Words and concepts are (in a certain sense) tools for communication and thought. Tools are a means of providing standard solutions for recurrent problems. Logically and technically, it is entirely possible that there be a tool for getting tennis balls out of milk bottles. It is solely because a solution to this problem is too infrequently required that no such instrument exists. If there were cultures with religions that worship egg-laying animals, or systems of transportation in which bicycles are important, the appropriate vocabulary and correspondent categories would have arisen in those cultures. From a logical perspective, the categories produced by a natural language often are rather confused and crazy. What counts in evolutionary processes is not logic, but utility. Linguistic evolution is ad hoc and shamelessly utilitarian. (Critics of language seem to have a particularly hard time with this fact.)

[5] Trans. K.D.

Let's take a look at the German category 'Vieh', for example. In the Middle Ages, the difference between 'Tier' ('animal') and 'Vieh' ('live-stock') was that animals living in the wild were called *Tier* (cf. English *deer*), while domesticated barnyard animals were called *Vieh*. Due to the progressive technological abstraction of our way of life, along with increasing urbanization, this distinction has become obsolete in today's German. 'Tier' has become a biological category, that is, 'animal'; the semantics of the word *Tier* include no conditions for use[6] which involve human dealings or human utilization (in contrast, for example, to the word *Wild* [*game*], which can be applied to any animal that is seen by hunters as being huntable, from quail to elephants). For modern speakers of German, the category 'Vieh' has become rather vague: it includes domesticated animals, but not all of them, it seems. At the end of the nineteenth century, Wilhelm Busch, the author of popular children's verse such as *Der Struwelpeter*, still referred to the Widow Bolte's *Federvieh* ("feathered livestock"). Today, however, I would not say that a goose breeder practices *Viehhaltung* (that he *raises livestock*); in referring to "newfangled" domesticated animals, such as ostriches or llamas, I'm not sure what I would say. I don't even know if horses belong to the category 'Vieh'. It could be that 'Vieh' is limited to domesticated animals that are meant for human consumption. Such uncertainty in classification is an uncertainty in regard to the use of the word *Vieh*. A lack of communicative contact with more knowledgeable speakers, and a lack of frequent active and passive use of the word *Vieh*, have the effect that I limit my own active use of *Vieh* to cases in which I am fairly certain that it applies—and that means cattle. Hence uncertainty leads to self-restriction in the use of a word; the uncertainty of many leads, cumulatively and gradually, to restricted use, and thus to conceptual constriction.

An example of a rather "wild" category in British English is that of 'tea'.[7] The rules of use for the word *tea* are such that, for this category,

---

[6] Although, in certain isolated expressions, the old usage shimmers through: in the zoo, there are *Tierställe* (*Ställe=stalls*), even for cattle; on the farm, they are called *Viehställe*.

[7] In the original text, German 'Salat' ("salad" and/or "lettuce") is used as an example of a "wild" category. Since English 'salad' is not as wild, 'Salat' has been replaced with 'tea'. Thanks to Catherine Cole for sharing her knowledge about this category—K.D.

there exist neither uniform criteria nor sharp boundaries for what falls under it and what does not. Having said this, we note that the use of the word *tea* nevertheless causes no problems for English speakers. They usually do not notice how chaotic and ad hoc their use of this word is, when its rules of use are considered from a logical perspective. Tea, *Thea sinensis* or *Camellia sinensis*, is a shrub that grows in Japan, India, Sri Lanka, China, etc. Tea is also the beverage that can be made, by infusion, from this plant's leaves. Further, tea is a light meal, with or without tea, towards late afternoon; finally (particularly in the north of England), tea is the evening meal, even if the accompanying beverage is a glass of milk, juice, or beer. The connection between the plant *tea*, the beverages called *tea* and the meals called *tea* is anything but clear. It is quite clear that the addition of hot water to tea produces tea, but *tea* might also mean scones in the afternoon or sausages in the evening, whether tea is drunk or not. The scones and sausages are not tea, but the meal at a certain time is. Tea must not include tea in any form; nor must a tea break or a tea dance.

One might think that the word *tea* is ambiguous, in the way that the word *club* is.[8] However, our feel for language (and not only that) contradicts this assumption. There is also a fairly dependable test: with really ambiguous words, an *obligation to dispel ambiguity* comes to bear. Pinkal calls this a *"Präzisierungsgebot"* or "specification requirement" (Pinkal 1985: 52 ff.).[9] However, no such obligation comes to bear with words that have varied or unclear extensions. A person who says *I've bought myself a club* may not leave open whether he's talking about an entertainment establishment, an implement for playing golf, or (in the US) a security device for his car. However, a person who says *I've bought myself a weapon* does not have to specify whether he means a tank or a hunting knife. We will not understand the first remark if we cannot dispel its ambiguity. But we understand the second remark even without knowing what kind of weapon is meant.

Teatime again. You cannot say *I've had lots of tea today* and mean food in general. However, the use of *tea* to mean a meal is not metaphorical, as it may be in the phrase *tea and sympathy*, or as it is in the expressions *a storm in a teacup, not my cup of tea, not for all the tea in*

---

[8] The original German example is *das Schloß* ("castle" or "lock")—K.D.

[9] Trans. K.D.

China, *Texas tea* (that is, *oil*) or *Long Island Iced Tea* (a cocktail of white rum, tequila, gin, vodka, Triple Sec, lemon juice, and cola, but certainly no tea!). Camomile tea and peppermint tea are also tea in a non-metaphorical sense, even though camomile flowers and mint leaves do not belong to the category of plants called *tea*. Tea towels are used for drying all sorts of dishes, not only tea cups, teapots and teaspoons; teaspoons, in their turn, can be used to eat or stir a number of things other than tea. A tea wagon may be used to transport various edible things and the utensils needed to eat them, not just (or even necessarily) tea; lunch in a tearoom need not include tea; and tea kettles are used to boil water, not tea.

The rule of use for the word *tea* seems to consist of a disjunction of usage conditions. *Tea* can be used to denote certain plants, certain beverages or any one of certain meals at certain times of day. Though the components of the meal are not included in the basic category, the things eaten at those times are nevertheless, in combination, called *tea*. This means that 'tea' is at one and the same time a category that classifies, first, certain plants; second, beverages made by infusion; and third, certain meals taken at certain times of day. It is a category that arose in the course of everyday life and communication, and it is handed down without the slightest consideration of clarity or logic. It is confused, has fuzzy boundaries and family-resemblance structure, as well as prototype structure—and yet, the use of the word *tea* causes no difficulties in everyday life.

The examples *Vieh* and *tea* are meant to demonstrate that the categories we cognitively and communicatively wield, day in and day out, are far from fulfilling the Fregean "requirement that a concept have sharp boundaries" (Frege 1979: 195; cf. Chapter 3), but present us with not even the smallest cognitive or communicative problems.

Categories and concepts are units of thought. They are engendered by the rules of use of the words we use to denote them. We do not first learn the concept 'tea', and then, in a second step, as it were, to denote this concept with the word *tea*; rather, we learn the rule of use of the word *tea* in our ordinary communication. As we learn this, we learn to differentiate between tea and non-tea, with a certain amount of tolerance for fuzzy boundaries. In scientific discourse, the opposite can occur: one is forced in the course of research to introduce new categories for which no common terms yet exist, and to come up with catchy and fitting words to name those categories. But such cases are the exception to the rule.[10]

As far as I know, the connection between concepts and rules of use is largely unexplored. The explanation of this connection is nothing less than the explanation of the connection between semantics and cognition. "Cognitive linguistics" is a discipline that studies the correlations between language and cognitive units, structures and processes. There are currently two major tendencies in the area of so-called "cognitive semantics"—one which identifies semantic structure with cognitive structure, and one which replaces this idea with a two-step model. I judge both models to be inadequate; my reasons for this are as follows. Even the two-step model assumes linguistically dependent semantic form and linguistically independent conceptual structure. I am in agreement with this model in so far as I am convinced that a theory of concepts cannot be a theory of linguistic semantics. The problem is its assumption of linguistically independent concepts, as well as a representational notion of semantics. According to this theory, signs represent semantic forms. It is not necessary to repeat here the reasons for rejecting this view. As far as I am aware, no substantiating arguments have been attempted for the first model, that of identification. At best, it is a *façon de parler* that boils down to terminological duplication. Cognitive categories, such as concepts, are equated with linguistic categories, such as meaning, without further explanation.[11] A prototypical representative of this tendency is Ronald Langacker. In his well-known essay on subjectification, he writes:

Inspired by formal logic based on truth conditions, semantic theory in the twentieth century has for the most part presupposed an *objectivist* view of meaning. Indeed, semantic textbooks often devote considerable space to explaining why the student is wrong, if not hopelessly naive, in supposing that a meaning could be anything so mysterious as a thought or concept (for example Kempson 1977:

---

[10] Such a case is noted in Chap. 7, n. 5. As another example, a new conceptual and cognitive category has arisen for a phenomenon that has existed for at least two decades: channel surfing, or rapidly changing television channels by remote control. With the use of the "catchy" expression *channel surfing*, a diffuse phenomenon becomes a practical cognitive and communicative concept—one that has been further extended to the electronic realm with the expression *surfing the Net*.

[11] "Thus every meaning is a concept, but not every concept is a meaning" (Schwarz and Chur 1993: 26, trans. K.D.).

15–20; Palmer 1981: 24–28). Recent years have nevertheless witnessed the emergence and continued elaboration of a reasonably explicit, empirically grounded *subjectivist* or *conceptualist* theory of meaning—in short, a true *cognitive semantics*. (Langacker 1990: 5)

The quotation from Langacker contains two misleading suggestions: first, he tries to awaken the impression that the only way to avoid an objectivist, truth-functional notion of semantics is to situate meanings in the head of the speaker; second, he implies that scholars are "objectivist" who hold as naive the assumption that thoughts or concepts should be equated with meanings. Neither of these implications applies, at least not to the authors he names. The non-objective aspects of meaning, such as subjectivity, perspectivity or evaluativity, are nothing other than rules of use in which the speaker's views, perspectives and values introduce conditions for the use of the respective words. The difference between the meanings of the words *stingy* and *thrifty*, for example, is that the speaker should choose *stingy* to express disapproval of the characterized disposition or behavior, and *thrifty* to show approval.

To escape the weaknesses of objectivism, it is not necessary to resort to the *Flucht in den Kopf* ("flight into the head"), as Feilke has aptly characterized the efforts of cognitive semantics (1994a: 19). Cognitively oriented semantic theories contain two fundamental errors: they are, for one, representationally conceived, with all the resulting problems; furthermore, they employ circular arguments. From observations of linguistic circumstances, the existence of corresponding cognitive structures is inferred—structures that are then used to "explain" the observed linguistic circumstances. Mark Johnson exemplifies this circularity with perfect clarity in his programmatic essay entitled "Philosophical Implications of Cognitive Semantics" (1992). I will try to summarize the basic ideas of what he calls "cognitive semantics" in four theses.

The first I would like to call the thesis of the "metaphoricity of knowledge." It runs as follows: our knowledge, our thought, our understanding and our experience are essentially imaginative, that is, metaphorical and metonymical in nature. "Human beings are fundamentally *imaginative* creatures" (Johnson 1992: 350). Our apprehension of the world is essentially metaphorical. "Meaning, metaphysics and morality are all irreducibly metaphorical" (Johnson 1992: 362).

The second central thesis is that of "systematic metaphoricity": the metaphors with which we *grasp* the world (to provide an immediate example), the *metaphors we live by*,[12] are not of a private and idiosyncratic nature. There are metaphorical patterns that appear to be largely temporally and culturally dependent. "Our actual experience is largely structured by systems of metaphors" (Johnson 1992: 350). Lakoff and Johnson call such systems "image schemas." "Image schemas are structures of imagination" (Johnson 1992: 349). They structure our experiences and our knowledge.

The third thesis will be called the "priority of bodily experience." "Cognitive semantics gives a central place to the role of our bodily experience in the structure of our conceptual systems" (Johnson 1992: 347). We use basic bodily experiences metaphorically, as a source of images for *grasping* the world.

The fourth and last thesis is that of "reflection." It states that our language reflects the way that we form categories; as Dirk Geeraerts writes in his editorial statement in the first issue of the journal *Cognitive Linguistics*, "the formal structures of language are reflections of general conceptual organization, categorization principles, processing mechanisms, and experimental environmental influences" (Geeraerts 1990: 1). Mark Johnson writes that "we try to understand language, and meaning in general, as grounded in the nature of our bodily experience and activity" (1992: 348). The fourth thesis, therefore, simply states that the claims of the first three theses somehow manifest themselves in language.

If we examine the four theses of so-called cognitive semantics together, it becomes clear that what we are dealing with is, first and foremost, a theory of cognitive structure, of conceptual acquisition. Language is only peripherally discussed. The fourth thesis, which finally brings language into play, is astoundingly trivial. Evidently, its only function is to make possible an answer to the question "How do you know what you have asserted in the first three theses?" To the questions, "How do you know that we are 'imaginative creatures', that our system of metaphors consists in the 'structures of imagination', that our knowledge is essentially metaphorical, that bodily metaphors play a predominant role, and so on?" the only answer is, "I know because I have discovered that our language is systematically metaphorical and that

---

[12] As reads the title of Lakoff and Johnson's well-known and fascinating work (1980).

bodily metaphors play an important part in naming inner and abstract events." (I will return to the question of the systematization and bodily nature of metaphor in Chapter 15; here, my sole concern is the argumentative structure of the theory.) If the semantic structure of language is the exclusive source of knowledge about cognitive structure, it is not admissible to turn cognitive structure around for the substantiation or explanation of the semantic structure of language. Cognitive semantics uses the unknown to "explain" the known. In other words, diachronic and synchronic semantics are practiced under the name *cognitive semantics*, and knowledge about the semantic structure of language (which I do not mean to devalue) is made out to be knowledge about the cognitive structure of the speakers of the language. Cognitive semantics thus proves to be a *façon de parler*, a way of using cognitive metaphors to talk about rules of use. In regard to its central points, its argumentative structure is *petitio principii*.

6

Types of Concept versus Types of Rule

I will now attempt to illustrate, with four central examples, the difference and connection between types of concept and types of rule of use. First, though, it will be necessary to agree on a working terminology.[1]

The classic idea of a concept is one that is well defined and has sharp boundaries. A correct definition of a concept is called its **intension**; the class of *existing* objects that fall under the concept is its **extension**; the class of all *possible* (past, present and future) objects that fall under the concept is usually called the concept's **comprehension**. Therefore, the intension of a concept **classifies** its comprehension. To the extension of the concept 'car' belong all presently existing cars; its comprehension includes all past, present and future cars, as well as all possible cars. If a distinguishing feature is added to a concept's intension, its comprehension (but not necessarily its extension!) becomes smaller, and vice versa. As an example, the concept 'yellow car' classifies its comprehension, that is, the class of all possible yellow cars; the concept 'yellow car with radio' classifies the class of all possible yellow cars with radios. Since there might be some yellow cars without radios, the comprehension of the concept 'yellow car' is larger than that of the concept 'yellow car with radio'. Since it is not impossible that all presently existing yellow cars have radios, or that there presently exists not a single yellow car, the only thing that can be said about the relation between the two extensions is that the extension of the concept 'yellow car with radio' cannot be larger than that of the concept 'yellow car'; the two extensions also could be equal. The statement "The larger the

---

[1] The terminology recommended here follows that of C. I. Lewis 1952.

73

intension, the smaller the extension, and vice versa" is consequently false. The statement "The larger the intension, the smaller the comprehension, and vice versa" is true. The distinguishing features common to all possible objects that fall under the concept (that is, to all elements of its comprehension) are the **essence** or the **essential features** of the concept.

The first class of concept that we will examine is that which Frege had in mind. Frege's definition of concept (see Chapter 3) represents the classic view: a concept is such that it can be said of each and every object whether it falls under that concept or not. That is, the concept maps objects into truth values. The concept is defined by its essential features, that is, by the common characteristics of the elements that belong to the concept's comprehension. The concepts 'prime number' and 'Supreme Court judge' are examples of this type of concept, which I will call *Fregean concepts*. Few concepts that correspond to the expressions of natural language are of this type. Logicians sometimes view the vagueness of natural languages as a deficit. Actually, a certain degree of vagueness is necessary for ordinary use.[2] If the definition of the concept 'circle' were restricted to exactly those figures in which every point is exactly the same distance from the figure's center, no one would ever have drawn a circle, and most people would probably never even have seen one. If the line between 'red' and 'pink' were fixed at a certain wavelength, the words *red* and *pink* could no longer be used in yarn shops without a certain amount of difficulty. If water were defined as 'H_2O + maximum 2% impurities', it could be that water flows down the Thames on one day and not on the next (or maybe never), or that there is water near its source, but not further down the river. Naturally, precision is necessary and sensible in some areas; for everyday life, however, it would be downright inconvenient. In regard to this, Pinkal writes of a *Präziserungsverbot* or "prohibition of specification" (1985: 55).

This is the kind of concept that we will examine next. Such concepts have *fuzzy boundaries*. This means that it is basically not possible for the speakers of a language to draw a sharp boundary separating the elements which fall under the concept and those which do not. The speakers have a certain amount of decision-making elbow room; that is, these concepts

---

[2] See Pinkal 1985 on various types of vagueness and lack of conceptual definition.

tolerate fuzziness. The concepts 'water', 'sick' and 'house' are examples. Where is the line between sick and well? Between a house and a shack? It is not a contingent deficit in our knowledge that makes it impossible for us to answer these questions, but the logic of the concepts. Anyone who asks his gardener to pull out the bushes and leave the trees must create an ad hoc boundary between the two.[3] "You can *draw* one; for none has so far been drawn" (Wittgenstein PI § 68).

The third class of concepts that we will consider are those with *family resemblance structure*. The metaphor of family resemblance was coined by Wittgenstein (PI § 66ff.) to illustrate the logic of concepts whose comprehension is not determined by a common feature, but by a number of overlapping features. This metaphor is best metaphorically explained: if we say that the family Smith's five daughters resemble each other, it does not have to mean that there is one feature, say the nose, in which they all resemble each other. It could mean that the first daughter has similar eyes to those of the second and the fourth; that the second daughter's nose looks like that of the third; that the fifth has the same mouth as the first and hair like that of the third and fourth daughter. With such a constellation, we would really have the impression that they all look similar. "I can think of no better expression to characterize these similarities than 'family resemblances'; for the various resemblances between members of a family . . . overlap and criss-cross in the same way" (PI § 67). Family resemblance is obviously an intransitive relation of similarity. For "normal" resemblance, if *A* resembles *B*, and *B* resembles *C*, then *A* also resembles *C*. But this is not true of our five daughters: the first resembles the second by virtue of their eyes, and the second resembles the third because of their noses, but the first has no resemblance with the third (nor does the second with the fifth).

The five daughters Smith:

1   2   3   4   5

---

[3] Cf. Hare 1963: 28.

Wittgenstein's language example is the word *Spiel* (*game*). "Consider for example the proceedings that we call 'games'. I mean board-games, card-games, ball-games, Olympic games, and so on. What is common to all of them?—Don't say: 'There *must* be something common, or they would not be called "games"'—but *look and see* whether there is anything common to all" (PI § 66). This really does seem to be the case: when we look at chess, professional soccer, computer games, Russian roulette, Monopoly, ring-a-ring o'roses and other children's games, we find no feature that is common to all. It follows that we are not able to classify the comprehension of the word *game* "beforehand," because its classification is partly ad hoc. The class of games is everything that the language community calls *games*. Nothing would prevent us from counting competitive fishing or hunting as games, but we do not. Anna Wierzbicka thinks that "the time has come to re-examine his [Wittgenstein's] doctrine of 'family resemblances', which has acquired the status of unchallengeable dogma in much of the current literature on meaning" (1990: 356). She actually identifies seven features that are shared by all of the activities called *game* in English. Of course, this does not refute Wittgenstein's assertion about the German word *Spiel*, which can be translated into English not only by *game*, but also by *play*, *match* and *gambling*. "To repeat: don't think, but look!" (PI § 66).

As a fourth class, I would like to consider those concepts that are said to have *prototype structure*. Eleanor Rosch has demonstrated in a series of essays and empirical studies (1973, 1976, 1979) that test subjects judge differently as to what members of a category are good examples for that category. The classic example of this theory is the concept 'bird'. At first glance, it makes sense: for test persons from central Europe, for example, robins and sparrows are "better" representatives of the category 'bird' than hens and geese; the latter are in turn "better" representatives than ostriches and penguins. These subjects need less reaction time to determine whether the statement "A swallow is a bird" is true than to determine the truth of "A penguin is a bird."[4] People therefore judge certain elements of the extension of some concepts to be more prototypical than others.

These are, to begin with, the empirical findings of such studies,

---

[4] A listing of the various tests that were performed to determine and substantiate prototype effects can be found in Lakoff 1987: 41 ff.

nothing more and nothing less. But confusion reigns as to how they should be interpreted.[5] Do they allow conclusions to be drawn about the nature of meaning, or the semantic structure of the respective expressions with which the categories are denoted? Can conclusions regarding the nature of our cognitive retention of semantic structures be drawn from this evidence? Does it reveal anything about the way we learn concepts? All of these interpretations of the data have been considered, and Rosch has herself frequently modified her own. Opinions run from the view "that psychological categories have internal structure" (Rosch 1973: 140) to the theory "that . . . words have different prototypical structures, i.e., that they have different conceptual centres" (Geeraerts 1988: 214). In other words, even prototype theorists can't agree on what claims they are prepared to make about prototype effects: should they be ascribed to units on the ontological, the epistemological or the linguistic level? To say that robins are more prototypical birds than hummingbirds is to speak on the ontological level; ascribing words with prototype structure belongs to the linguistic level; and those of the opinion that our concepts have prototype structure are clearly talking on the epistemological level. A cautious interpretation of subjects' prototype judgments is provided by George Lakoff. "Our basic claim will be that prototype effects result from the nature of cognitive models, which can be viewed as 'theories' of some subject matter" (Lakoff 1987: 45). If I understand his statement correctly, it means something like this: people have a particular "bird theory," that is, a certain cognitive model of the concept 'bird', and this results in different assessments as to what is a "better" and what a "worse" bird. According to one such interpretation, prototype effects are not a characteristic of words or of meanings, but of certain common-sense views about birds. They are an effect of stereotypical views. Anna Wierzbicka implicitly refers to the connection between prototypes and stereotypes when she writes that "properties such as flying, feathers, and so on are presented as essential parts of the stereotype, not as necessary features of every bird" (1990: 362). We judge those objects to be prototypical that correspond to our stereotypes.

This description seems to me reasonable and sufficiently clear; furthermore, it is compatible with Lakoff's quoted view: we have a "bird theory," a bird stereotype; consequently, we judge robins to be more

---

[5] See Lakoff 1987: 44 ff.

prototypical than penguins. The bird that best fits our stereotype is for us the prototypical bird. As Wierzbicka has correctly observed, this has nothing to do with the question of necessary and sufficient conditions for classifying something as a bird, and it does not allow the conclusion that penguins (as the expression "a worse bird" would seem to imply) do a worse job of fulfilling the conditions for the intension of the concept 'bird' than more prototypical specimens do. According to this expression ("a worse bird"), a stereotype is an epistemological unit, and a prototype an ontological unit. The existence of stereotypes and prototypes results in what Lakoff calls "prototype effects": graded responses in subjects' prototype judgments.

The findings of prototype research are often overestimated.[6] To blame is, first, cognitivist overinterpretation; second, the tendency of cognitive semantics to equate cognitive categories with semantics; and finally, the tendency to overgeneralize the areas of application of prototype theory.[7] Wierzbicka (1990) presents good arguments for the inappropriateness of ascribing prototype structure, for example, to collective concepts like 'toy', 'furniture', or 'gift'. Certain features make a bird into a bird, but they don't make a ball into a toy or a gift. Not every ball is a toy; some balls are used for professional sports. You can't necessarily tell by looking at a ball whether it's meant to be used as a toy, or in a "real" game. 'Bird' is a taxonomic concept; 'toy' is a collective one (cf. Wierzbicka 1990: 355). The intension of 'toy' classifies things not by their features, but by their uses. The world can be classified according to birds and non-birds, but not according to toys and non-toys. A toy is anything with which people can play. It makes no sense to try to decide whether an air pump is better classified under the category of toys or the category of gifts.

Up to this point, I have used the term *subjects* with the express purpose of avoiding the word *speakers*. If I had said that speakers are the ones who make prototype judgments, I would have given away the upshot of my discussion—the question of the extent to which prototype judgments are dependent on the language spoken by the subjects, or on the language in which the questions are posed. The question of whether a watermelon is a more typical melon than a honeydew melon cannot be

---

[6] See M. Posner's (1986: 58) and Wierzbicka's (1990) critiques.
[7] See also Bickerton 1990: 34 ff.

asked, for example, in Catalan, Spanish or Turkish.[8] The question of whether celery is more typical celery than lovage is nonsensical in English, but makes complete sense in French.[9] This shows that prototype effects are not independent of language. A specific conceptual hierarchy must be present in the respective language in order even to formulate the questions. Languages classify things in a language-specific manner. Fennel, dill and anise belong to the same family of plants, but in English there is no superconcept to which they all belong. Only in a language that has the superconcept X can it be tested as to which of the three plants is the more typical X.

Even though concepts are not independent of language, they cannot simply be equated with meanings. Meanings are rules of use. Rules of use engender the categories that we use to classify our world, but they are not identical with those categories. In the course of language acquisition, we are *"abgerichtet"* ("trained"), as Wittgenstein puts it,[10] to a certain language and the form of life with which that language is interwoven. In learning the correct use of words, we acquire a certain classification of the world. In so far as the biological equipment of humans and their forms of life are similar, it is to be expected that classifications will also be similar beyond the boundaries of language and culture.

Let's take a look at the word *head* and the concept 'head'. If the concept 'head' is coextensive with the use of the word *head*, the following should be true: a head is everything and only that which is called *head*. In the following paragraphs, I would like to demonstrate that concepts and rules of use require different sorts of consideration. We have a relatively clear concept 'head'. Other than some confusion (unimportant here) about where the head stops and the neck starts—say, on a parakeet—'head' is a Fregean concept, at least in regard to vertebrates: it is clear what belongs to the concept and what does not. It is the part of the body where the eyes, nose, mouth (or beak) and ears can be found. For snails, worms, squid, and rock lobster, the decision is rather more difficult. The prototypical head is the human head. Now, the use of the

---

[8] 'Watermelon': Span. *sandía*, Cat. *síndria*, Turk. *karpuz*; 'honeydew': Span. *melón*, Cat. *meló*, Turk. *kavun*.

[9] 'Celery': Fr. *céleri branche*; 'celeriac': Fr. *céleri rave*; 'lovage': Fr. *céleri vivace*.

[10] It is a matter of training in so far as primary language acquisition generally must make do without explanatory instruction; see PI § 5 ff.

word *head* is considerably more diverse than the concept 'head'. This is because, in regard to humans, the use of the word *head* interacts with the use of the words *face, mouth* and *nose*. For example, the mouth is clearly a part of the head. But when I have a piece of candy in my mouth, I cannot describe the situation with the sentence *I have a piece of candy in my head.* With the expression *in my head*, we obviously refer to just one part of the head, namely the general area of the skull. Thus we can say that we have ears on our head, but not that we have a nose on our head. You can say that someone has a brain or sawdust in his head, but not molars or a tongue. A slap in the face is not a slap on the head, and a facial injury is not a head injury, even though the face is indisputably on the front of the head. The word *head* is clearly used, on one hand, to describe and classify the part of the body above the neck; on the other hand, to describe the part of the head around the area of the skull. In the sentence, *He hit him on the head, head* clearly denotes only a part of the head; head and face together make up the head. This sounds like a logical contradiction. One strategy to avoid it might be to say that *head* is ambiguous. But there are three problems with this strategy: first, there is no need to dispel ambiguity (that is, Pinkal's "specification requirement" does not come to bear; cf. Chapter 5). Second, sentences like *The backside of my head is a head* or *I have a head on my head* are decidedly not well formed. With truly ambiguous words, sentences like this don't seem so bizarre, as the following three examples demonstrate: *That glass is not glass. We play bridge near the bridge. He had a ball at the ball.* Third, the "inferior logic" of language is neither infrequent nor irritating, as can easily be shown: the length of the arm is measured from the shoulder to the tip of the middle finger. Does this mean that the hand is part of the arm? Or do our arms end at the wrist? Do our legs end at the ankle? Regardless of the answers to these questions, if *head* is ambiguous, then so are *arm* and *leg*, and the land of ambiguous words is well on the way to overpopulation. I surmise that it is wiser to accept the fact that certain aspects of certain expressions of natural language have meanings with ad hoc character. For as we saw in the above example, we have a relatively clear concept 'head', though its boundaries become fuzzy in reference to mollusks and crustaceans (and possibly other animals as well). However, in the cases in which the concept 'head' is clearest, namely in reference to humans, our use of the word *head* is most confused.

This type of confusion seems to be typical for so-called meronomies.[11] Within the lexical structure of a language, two types of branching hierarchical structures can be distinguished: taxonomies and meronomies.

A taxonomy structures classes into partial classes. A meronomy structures objects into parts. A typical example of (a part of) a taxonomy is:

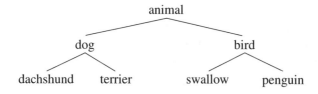

A typical example of (a part of) a meronomy is:

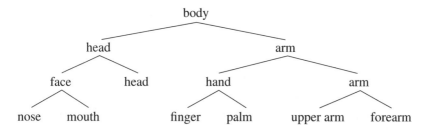

Meronomies are significantly different from taxonomies in a number of ways (see Cruse 1986: 177ff.). Here, I will discuss only two of these differences, those that are responsible for the confusion described above. The question of whether a penguin is a kind of bird, or a dog a kind of animal, can be answered by means of biological analysis and the application of classification criteria. But the question of whether one can say that the hand is a part of the arm cannot be clarified by the analysis of hands and arms. It is purely a question of language. Since a meronomy is not a hierarchy of classes, there are no division criteria in the sense of taxonomy's classification criteria. For the meronomy of body parts, at least, it seems to be typical that one and the same term of a hierarchy can be found on two ends of the same branch. If we adopt Cruse's terminology, we can say that the word *head* is used both as

---

[11] On the theory of meronomies, see Cruse 1986, chap. 8. The term *meronomy* is derived from the Greek *meros*, "part." I thank Petra Radtke for bringing my attention to the concept of meronomy.

a holonym (as a description of the whole) and as a meronym (as the description of a part of a holonym). In the case of taxonomies, speakers are relatively free in their choice of level.[12] Within a certain boundary, they have the freedom to choose the hyperonym (the term that refers to the superclass) or the hyponym (the term that refers to a part of the hyperonomic class). It is possible, for example, to say *I've bought myself a pet* if I've just acquired a hamster. (Though it might be a bit strange to say *I've bought myself an organism* if I've just purchased tomato plants for the garden.) With meronomies, however, it appears that speakers may not choose the term that refers to the whole (the holonym) when they mean only a part of it: my body reaches from the top of my head to the tip of my toe, but I don't wear a cap on my body. My arm reaches from my shoulder to the tips of my fingers, but I don't have fingernails on my arm. It follows that a term that is used both as a holonym and as a meronym is always interpreted in a meronymic sense, if such an interpretation is possible. This means that the terms of a meronomy tend to be interpreted in the more specific sense: *She has a wound on her arm* means that the wound in question is not on her hand. *He has a tattoo on his body* implies that said tattoo is not on his arm. At this point, I will interrupt these provisional considerations. To my knowledge, more detailed analyses of meronomic hierarchies are lacking. Let us return to our central line of argument.

The examples I have listed should make it clear, on the one hand, that concepts are not independent of language, and on the other, that concepts cannot simply be equated with meanings. Concepts are engendered by meanings. They are the units of our thought, formed by the rules of use of our language. "It is one of the commonest mistakes in philosophy . . . to suppose that all rules determining meaning have to be of the same kind, i.e. that all terms have meaning in the same sort of way," notes Richard Hare (1963: 7–8). I would now like to show that the four types of concept described here (Fregean and fuzzy concepts, concepts with family-resemblance structure and prototype structure) are engendered by linguistic signs that have different types of meaning-determinative rules of use. Four types of rule of use correspond to these four types of concept.

---

[12] Thanks to Petra Radtke for her observation about different kinds of restriction in regard to choice of level.

There are words whose use we acquire and retain through explicit definition. A prime number is a whole number that is divisible by 1 and by itself. I learned this in grade school, and these are my criteria for deciding whether a number is a prime number or not. I try to use the term *prime number* only in reference to, or to characterize, numbers that fit this definition. The concept 'prime number' corresponds to rules of use whose criteria are exclusively truth-conditional features. Such rules of use produce Fregean concepts.

I did not learn the use of the words *water* or *house* by means of explicit definition. We use *water* to refer to what comes out of the tap, what we drink, what we wash and bathe with, what flows in rivers, lakes and seas, what comes down as rain, and so on. Water is good for swimming, drinking, washing, watering plants, etc. The criteria for the use of the word *water* include not only the features of the liquid that is so named, but also its use and appearance. Rules of use whose criteria for the respective word are the indicated object's uses typically produce concepts with fuzzy boundaries, that is, fuzzy concepts, since the range of the object's usefulness is itself usually rather fuzzy. Many rules of use have both the object's features and its uses as criteria. The meaning of the word *house* is one example of this. I'm not sure if mobile homes and churches (as in "house of God") are houses, but I'm fairly certain that igloos and teepees are not. Houses are meant for living in, as igloos and teepees are, but unlike them, houses are, to some degree, solidly built and relatively bound to a certain place for a certain amount of time.

We do not learn the meaning of the word *bird* by means of definition; nor do we use the word to indicate animals that are used in a certain way (in contrast to, for example, *livestock* or *game*, whose rules of use produce fuzzy concepts). Rather, we learn the use of the word *bird* by means of typical examples: we call those little feathered animals that hop and fly around in the back yard *birds*, along with all animals that are similar in relevant ways (cf. Bickerton 1990: 34). Rules of use of this type produce concepts with prototype structure. What count as relevant similarities is something that children learn gradually in the course of time; the "strange" specimens, such as penguins and emus, they learn to subsume explicitly and ad hoc. Thus the rule of use for *prime number* is similar to that of *bird* in that both have features of the object as criteria for the use of the word. However, we were given the rule of use for *prime number* explicitly, whereas for the word *bird*, we have to work it out inductively, a process accompanied by all the correspondent uncertainties of over- and undergeneralization. For the meaning of the expression *prime number*, we do not learn "7 is a prime number, as well as everything that is similar to 7 in a relevant way." Seven may indeed be the most frequently named prime number, but it is not a prototypical prime number in the way a sparrow is a prototypical bird, or a fish with the size and shape of a herring is a prototypical fish. When the idea of prototypes is applied to concepts that classify their comprehension according to the object's uses (if a hammer, for example, is a more prototypical tool than a pencil), one should at least be aware that it is necessary to distinguish between two different types of prototype structure.

Imagine that we are studying how the men of a small tribe in the South Pacific perform bungee jumping. How might we decide if their actions are a game? What kind of information would we need? If they do it for the pure joy of a free fall, we could call it a game; however, it could also be a sport. What if they get money from the crowd for their jumps, or if they have to jump in order to marry? What if it is a rite that one performs upon turning 40, or if they're all professional bungee jumpers? As I see it, it would be impossible for us to decide if it is a game or not. We might ask ourselves if we would call it a *game* if we were to do such a thing. But that would not help us in the least with our decision. Competitive fishing is not called a game, as far as I know, but I think that bullfighting could be. Russian roulette is a game; a pistol duel is not. Playing the stocks for thrills might be called a game, if we stretch it; and speculating with venture capital can be a game, too.

The rule of use for the word *game* is guided by a number of prototypes that we learn, ad hoc, to designate as games. As children, we learn that Monopoly is a game, that soccer is a game and that "playing house" is a game. We are able to learn this without having to suppose among them any common features whatsoever. Additionally, almost all children's activities that serve no life-sustaining purpose we also call *games*. In calling a number of prototypes *games* ad hoc, we end up with a disjunction of features that can easily be recombined, as in: "An activity is called a *game* when it is practiced for its own sake and is fun, or when it has a lot of rules and a winner, or when there's a chance or a challenge to be taken, or when it serves as practice in preparation for another activity, etc., along with all activities that are similar to these in a relevant way." Such a rule can easily be expanded with the addition of positive or negative ad hoc rules, such as: "Activities that serve a religious purpose cannot be called games." Rules of use of this sort produce family-resemblance structure. We may assume that most languages do not have many words with such disorderly rules of use. Like other disorderly aspects of language, such words require relatively a high frequency of use and interpretation-aiding contextual integration, in addition to a high degree of tolerance and acceptance on the part of the speakers. If I read "iced peach tea" in a café's list of beverages, I would accept its designation as *tea* without question, because of family-resemblance structure (and a certain amount of charity towards the authors of the menu)—even though I ordinarily might not call such a drink *tea*.

To summarize, we can say that there are rules of use that employ clearly recognizable features of the object as criteria for word use; these produce **Fregean concepts**. Rules of use that employ the uses or usefulness of the reference object as criteria produce **fuzzy concepts**. Rules of use that have prototypical examples of the reference object and relations of similarity as criteria for use produce **concepts with prototype structure**. Finally, rules of use whose criteria are a disjunction of prototypical examples of reference objects, together with relations of similarity, produce **concepts with family-resemblance structure**.

Concepts are functions that map objects into truth values. This is what we learned from Frege (see Chapter 3). Is this definition generally applicable, or only for the concepts that Frege has in mind, namely those that "have the property of yielding a genuine sentence when saturated by any meaningful proper name," and which therefore "must yield the proper name of a truth value" (1979: 195)? We have seen that most ordinary concepts do not have "sharp boundaries" (Frege 1979: 195). Nevertheless, I believe that Frege's definition can be generalized, if only we divest it of the requirement of sharp boundaries. What does it mean to say that a concept maps objects (in the broadest sense of the word) into truth values? It means that anyone who knows the concept 'house' can say of every *x* whether the statement *x is a house* is true or false. Colloquially, one might say that anyone who knows the concept 'house' knows what a house is. This is exactly the case, regardless of the fact that there are "objects" for which I am unsure whether I should *term* them houses or not. The rule of use for the word *house* allows the speaker a certain amount of freedom in deciding whether she can call a mobile home a *house* or not. *Freedom* of decision does not mean the *inability* to decide. I know what water is, what a house is, whether I am sick or not, and so on. That is, I am capable of assigning a truth value to every completion of the functions *x is water*, *x is a house* or *x is sick*. The difference between the concepts 'house' and 'prime number' is the fact that, in some cases, I may decide if a mobile home belongs to the class of houses, but I may not decide if, for example, the number *o* belongs to the class of prime numbers.

Concepts with family-resemblance structure also map objects into truth values. Anyone who is familiar with the concept 'game' knows what's a game and what's not. In some cases, the speakers have some freedom of decision, and in some cases there are ad hoc rules. That there are no *uniform* criteria for deciding does not mean that a decision cannot be made as to whether something is a game or not.

With concepts that have prototype structure, another aspect comes to bear. The concept 'bird' undoubtedly maps objects into truth values, but the judgments are weighted, as it were. This prioritization does not concern the judgments themselves, but the degree of conformity of the category members with standard expectations, that is, with the stereotype. Since the question of prototypes concerns the prioritization and not the judgment, prototype structure is not precluded for any of the types of concept described here. A concept that has prototype structure can be a Fregean concept such as 'bird' (there are, in regard to the current state of evolution, no animals whose membership in the class of birds is dependent on the speaker's decision), or a fuzzy concept, such as 'tea' or 'house'. A concept with family-resemblance structure also necessarily has prototype structure. If family resemblance is defined by the absence of a common criterion and the existence of overlapping criteria, it should not preclude the possibility of concepts with family-resemblance structure and sharp boundaries. I am not aware of any such concept, but one could be defined.

7

Expression and Meaning

In the previous chapters, we have acquainted ourselves with different prototypical notions of linguistic signs. The quintessence of the exposition up to this point has been:

(1) Linguistic signs serve us to communicate, classify and represent.

(2) A theory of the representative capacity of linguistic signs provides no answer to the question of which property of a sign enables it to represent something (whatever that something may be), or more generally, by virtue of which property a sign is suitable for communication.

(3) This does not mean that theories of meaning as use and representational theories are mutually exclusive. Cognitivist theories are generally representationally conceived.

(4) The question "By virtue of which property is a sign suitable for communication?" can be answered only by a theory of meaning as use.

Until now, our discussion has considered only the established signs of a language. But how do signs emerge? How do new signs arise from old signs? How and why do signs change? At this point, we will turn to the question of the genesis and change of linguistic signs.

The signs of a language can come into existence through intentional, creative acts. In scientific discourse, it is common practice to create signs and intentionally modify them. Every non-redundant definition is such a creative or modifying act. We will not discuss these forms of genesis and change here, as they are relatively uninteresting for linguistic and sign theory. More interesting are the ordinary, everyday forms of genesis and change. They are typically produced by the speakers of a language, but neither intentionally nor knowingly. In almost all cases, the establishment of linguistic signs is a side effect of communicative endeavors. Linguistic signs are the result of communicative attempts, not their prerequisite! If the mastery of a fully established language were necessary for communication, it would be possible to explain neither how that language could have come into being, nor how children learn the language of their surroundings. Primary language acquisition clearly requires (among other things) that children can adequately interpret, at least to some extent, the communicative attempts of a particular language. Assuming that a child is able to understand his mother's utterances only after he has fully learned her language makes the mystery of language acquisition appear completely insoluble.

In accordance with the theory I presented in Keller 1994 (chapter 4), established linguistic signs are a phenomenon of the third kind: they are neither natural phenomena, like the "dance language" of bees, nor artifacts, like the Morse code and the pictographic alphabet created for the Olympics. Rather, they are the unintended results of a large number of intentional communicative acts. An adequate theory of language must not only explain and describe the functioning of language, but also come to terms with the fact that every so-called natural language is subject to a constant process of change. Such a theory must view language change as a phenomenon immanent to language use. Erica García demands that "our synchronic description should . . . ideally be such that language change would not require any extra linguistic explanation" (1985: 276). It follows that an adequate theory of linguistic signs must also view sign change as immanent to sign use. Linguistic signs are not stable entities that "suffer" change due to extraordinary adverse conditions; they are by nature dynamic and thus only rarely remain unchanged over long periods of time. In other words, their unmarked state is change, or, as Anttila and Embleton write, "Change is the essence of meaning" (1989: 157).[1] The theoretical basis of a dynamic sign theory consists in, first, an evolutionary conception of language (see Keller 1994: chapter 6), and second, the view that the meaning of an established sign

---

[1] This is also the central theme of Michael Shapiro's writings on linguistic sign theory (cf. Shapiro 1991).

is the rule of its use in the respective language. The view called a *theory of meaning as use* was presented in Chapter 4. We will now take a more detailed look at linguistic signs, namely at the aspect of their communicative instrumentality. For the relevant location of the process of sign genesis and change is not to be found in our heads, but in the situation of use. Signs develop and change in the course of their communicative deployment.

The word *communication* is used in extremely diverse ways. Practically every form of influence that one system has on another can be called *communication*: animals, brain cells etc.—all of them can communicate. Just about any interpretively useful event can be called *communication*; in that case, a hook to the jaw is communicative, as is wearing a tie, or blades of grass waving in the wind. I will use the word *communication*, as is common in linguistics and the philosophy of language, with a very specialized meaning: *communication* will denote every intentional behavior, performed in an open manner and with the aim of bringing an addressee to recognize something. Precise definitions of *communication* are very complex. Roland Posner (1992: chapter 3.3) presents one on the basis of the Gricean definition[2] of what it means to "mean" something and shows how communicative acts can be theoretically construed from less complex acts. Here, the following informal characterization shall suffice: communication in the sense relevant to this text is *influencing others*, specifically, by giving them to understand—through signs (in the broadest sense of the word)—that to which one wants to lead them, in hopes that this knowledge may be reason enough for them to let themselves be influenced in the desired way.[3] In our context, the important thing about this definition is that, first and foremost, communication is a form of influence; second, that such influence can be qualified as communication only when it takes place by way of cognizance. Under certain conditions, the imperative *Go down the stairs* is not much different, as regards the intended goal, than a kick. Both forms of influence can bring forth the desired reaction from the addressee, namely the act of going down the stairs. But only the imperative is communication in the sense intended here. For it is true only of the imperative—and not of the kick—that the desired influence comes about through the addressee's

---

[2] See Grice 1957, 1968, and 1969.
[3] This is one possible reformulation of Grice's notion of meaning.

recognition of what the other wants him to do, *and* that exactly this knowledge is reason enough for him to let himself be influenced in the desired way. For the influence in the form of a kick, the conditions before the *and* of the previous sentence can very well apply; the conditions after the *and* definitely do not. As Philipp Wegener wrote in 1885, "The purpose of our speaking is always to influence the will or the understanding of another person in the way that seems to the speaker to be valuable" (Wegener 1885: 67).[4] Communication is aspiring to influence others while retaining respect for their freedom of choice.

Communication is thus letting others perceive something which, along with their previous general and situation-specific knowledge, allows them to recognize what one wants them to recognize. Of course, the goal of such influence does not have to be anything dramatic. Even if I just say *hi* to someone, a desire is present to influence her in the sense described here: I want to get her to recognize, for example, that I have seen her; since failing to greet someone can be an affront under certain conditions, the least that I might want her to recognize with my greeting is that the state of our acquaintance has not changed.

The means that one uses in attempting to get others to recognize what one wants them to recognize are generally called **signs**. Signs, therefore, are clues with which the speaker "furnishes" the addressees, enabling and leading them to **infer** the way in which the speaker intends to influence them. Signs are not, as I have already hinted, containers[5] used for the transport of ideas from one person's head to another. Signs are hints of a more or less distinct nature, inviting the other to make certain inferences and enabling that other to reach them. "Thoughts do not travel" (Sperber and Wilson 1986a: 1). The process of making such an inference is called **interpretation**; the goal of this process is **understanding**.

Communication, then, is an act that consists of giving the other hints that put into motion by that person a process of interpretation, the aim of which is discovering the desired goal of the attempted influence, that is, understanding the speaker's act.

Even at this early stage, it is necessary to distinguish between two

---

[4] Trans. K.D.

[5] On the fateful consequences of the conceptualization of communication as a conduit operation, see Reddy 1979. For a critique of the view that communication involves the packing and unpacking of "contents," see also Sperber and Wilson 1986a: chap. 1.

perspectives: that of the speaker[6] and that of the addressee. That which has been described so far is the speaker's perspective, and is true, as stated above, only for intentional communication. From the perspective of the addressee, the question of significance looks somewhat different, because not everything interpretable, nor everything that actually is interpreted, must have been communicated. This is true in a double sense. First, events can be interpreted that clearly have no communicative purpose: fingerprints, storm clouds, measles spots, and so on. Second, every communicative act has non-communicative side effects, and nothing prevents the addressee from making them into objects of interpretation: tone of voice, handwriting, volume, accent, and so on. Thus there is an asymmetry between communication and interpretation. The addressee's interpretive attempts are not restricted to a boundary formed by the speaker's intentions (cf. Keller 1994: 96ff.). The addressee can go beyond those intentions; every interpretation based on the criticism of language makes systematic use of this possibility. The role of the addressees in the game of communication is solely the attempt to get at (that is, interpret) what the speaker intends them to recognize. Whatever the addressees interpret over and above this is their own doing; the speaker cannot be accused of having meant it. On the other hand, the speaker must go on the assumption that the addressees will recognize only that which the speaker's signs make easily accessible. Even if I tend to speak with a Texas accent, I cannot use this tendency to back up a reproach like "But I *told* you I'm from Dallas!" However, I can use my accent—at my own risk, as it were—to get this across to others. The asymmetry of communication and interpretation is very important for the genesis of signs. Humans not only **use** signs for the purpose of exerting influence, they **make use of** things, events, and so forth, **as** signs. They use perceptible things in the world to infer that which is only indirectly perceptible, and to lead others to the same inferences. Things can become signs through exploitative use. The most fundamental principle of every kind of sign use is that directly perceptible things are used to

---

[6] It would be more appropriate to say, rather than *speaker*, something like *communicant*, since a communicative act must not be verbal; nor must it be stated in formal language. For example, people can wave their hands to warn others of danger. For purposes of brevity, a waving person is also called a "speaker." This is an example of a concept for which there is no established expression available (cf. Chap. 5, n. 8).

infer (from the perspective of the addressee) that which is not directly perceptible; or (from the perspective of the speaker) to encourage another to make inferences that are not directly perceptible.

Every sign has two sides, expression and meaning, and they are joined in the act of semiosis. This description, which goes back to Saussure (1960: 66), is misleading for two reasons. For one, talk of semiosis encourages the inadequate view that what is combined in semiosis must have existed independently before the connection was made.[7] Now, theorists of semiotic connection usually deny the pre-semiotic existence of semiotic partners, but neglect to explain why the logical inconsistency—inherent in speaking of the connection of two units which, unconnected, do not exist—does not bother them. Second, talk of two sides—even if they are said to be as indivisible as the two sides of a piece of paper (Saussure 1960: 113)—encourages the reification of meaning. Of course, theorists of dualistic conceptions of signs are not to blame for this. They really did have a reified notion of meaning. The *signifiant*—an *image acoustique*—is held together with the *signifié*—a *concept*—by a bond—a *liège*, writes Saussure (1960: 67). A black tie, for example, is a sign in Germany; wearing it is (among other things) a sign that the wearer is in mourning. I would find it misleading if someone were to say that my tie has two sides that are combined in the act of semiosis and held together by a bond. Of course, such a manner of speech can be rescued by an appropriate interpretation of its metaphoricity. But it is easier simply to avoid it. Rather than talking of sides, I will talk of the two aspects of signs.

Every sign has two aspects, that of perceptibility and that of interpretability. The uses of signs are thus sensually perceptible things, circumstances, acts or events that are held to be interpretable. Interpretability must not be the primary function of that which is regarded to be a sign, but it must be one of its functions or possible uses. The primary function of a car, for example, is transportation, but it can also serve as a sign, signifying its owner's affiliation with a particular group.

Sometimes it is unclear, or disputable, whether something is a sign or not. This uncertainty can have two sources, either the aspect of interpretability or that of perceptibility. "Signs from above" and stellar constellations come to mind, for example. In such cases, the question of

---

[7] In regard to this, see Hjelmslev's critique of Saussure 1963: 48ff.

interpretability is often a matter of dispute. Those who hold these things to be signs must believe that they are interpretable, or (an even stronger assumption) that they exist to be interpreted. Sometimes, amazingly, even the question of perceptibility comes up. Consider auras, conversations with the dead, ground radiation, hidden water veins, godly messages, and so on. Here again, whoever believes that these things are signs must also believe them to be perceptible.

If one of these two aspects is lacking, it is not as though we have a sign that is somehow incomplete; rather, the thing in question is just not a sign. (This is the point of the theory that the two "sides" of a sign are "indivisible.") Trivially speaking, something that lacks the aspect of perceptibility cannot be a sign. The question of interpretability cannot arise in regard to things that are imperceptible. Analogously, something perceptible but not interpretable is also not a sign.

At this point, I would like to make the following terminological stipulation:

> The property by virtue of which a sign is perceptible will be called **sign expression**; the property by virtue of which a sign is interpretable will be called **sign meaning**.

This stipulation has two important consequences.

(1) Expression and meaning are defined as aspects of signs. Consequently, everything that is not an aspect of the sign itself does not qualify as a candidate for the meaning of the sign. Thus meaning is situated neither on the ontological level, as it is in Frege's or in naive-realistic common-sense theories, nor on the epistemological level, as it is in Saussure's or cognitivist theories. Rather, meaning is where it belongs: on the linguistic level.

(2) According to this, an expression is always the expression of a sign, and meaning is always the meaning of a sign. "An expression is expression only by virtue of being an expression of a content, and a content is content only by virtue of being a content of an expression," writes Louis Hjelmslev (1963: 48–9), calling this relation of mutual dependency *solidarity* (1963: 24).[8]

The second point needs some explanation. Its thesis is that there can be no meaning without expression, and no expression without meaning. We

---

[8] Cf. also R. Posner 1991: chap. 4.1.

will begin by considering the first part of the thesis. Trivially speaking, perceptibility is a condition of intepretability for the thing that is to be interpreted. There is, by definition, no case of a meaning for which there is no expression.

The first part of the thesis is thus a truism. Its second part, however, is more problematic: what's wrong with viewing a random string of letters, say *nobenish*, as an expression without meaning? The answer is as follows: if *expression* is not defined as the expression of a meaning, there is no criterion for identity. Consider this game: I make a gesticulatory movement, and you have to imitate it. If you make a mistake, you are penalized. (Games of this kind are played by children, and in another version, as I understand it, by some fraternities, as a drinking game for initiating the "pledges.") The point of such games is that other players have no chance of winning, because they never know what belongs to the movement and what does not: I raise my glass. Is the fact that I have my pinky extended important? Does it belong to the movement to be imitated? What about the fact that I have my left elbow on the table? The players have no criterion for deciding. The same is true of the "meaningless expression" *nobenish*: if *nobenish* is an expression without meaning, are NOBENISH and "nobenish" identical expressions? Or are we dealing with different expressions? Are they homographic or homophonic expressions? There is no criterion for deciding this. For the identical is only identical in regard to a certain aspect. The aspect in which different representations of a sign are identical is its meaning. This is why expression and meaning "need" each other in order to exist. The expression needs the meaning as a criterion of identity, and the meaning needs the expression for materialization. Of course, for a really innovative expression, used for the first time, this does not apply. If I make a gesture at the train station to warn you of a pickpocket approaching from the side—a quick movement of my eyes and a simultaneous grab at my pocket—it is a gesture that follows no conventional rules. Its constitutive parts have not been established, nor what would count as a repetition of the same gesture. Its salience[9] and contextuality must make clear its purpose, namely to be interpreted, thus producing its identity and identifiability.

Our definition of expression and meaning says that expression is that which makes the sign perceptible, and meaning is that which makes the

---

[9] On the concept of salience, see Lewis 1969: 38, 159.

sign interpretable. It is very important to point out that this definition deals with potentialities. The expression is not what we perceive, but what makes the sign perceptible. The meaning is not what we interpret, but what makes the sign interpretable. When I see NO, I perceive something different from what I perceive when I see *No* or **No**. But I still see the same sign three times, namely in three different realizations. What makes this sign perceptible is the fact that there are rules for its realization—rules of phonological, phonetic and, if applicable, orthographic and graphemic nature. To know the expression of a sign is to know the rules of its realization.

The same goes for meaning. That which makes a sign understandable is not to be confused with "that which is meant," that is, denoted or meant by the speaker. The denoted object, or that which is meant by the speaker, are not parts of the sign. Ideas, thoughts and intentions are not aspects of signs. Intentions are realized with signs, just as wishes can be realized with money. But intention is as much an aspect of a sign as a wish is an aspect of a coin—namely, not at all. Ideas and thoughts can be communicated **by virtue of** sign meaning. If I want to communicate a thought to you, I choose a sign that is suitable for the communication of that idea. If and when you have understood the thought that I wanted to communicate to you, this was by virtue of the fact that you knew the meaning of my chosen means; on the basis of this knowledge (and other assorted assumptions), you drew the inferences to which I wanted to lead you.

We can put it like this: anyone who knows the meaning of my words, including their syntactic connections, has a fairly good chance of understanding what I mean, that is, my thoughts and ideas. But that which puts the addressee in a position to get at my thoughts, namely, the meaning of the signs, is not identical to my thoughts; rather, it is the means and possibility of their communication. If meaning were something to do with thoughts or cognition, if it were something mental, it could not be an aspect of signs. For language, and thus signs, have no spirit, no psyche and no intentions; just as the rod feels no pain. As above, "Cut the pie any way you like, 'meanings' just ain't in the head!" (Putnam 1978: 65).

PART III

Sign Emergence

8

Basic Techniques of Interpretation

Considered in their communicative aspect, signs are, as we have seen, an aid for inferring something not directly perceptible from something that is. This is as seen from the perspective of their interpreter. From the perspective of the speaker (in the widest sense of the word), signs are a pattern for the production of perceptible things, things given to the interpreters to bring them to infer the way in which the speaker intends to influence them. The ability to interpret is primary. The ability to communicate makes systematic use of the ability to interpret. The communicating person exploits the interpretive ability of the addressee for his or her, the speaker's, own gain.[1] Interpretation is (among other things) making inferences on the basis of systematic, or supposedly systematic, connections. In deciding to call *meaning* that which makes the interpretation of signs possible, we do nothing other than call *meaning* exactly that which serves the interpreters as the basis for their inferences. Thus we will view meaning as the systematic connections by virtue of which signs are interpretable.

What are the systematic connections that come into question for this role? There are exactly three: the connections that we use for interpretation can be causally based, similarity based, or rule based. In other words, we are able to make causal, associative and/or rule-based inferences. *Quartum non datur*. I would like to call these three procedures the **basic techniques of interpretation**. As we will see, they play a

---

[1] "Each sign must have its peculiar Interpretability before it gets any Interpreter" (PW 111). Cf. also Sperber and Wilson 1986a: 176: "Human external languages are of adaptive value only for a species already deeply involved in inferential communication."

decisive part in the "life" of signs. Interpreting spotty skin as measles, or waving blades of grass as a sign of wind, is a causal inference; interpreting a picture of a pig with a red slash over it (as can be found accompanying the meals on some flights to countries with Muslim populations) as a sign for food that complies to Muslim standards, is an associative inference; interpreting *bye-bye* as a parting greeting is clearly a rule-based inference, drawn by someone who knows the rules of use of the expression and employs them to infer exactly this.

Following an accepted nomenclature, I would like to call the three basic techniques of interpretation the **symptomic**, the **iconic** and the **symbolic techniques**. Correspondingly, **symptoms** are signs that are interpreted with causal inferences, **icons** are signs that are interpreted with associative inferences, and **symbols** are signs interpreted with rule-based inferences. With this, I have adopted several expressions that others, mostly Peirce and his followers, have previously employed. Peirce's terms are *index*, *icon* and *symbol*.[2] My partial adoption of Peircean terminology might lead to the assumption that my intention is to interpret Peirce, and consequently to the accusation that I interpret him incorrectly. However, I intend to provide neither an interpretation nor a reformulation of Peirce. His theory of signs is probably one of the most elaborate representational sign theories around: "A sign, or representamen, is something which stands to somebody for something in some respect or capacity." In the following paragraphs, I will contrast his definitions of *index*, *icon* and *symbol* with, respectively, my definitions of *symptom*, *icon* and *symbol*.

Usually, these three types of signs are distinguished and defined within the framework of a representationally conceived theory of signs. The basis of their definition is thus the kind of relations that hold between the sign and its denotatum.

"*Aliquid stat pro aliquo*," reads the scholastic definition of signs: something stands for something else. Ever since, sign theorists have concerned themselves with the relation of "standing for," and searched for adequate candidates for its arguments: what stands for what? Some of the answers have been, for example, that the sign stands for an object; that the sign stands for a concept; that the expression stands for the meaning;

---

[2] A good and readable presentation of Peircean sign theory is provided by Nagel 1992. See also Lyons 1977: chap. 4.2.

that the expression stands for a concept; that the expression stands for an idea or an association; that the expression stands for an object as mediated by a concept; and many more (cf. Lyons 1977: 96ff.). There are two main reasons for the wide variety of offers.

(1) The sign is not always systematically distinguished from its use. Or, to put it differently, the sign is said to have properties that it has, at best, only with certain uses.

(2) "Standing for" is an unexplained metaphor; it would have to be subjected to clear interpretation before a search for candidates for arguments in support of this relation might begin.

The metaphor of standing for is probably the basis of the observation that signs are used to infer something not directly perceptible, or not directly obvious, from something that is. Therein lies the point of sign use, as it were. Representational conceptions of signs reify both aspects of sign use, construing their perceptibility as a replacement or representative of that which is not directly perceptible: the expression stands for that which is meant. But signs make inferences possible. Otherwise it is like saying that the premise stands for the conclusion. According to the theory of signs that I propose here, it makes no sense whatsoever to say of signs that they stand for something, not even charitably or in a metaphoric sense. At best, the metaphor of "standing for" can be used, if charitably interpreted, to indicate the relation in which a certain use of a sign stands to that which is meant or denoted. Some linguistic signs can be used to "stand for something." In the utterance made on May 28, 1997, "Robin Cook indicated that he intends to discuss the matter with the prime minister," one could say, metaphorically and reifyingly, that *prime minister* stands for Tony Blair. That is to say, in this utterance, the sign *prime minister* is used to refer to Tony Blair. When a sign "stands for something," as in this case, it is by virtue of its meaning. Therefore, we may not say that a sign stands for its meaning. Rather, meaning is that which enables the sign to be used for the purpose of referring to something. The sign itself, when not in use, stands for nothing at all, just as an unused whip causes no pain.

Sometimes it is said that a sign has meaning only when used. (From this it follows, incidentally, that there are signs without meaning: namely, every sign that is not momentarily in use.) This notion is a result of the notion that signs stand for something. For if they stand for something, they do so only when they are used. Linguistic signs (and other symbols), according to my theory, certainly have meaning even when they are not momentarily in use. After all, it is meaning that makes a sign usable in the first place! Chess pieces still have meaning, that is, a function in the game (not in a particular round!), even if they are lying in a box. Signs have meaning in the language, not in the uttered sentence (cf. Wittgenstein PI § 559). Near the end of this chapter, I will introduce the term *sense* for what a speaker means with the use of his or her signs in a particular sentence.

Let us return to the three types of sign I have defined by means of the three basic techniques of interpretation. The reason for my excursus about the relation of "standing for" is that symptoms, icons and symbols are usually defined according to the kind of relation in which the sign stands to the denotatum. People assume that symptoms, icons and symbols each stand for things in different ways, and try to make these differences definitively useful:

(1) The relation of a symptom to its denotatum is that of naturalness.

(2) The relation of an icon to its denotatum is that of similarity.

(3) The relation of a symbol to its denotatum is that of arbitrariness.

This is a somewhat crude characterization of the attempt to define these three types of sign according to relationships of representation. It is further assumed of the relation of arbitrariness, for example, that it exists "within" the symbol, so to speak; that is, between the "expression side" and the "content side" of the symbol. Or it is assumed that arbitrariness is a relationship between "the sign and its signification" (Lyons 1977: 100). As I will later undertake a more detailed consideration of the concept of arbitrariness, this brief reference will suffice for now.

The attempt summarized above to define three types of sign is inadequate for two reasons: first, the relation of representation is inappropriate, as I have frequently emphasized; this is especially true of symptoms, as I will demonstrate shortly. Second, the postulated underlying relations are non-homogenous; naturalness, similarity and arbitrariness are not on the same level.

The three types of sign in my proposed definition are distinguished solely by the techniques of their interpretation. Consequently, something that is an icon for one person can be a symbol for another. The speaker

may use a sign that is already a symbol for her, but which is still interpreted by the hearer as an icon. The deciding factor is the chosen technique of interpretive inference. The change of a sign from one type to
another, such as an icon becoming a symbol, is a change in the chosen
technique of inference. That is, in order to explain how a symptom or an
icon, over a certain period of time, becomes a symbol, one must demonstrate how causal inference is replaced over the course of time with associative or rule-based inference. Before I do this, I would like to examine
each of the three types of sign in succession. Talk of three types of sign
is slightly reifying, but practical. This reification is unproblematic,
I think, as long as we keep in mind that our primary concern is the three
techniques for the interpretation of sign expression.

   Symptoms are, in a certain sense, the simplest and most archaic signs.
Other animals, not just humans, are capable of making causal inferences. Baboons that live in the steppe, for example, are able to interpret
certain movements of blades of grass as a sign of danger, namely, as a
symptom of approaching big cats (Sommer 1989: 150ff.). The red spots
that "mean" measles are probably the most frequently cited example
of a symptom in the literature on linguistics (Grice 1957). Symptoms
also play a role in human communication: blushing is a sign of embarrassment, trembling a sign of fear, a loud voice a sign of anger, tears a
sign of sadness, a smirk the sign of *Schadenfreude*, and my accent a
sign of origin.

   Symptoms are signs only in a certain sense, for they are not intentionally used. They are just "there," and intentional use often changes their
character. In that case, as we will see in Chapter 11, they cease to be
symptoms. Symptoms are not there for the express purpose of communication. Rather, it is their interpretive use that makes them into signs. The
ability to interpret is more basic than the ability to bring someone to a
certain interpretation. The second of the two abilities implies the first.
Symptoms are therefore more elementary signs than icons and symbols.

   If the metaphor of "standing for" is anywhere completely wrongly
applied, it is in regard to symptoms. This is because spots—to stick with
the example of measles—do not, of course, "stand for" measles; they
are just a part of the disease. Moving blades of grass do not "stand for"
approaching lions; rather, the lions make the grass move. Trembling is
a part of my fearful behavior, blushing a part of my embarrassment. (In
such cases we can be deceived by outmoded, dualistic views, according

to which fear and embarrassment are "really" mental and not physical phenomena. According to this notion, the body is just a reflection of the soul.)

The assumption that a part is always a sign of the whole would lead to veritable sign inflation. This makes it clear that symptoms are not symptoms per se, but that they become symptoms only through their interpretive use. My left foot is a part of my self. It would be inappropriate to assume that I walk around on symptoms. However, if just this foot were sticking out of an avalanche cone, I would gladly accept its interpretation as a symptom of me. Jaroslav Jiránek argues that this applies to "every kind of sign, not just 'symptoms' " (Jiránek 1992: 374).[3] Every sign becomes that kind of sign "only in the case" that it is interpreted as such. If we take this idea literally, it follows that a sign ceases to be a sign when it is not interpreted as such. Do the traffic signs in a deserted street at 3 a.m. cease to be signs until someone comes along and happens to see them? This would be a strange theory indeed. But for symptoms, it is absolutely true! After my happy rescue from the avalanche, my left foot ceases to be a symptom of my self, until someone again interprets it as such.

The notion that signs are only signs when interpreted as such could be charitably interpreted and understood as follows: signs are signs only when they are in use as signs within a group. In fact, this is true of symbols, but certainly not of symptoms! Symptoms are precisely *not* "in use" in the sense that symbols and some icons are. No matter how you look at it, there is an essential asymmetry between symptoms and other signs. The point of each and every sign consists in being used to infer the less-than-obvious from the perceptible. Icons and symbols are created for this purpose, while symptoms are not. Doctors use perceptible spots to infer the imperceptible remainder and thus the whole, the disease. They infer the whole from a part. With this, spots become symptoms.

Thus we may provisionally assert that a part is a symptom of the whole in situations when the part is used to infer the whole.

To recall the goal of our analysis: in what does the meaning of a sign consist? We decided to call *meaning* the systematic connections by virtue of which a sign is interpretable. What it is that enables doctors to infer that someone with spots is sick with measles? It is their knowledge that

---

[3] Trans. K.D.

spots are a part of the appearance of measles. The meaning of the spots consists in the fact that they are part of the disease of measles. More generally put, the meaning of symptoms consists in the fact that they are a part of a whole. The systematic connection that we are looking for, the one that enables us to use phenomena like spots, trembling or blushing as signs and, as symptoms, to "understand" them, is the part-to-whole relationship.

However, there is another kind of symptom, the meaning of which is not the part-to-whole relationship: fingerprints, footprints and accents are a few examples, and there are numerous others. My accent can be interpreted as a symptom of my regional origin; finger- and footprints can be symptoms of the presence of the person who left them. Again, it is not that my desk is full of symptoms when it is covered with fingerprints, but if the fingerprints become the object of interpretive attempts, they can be symptoms. In such cases, their interpretability is not based on a part-to-whole relationship, but on causation. The meaning of a fingerprint interpreted as a symptom consists in its being the effect of the responsible party's causation. For the interpretation of such signs, the interpreter of the sign uses the causal chain "causative agent/cause/effect." The technique of interpretation is that of causal inference.

A special case of the cause-and-effect relationship is the means-to-end relationship. It, too, can be used for interpretation. If I see someone with a fishing rod standing on a river bank, I will take all of this as a symptom for the goal of catching fish. From an employed means (the fishing rod), I infer the end (catching fish) pursued with that means. The employment of linguistic means is also a symptom of the desired end. We will discuss this point in detail in Chapter 13.

Symptoms can thus be subdivided into three types: those whose meaning is the relationship of part-to-whole, of cause-and-effect, or of means-to-end. If we are willing to agree that all three types of inference may be called causal, we may summarize with the following definition:

> Symptoms are signs whose technique of interpretation is that of causal inference.

Charles Sanders Peirce defines an index—which corresponds to what I call *symptom*—as follows: "An index is a sign which would, at once, lose the character which makes it a sign if its object were removed, but would not lose that character if there were no interpretant" (Peirce 1955:

104). In order to understand this statement, a terminological annotation is necessary. A sign, writes Peirce, creates an interpretant in the mind of the addressee (CP 2.228). In the Peircean model, the interpretant of a sign is a mental correlate of the sign and itself has sign-like quality. The interpretant is the mentally represented correspondent of the sign, and enables the sign user to denote with it the object for which the sign stands.

Back to Peirce's definition. In a simplified reformulation, it states that an index would not be an index if that for which it stands did not exist. But it would still be an index even if there were no one who used it as a sign. The first part of this definition is trivial; the second I hold to be inadequate. Its triviality can be easily demonstrated by contrasting it with my definition of a symptom. Since the "character which makes it [the index] a sign" is the part-to-whole relationship, the cause-and-effect relationship or the means-to-end relationship, the first part of Peirce's definition states, in the spelled-out version, that a part would not be a part if the whole did not exist; that an effect would not be an effect if there were no cause; and that a means would not be a means if there were no end. In my opinion, the inadequacy of the second part of Peirce's definition is due to the fact that he attributes the status of an index to everything that fulfills the first condition, even if that thing is not employed by the sign user as an index. Consequently, everything that exists and which is the case is an index of everything that stands to it in one of the three aforementioned relationships. I assume that, for the sake of symmetry, that is, for the elegance of his system, Peirce also regards potential indexes as indexes. To avoid the world being overrun with symptoms, I have argued that an object (in the widest sense) only becomes a symptom with its interpretive use; in other words, that symptoms exist only as symptomic occurrences.[4]

Returning to my proposed definition of symptoms, I would like to add two necessary remarks.

(1) If one says, as is common, that symptoms are natural signs, this clearly cannot be taken to mean that symptoms themselves necessarily belong to the sphere of natural phenomena. Fingerprints, footprints and accent are results of human actions. Those who call them natural signs evidently mean to emphasize that a causal relationship is the only one necessary for their interpretation.

----

[4] On the Peircean concept of index, see Goudge 1965.

(2) The concept of symptom can be expanded to the desired degree
by adding the interpretation of non-causal contingencies as a criterion: if Peter's bicycle is not standing in front of his house, it is a
symptom that he is not at home. I have decided not to include in
the class of symptoms such signs as have an overtly ad hoc character and which are the object of pragmatic inferences. These
signs are a kind of circumstantial evidence, and though they may
serve to justify suspicions, they lack symptomic character. They
play no role in sign dynamics. I admit, however, that there can be
a continuum between symptoms and evidence of this sort.

To summarize our explanation of the concept of symptoms, we will say
that everything that is the case can become a symptom of what can be
causally inferred from it, that is, if it is made by the interpreter to be the
premise of an inference. Symptoms differ from other kinds of signs,
namely icons and symbols, in the following five ways.

(1) Symptoms have no "sender"; there is thus no one who means
something by a symptom.[5]

(2) Being a symptom is not a quality of a thing. Rather, things are
raised to the status of symptoms by virtue of their interpretive use.

(3) Symptoms therefore exist only as symptomic occurrences. A dictionary of symptoms, after the manner of a dictionary of symbols,
is not possible.[6]

---

[5] One supposed exception is the windsocks that are sometimes hung on highway
overpasses, giving drivers the possibility to judge wind speed and direction. Couldn't
we say that the motorist is the windsock's addressee, and that it is used as a symptom
for the current weather conditions? No; for the windsock itself is not a symptom. Its
movement is, and this has neither sender nor addressee. A similar case is the following:
A person gets home from work and calls out from the hallway, "Where are you?" The
addressee answers "Here!" from the living room. The one in the hallway now knows
where the other person is, because a causal inference can be made of the direction from
which the answer came. But the meaning of the word *here* allows no interpretation of
the speaker's position in the house, as *I am here* is an analytically true sentence. Only
the direction from which the answer came is interpretable, namely, with symptomic
methods.

[6] Medical lexicons of symptoms are basically lexicons of diseases. The criterion for
inclusion or exclusion is the existence of "nosologic entities," that is, uniform and easily
characterized symptoms that are subsumed to a "certain illness group" by means of an
organizing principle (Hadorn and Zöllner 1986: p. x).

(4) The question "Of what is the symptom a symptom?" is principally open. A symptom can be interpreted as a symptom of anything causally inferable from it.

(5) 'Symptom', in contrast to 'symbol', is a relational concept (like 'girlfriend', 'evidence', or 'brother'). That is, it makes no sense to call something a symptom without saying of *what* it is a symptom. (This follows from points 2–4.)

Icons are true signs. Unlike symptoms, they are communicative means. Communicative means are means employed by the sign user to influence the addressee according to the Gricean model; that is, to exert influence by giving the addressee to recognize, by means of signs (in the broadest sense), what one wants him to do, in the hope that this recognition may be his reason for letting himself be influenced in the desired way (cf. Chapter 7). Any thing or phenomenon in the world can become a symptom by virtue of its use by an interpreter for the purpose of interpretive inference, even though no sign user, in the sense of a "sender," is involved. But natural things or artifacts become icons through their use for the purpose of communication. Colloquially, one might say that it is through the "sender's" doing that something becomes an iconic sign, while symptoms are created exclusively through an interpreter's doing.

Typical iconic signs are, for example, the stylized "man" and "woman" on toilet doors, the pictograms for the Olympic games, the *U* in *U-turn*, and the aforementioned crossed-out pig for food that complies to Muslim standards. The word *cuckoo* is no longer an icon, but a symbol whose iconic past is still evident. However, I will deal with such transitions later.

Representational notions of signs usually define icons with the help of the relationship of similarity, or homomorphy, supposed to exist between the sign and that which is meant (cf. Jiránek 1992: 374). But there is no resemblance whatsoever between a men's toilet and the stylized depiction of a man on its door; just as little as the resemblance between the sound [kú:ku:] and the bird that we call *cuckoo*. The degree of similarity between the image of a crossed-out pig and the fact that the meal offered on the plane complies to Muslim standards is not exactly overwhelming. In other words, it is simply not true that the similarity of the sign and its denotatum is a necessary condition for iconicity (which it should be, if it is a defining criterion). Nelson Goodman clearly demonstrates that similarity alone is not adequate: "a Constable painting of Marlborough Castle is more like any other picture than it is like the Castle, yet it represents the Castle and not another picture" (Goodman 1968: 5). The concept of similarity is not entirely wrong, but it may not be taken too literally. For it is not specified how strong or direct the resemblance must be. The determining factor is not similarity, but rather the fact that the sign is capable of fulfilling its purpose: it must have the ability to call forth the "speaker's" intended *association* in the mind of the addressee. Similarity is certainly a good trigger for associations, but it does not make an icon into an icon. This is accomplished by the technique of interpretation, the associative inference. For this, even a very "far-fetched" similarity can be sufficient. The similarity can be (a) phonetic, graphic or gesticulative, (b) direct or indirect, and (c) strong or weak.

With *U-turn* the similarity is graphic, direct and fairly strong. In the case of *cuckoo*, the similarity is phonetic and indirect, but relatively strong; indirect because, rather than there being similarity between the sound and animal it denotes, it is between the sound and the call of the animal it denotes. The similarity in the case of the toilet icons is graphic, indirect and largely weak. It is indirect and weak because there is no similarity between the graphic representation and its denotatum, namely, a men's or women's toilet; rather, similarity comes to bear (for example) between the graphic representation and the stereotypical manner of dress of the people who are to use the toilet.

Icons work as impulses for association. With the use of an icon, the producer of the sign expects the addressee to infer a reasonable interpretation of the occurrence of the sign, by way of association[7] with the graphic, phonetic or gesticulative expression of the sign; that is, the sign user expects the addressee to try to figure out, through association, what plausibly could be meant. Since the interpreter needs no special knowledge or rules in order to do this, but only a naturally human faculty of association, icons can be used and understood more or less independently of language and culture. The most common form of iconic

---

[7] There is another, technical use of the word *association*, as in *an associated member of the commission*, which is not intended here. Association in this technical sense comes to bear precisely in regard not to icons, but to symptoms and symbols: a cause is associated with its effect, and a symbol is associated with a rule of use. Here, I use *association* strictly in the psychological sense, meaning a free play of ideas. Thanks to Sheila Embleton and Raimo Anttila for drawing my attention to the ambiguity of *association*.

communication is "talking with one's hands" in a foreign country. Cultural knowledge may come into play in so far as the iconic expression must itself be correctly interpreted before it can be the starting point for further interpretive efforts. In order to associatively infer from a stylized figure wearing a skirt that the door on which it is found leads to a women's toilet, one must know, for example, that men in that culture do not wear skirts.

To recall our central question once again: of what does the meaning of an icon consist? It consists of exactly that systematic connection that enables its interpretation. Its meaning is the similarity, of whatever kind it happens to be, that calls forth the association or chain of association with that which is meant. Note that this thesis does not claim that there is similarity between the icon and its meaning. It says that similarity *is* the icon's meaning! This is because similarity is what makes the icon interpretable.

As we have seen, a lexicon of symptoms is not possible. Since anything can serve as a symptom of whatever is causally inferable from it, and since symptoms cannot be intentionally used without losing their symptomic character, there can be no fixed repertoire of symptoms, intended and ready for use. Is a lexicon of icons possible? More so than one of symptoms. Repertoires of iconic signs in use evidently exist, but such ready-to-use repertory icons are highly unstable characters. If a certain frequency of use comes to bear, they are, as we will see, practically damned to become symbols.

Association become habitual ceases to be association.

A fundamental characteristic of icons is that they can be created ad hoc. If, for example, a colleague leaves his eyeglasses in my office, and from my window, I see him getting into his car, I can make a gesture pointing to my own glasses to indicate to him that he has forgotten his. The message "You left your glasses in my office" is conveyed iconically by means of the reference to my glasses. This example illustrates the above assertion: the sign doesn't "contain" the message; it's not transporting anything. Pointing to my glasses is a means of getting the other to recognize something. It is an interpretive key in the form of an associative impulse, and I give it to the addressee in the hope that, with the help of this key and his knowledge of the situation, he will be able to infer my intent. With such a key, I appeal to his associative ability. Plato's notion that the image-like quality of an expression enables the addressee to recognize what the speaker is thinking, his initial theory that "the signification of words is given . . . by likeness" (Plato 435b; cf. Chapter 1), would be correct—if our communicative means were icons and icons only. It is clear in the example of the forgotten eyeglasses that the possible interpretations of an iconic expression are fundamentally open. With the same gesture, but different situational conditions, I could mean to convey the message, "Don't forget to pick up my glasses at the optician's," or many other things. The interpretation of an icon is highly dependent on context.

For the purposes of contrastive explanation, I would like to include here a description of the Peircean definition of icons. "An *icon* is a sign which would possess the character which renders it significant, even though its object had no existence" (Peirce 1955: 104). The Peircean index, we learned, loses its indexicality if the denoted object does not exist. This is because (for example) a part (trivially) ceases to be a part if the whole no longer exists. An icon retains the qualities that make it a sign even if it has no denotatum. I will illustrate this thought by means of example. Imagine drawing a picture of your parents' house on a piece of paper. With this, you have produced an icon, in the Peircean sense, of their house. The drawing is an icon by virtue of its similarity with the house. The same drawing could just as well be a creative drawing of a nonexistent house. Whether the house is "reproduced" in the drawing, or freely created, the characteristics of the drawing are the same. In one case, however, the drawing is a sign, and in the other it is not. It does not lose its characteristics when it loses its sign character. So far, this idea is correct. Elsewhere, though, Peirce seems to maneuver himself into direct contradiction, when he says, "It is true that unless there is really such an Object, the Icon does not act as a sign" (CP 2.247). It follows that there are icons that are not signs; and this contradicts his definition of the icon *as* a sign: "An Icon is a sign" (CP 2.247).

I would like to return to my concept of icon and summarize: a thing (a gesture, figure, sound, etc.) becomes an icon when it is used to bring an addressee to a certain recognition by means of association. To a modest extent, one may speak of iconic repertories, whose members, however, are gravely endangered. Anything that is in a position to bring forth associations can be used, in appropriate circumstances, as an iconic sign.

With this, we have come to the third type of sign. **Symbols** are signs that are defined, according to the teachings of representational semantics, by the fact that they stand in a relation of arbitrariness, that is, a relatively arbitrary relationship to that which they mean. We have decided to call *meaning* that which enables the interpreter to make an interpretation. For symptoms, this is the relationship of causality; for icons, that of similarity, in the broadest sense of the word. In what does the meaning of symbols consist? In their arbitrariness? That cannot be, for inferences cannot be made from arbitrary relations. Indeed, the very word *arbitrary* indicates the impossibility of resolution. Symbols really are arbitrary, in a sense that requires further explanation, but this property is not interpretively useful for the addressee. This shows that the concept of arbitrariness is not on the same level as that of naturalness or of similarity.

What makes a symbol interpretable is the rule of its use in the language (cf. Chapter 4). Here, too, a comparison with the Peircean definition is helpful: "A *symbol* is a sign which would lose the character which renders it a sign if there were no interpretant" (Peirce 1955: 104). This characterization of the symbol would be fully compatible with my understanding of the concept if one were prepared to view the rule of use of the sign as its interpretant. At first glance, one might gain the impression that the following assertion could be interpreted in this sense: "A Symbol is a Representamen whose Representative character consists precisely in its being a rule that will determine its Interpretant" (Peirce 1955: 112). We recall that the interpretant is the mentally represented correspondent of the sign, and allows the sign to be interpreted. "Significance is interpretability," writes Thomas Short in the course of his description of Peircean semiotics (1988: 82). But viewing the interpretant as the rule of use of the sign would not be in the Peircean spirit, as becomes clear in other passages: "A *Symbol* is a sign which refers to the Object that it denotes by virtue of a law, usually an association of general ideas, which operates to cause the Symbol to be interpreted as referring to that Object" (Peirce 1955: 102). The Peircean representant *is* not the rule; rather, it is the mental correspondent of the sign, connected to it by means of a rule. Peirce stays consistently within the bounds of the representational notion of signs, while avoiding a regression to a "label theory" of meaning. For the mental correlate of the sign, the interpretant, is not construed as presemiotically existent. A complete understanding of the Peircean conception of signs requires an understanding of his entire theoretical construct. Therefore, I will leave it at this reference to the Peircean definition of the symbol, and return to my own suggestions.

To know what a symbol means is to know under which conditions it is usable for the realization of which intentions. If someone says to me "Hey you, come over here," I can interpret what he intends me to do, since I know what one usually intends to get people to do with the utterance of this sentence. Its meaning is not "that I should come over here," or anything like it. "That I should come over here" is (possibly) my interpretation, which, thanks to meaning, I am able to reach. The meaning is not what the other wants from me, but that which allows me to "guess" what they want from me. What another wants from me is not an aspect of the English language and therefore cannot be a part of the meaning of its signs. The rule of use, the mutual knowledge of the conditions in which, and the purpose for which, the symbol is usable, is what puts the interpreter in the position to infer the nonobvious from the perceptible. The nonobvious is the intention of the speaker. The goal of the interpreter is to figure out that intention; the means to do so is the inference made on the basis of knowledge about the rules of use of the employed signs. If everything goes as planned, what the addressee understands is just what the speaker means. I will call what the speaker means the **sense** of the utterance. Thus I will call the sense of an utterance that which interpreters come to recognize when they have reached their interpretive goal. By way of sign meaning, the interpreter tries to decipher the sense of the use of those signs. The object of interpretation is the uttered sentence with its meaning; the goal of interpretation is the sense of the utterance. The sense of the occurrence of a symbol is the communicative intention that the speaker pursues with the use of that symbol. The sense of my use of *I*, when I say *I*, is not I! Rather, the sense of my use of *I* is my intention to refer to myself with this utterance. The sense is the reason for the employment of linguistic means, not the object that the sign "stands for." However, the recognition of the intended object, that is, the fixation of reference, is a part of the recognition of the communicative intention.

Thus the interpretation of the use of a symbol is *not* the attempt to find out the meaning of the symbol; rather, it is to figure out the sense of the occurrence of this symbol on the basis of knowledge of its meaning. If I do not know the meaning of the symbol, that is, if I do not know to what end it is normally and normatively used, I will not be able to figure out to what end you use it in a particular utterance.

The game of chess is appropriate here—as in other cases (cf. Wunderli 1981)—as a descriptive analogy: when someone says, "Aha, he wants to take my bishop with his rook," she gives you to understand that she believes she has understood the sense of the move. For this, she must be familiar with the "meaning" of the bishop, that is, she must know which moves may be made with the bishop and which may not. Anyone who does not know the rules of use of the bishop will not stand a chance of understanding the sense of the moves involving the bishop. Like the sense of an utterance, the sense of a move is the end to which that move is undertaken.

The interpretation of icons is highly dependent on situational or contextual knowledge. The act of pointing to my eyeglasses allows an endless number of interpretations. A photograph of a man pointing to his glasses is not meaningfully iconically interpretable without knowledge of the specific circumstances. The number of possible interpretations of the utterance "You left your glasses in my office" is considerably lower. Certainly, the glasses might be wine glasses, and the party to which "you" and "your" refers also is not fixed. Furthermore, the utterance might be ironically, metaphorically or otherwise nonliterally meant. But in comparison to iconic communication, symbolic communication has a very narrow field of possible interpretations.

Meanings are keys for interpretation. The addressee of the utterance, "You left your glasses in my office," knows, if he speaks enough English, that the word *glasses* is used to denote a certain sight aid or drinking vessel, that *your* can be used to denote the connection of the glasses to the addressee, and so on. These interpretive tips reach the addressee in a certain situation. They both complete and actualize the addressee's situational knowledge, allowing him to broaden it in regard to what the speaker would like him to recognize. That is, the interpretative tips allow the addressee to interpret the speaker's utterance. The reverse situation is more common: the hearer completes the linguistic knowledge given him by the semantics of the uttered sentence with relevant situational knowledge. In this way, the context or situation restricts the number of possible interpretations in regard to what is intended. But this scenario stands the process of interpretation on its head. In order to filter out the relevant parts of their situational and general knowledge, addressees must first be able to make an adequate interpretation of the utterance. But in that case, they could spare themselves the effort of completion. Rather, hearers attempt to fit the utterance directed to them into their situational knowledge, which is a part of their general knowledge. And if the utterance doesn't fit, it must be made to! It is reinterpreted until it fits. I always carry my situational knowledge with me. Every piece of information that is new to me must be integrated with as few gaps as possible, as must any utterances directed to me. The art of interpretation consists in, on the one hand, finding the slot in the system of previous knowledge where the newly arrived information fits, and on the other hand, "bending" the newly received utterance "into shape," reinterpreting it until it really fits into the slot.[8] The interpretation of an uttered sentence is like the establishment of truth in a trial based on circumstantial evidence. Meanings are circumstantial evidence provided by speakers to addressees, hopefully enabling them to guess the sense of the utterance on the basis of their familiarity with rules of use and their situational or contextual knowledge. "Meaning" and "sense" are completely different categories. The sense of an utterance is the objective pursued with its use; the meaning of a word is its rule of use. Knowing how to use a hammer would be knowing its meaning. Understanding why someone uses a hammer to pound a nail into a wall would be knowing the sense of using a hammer and the sense of this action.

---

[8] On the role of context in interpretation, see Sperber and Wilson 1986a: 137 ff.

9

Inferential Procedures

Communication is a risky business. How can I make sure that you will interpret my sentences in the way in which I mean them? How can I make sure that I have understood your utterances in the sense in which you mean them? One answer might be that it is like a game of chess. "To have a meaning is to have a place in a language game" (Rorty 1989: 18). Chess has rules. I know them, and so do you. I interpret your moves, and you interpret mine, on the basis of our knowledge of the rules. But that's not how it works in the game of communication. Here, the chess analogy fails.

Why is it inadequate? The answer is that the rules of chess apply strictly and timelessly, as it were; furthermore, they are codified. They exist as formulated rules, and in this sense, one can say that the rules of chess exist independently of whether you and I or anyone else knows them. It is somewhat different with the rules of a language. They do not apply strictly, they are not codified, they do not apply for all "players" in the same way, and many of them are subject to permanent historic change. Thus it is misleading, in a way, to say that there are rules of use for words like *tea* and *but*—rules that you and I both know. The rules do not exist outside and independently of those who follow them. For those who follow them are also the ones who produce, perpetuate and some-times change them, through use or partial violation. (Incidentally, though, rules do not necessarily have to be broken in order to change. It suffices when, in the course of time, peripheral uses become central.) I am not able to speak German because I know the rules of German; rather, to be able to speak German is to know the rules. Talk of the rules of our signs is a somewhat reifying and abbreviated description of the fact that, in regard to our use of signs, there exists a more or less common practice upon which we rely until there seems reason not to. The answer to the question posed above is therefore that I can be sure neither of being correctly interpreted by you, nor of correctly understanding you! As long as everything goes well in practice, we assume that we have correctly understood each other. There is no other criterion. Checking back to be sure can reduce the risk, but it will not do away with it. For even affirmative answers must be interpreted.

Now, if rules of use consist in nothing other than common practice and mutual expectations, and the trust in the commonality of practice, is it not simply wrong to say that meanings "ain't in the head"? This is James Hurford's question: "Outside the individual language user, are these rules realities in any sense?" His theory is that rules must be reducible to individual-psychological concepts: " 'To be familiar with a rule' or 'to know a rule' simply means to be in a certain mental state" (Hurford 1992: 369).[1] With this, he affirmatively refers to Chomsky's reply to Kripke's analysis of Wittgenstein's argument against the possibility of a private language.[2]

To give away the punch line:

(1) I share Hurford's opinion that the concept of rules must be reconstructed according to the principles of methodological individualism.[3]

(2) I am not of the opinion that "to know a rule" simply means to be in a certain mental state.

Let us examine these opinions in turn.

The principles of methodological individualism claim that assertions about collective phenomena are permissible and have explanatory power only if they can be traced back to assertions about individuals. 'The people's desire for peace' is an example of such collective concepts; it is useless (or even dangerous) as long as it is not stated how the desire

---

[1] This and all following quotes from Hurford 1992 are my translations (K.D.).

[2] Chomsky 1986: 224 ff., Kripke 1982. My commentary on this controversy can be found in Keller 1992: 387. Since Chomsky's remarks do not really deal with Wittgenstein's private-language argument, I will refrain from repeating his and my comments here.

[3] On methodological individualism, see Hayek 1948: 3 ff.

of the people for peace relates to the desires of the group's individual members. Ideologues often use the emptiness of these concepts for their alleged arguments, as in the appeal to 'the interests of the working class' or other collectives. But these concepts are also employed in linguistics, mostly through sheer ignorance. 'The English language' is a collective concept, one that is also useless unless the relation that holds between the English language and your and my language is specified. If one were to assume that the English language is the average of all English speakers' competencies, the one with the least competency would dictate the boundary of the notion, as it were. This would not be appropriate. If we were to assume that the English language were the sum of all English speakers' competencies, vast numbers of idiosyncrasies would have to be included, idiosyncrasies that we would not really want to regard as parts of the English language. So what is the English language, then? What is true of the concept 'the English language' is also true of 'the rules of the English language'. Because of this problem, Noam Chomsky has consequently formulated (as have others) a linguistics in which the concept of language in this hypostatized sense has no place (Chomsky 1986, 1992; for discussion, see Keller 1994: chapter 5.4). His doctrine states that only the competencies of the individual speaker truly exist. With this, however, a number of interesting and even essential questions are excluded from linguistics. The baby has been thrown out with the bathwater.

Up to this point, I concur with James Hurford. He, too, does not care to "go as far as Chomsky" (1992: 371), and refrains from giving up the concept of language in the sense of 'community language' and 'community norms'. But it does not follow from the reasonable doctrine of methodological individualism that every collective concept *must* be rejected. They just have to be "tied in" on the individual level. One of the arguments against individualism is that its claims must be rejected because there are concepts that are irreducibly collective: the fact that the average German has 2.3 children does not apply to any individual, for example. Also, the doctrine of individualism is to be rejected on the grounds of the concept of sum (expressed in the catchphrase that states something is "more than the sum of its parts"), one of the famous Ehrenfels criteria. But this argument is weaker than the sum of its parts. Statistical claims are permissible precisely because the path from individual assertions to the statistical assertion is known and spelled out. In fact, an explanation of the phenomenon of oversummation requires that the point of departure is assertions about individuals, and that the synergetic accumulation is derived from the interaction of individual elements.

Hurford is of the opinion that the concept of rule is like "an infectious disease. AIDS infects the blood of individuals; a community as such has no blood, except in a derivative sense. Therefore, communities can't get AIDS; only their members can" (1992: 371). The analogy is not convincing. Even though it is true that a population cannot get sick, it can have a certain degree of contamination. Again, the concept of degree of contamination is permissible because epidemiologists determine the degree of contamination of a population from the infection or non-infection of its members. The question to be asked in regard to rules is not binary! It is not: "Are rules identical to individual states of knowledge, *or* is 'rule' a collective concept, meaning that rules exist 'outside' of individuals?" Hurford erects just such a dichotomy. But the decision to be made is actually ternary:

(1) Are rules identical to certain states of knowledge of individuals?

(2) Is 'rule' a collective, holistic concept, meaning that the "existence" of rules is to be found "outside" individuals?

(3) Is 'rule' a collective concept that can be derived according to the principles of methodological individualism, such that collective knowledge may be linked to individual states of knowledge?

I am of the opinion that the answer to the first two questions is no, while the answer to the last question is yes. Rules are conventions in David Lewis's sense (1969: 78).[4] Hence 'common knowledge' is, on the one hand, strictly individual, but on the other hand, it may not be too sharply defined.[5] If taken exactly, a rule of language is never an object of collective knowledge in the strict sense. Language users proceed silently from the hypothesis that the ways of using a certain expression are sufficiently and relevantly in agreement. Lewis's definition of convention is, to put it very simply, a regularity in behavior within

---

[4] See Chap. 10 for a more explicit description of Lewis's definition of convention.

[5] For an individualistic definition of "collective knowledge," see Keller 1974: 103 ff. On the question of the necessary vagueness of its definition, see Sperber and Wilson 1986*a*: 38 ff.

a group, one to which everyone conforms, to which everyone expects everyone else to conform, and in regard to which the reason of every individual for conforming to exactly this behavioral regularity is the expectation that everyone else will, too. (Otherwise, one might just as well choose a different behavioral regularity.) Collective knowledge must exist in regard to this expectation, that is, everyone must know of it, and must know that everyone else knows of it.[6] In order to get around the rigidity of the concept of "knowledge," Sperber and Wilson suggest choosing the concept "mutual manifestness" instead of "mutual knowledge." According to this suggestion, *Peter knows that the phone is ringing*, for example, should be replaced by *It is manifest to Peter that the phone is ringing*. "The notion of a mutually manifest assumption is clearly weaker than that of a mutual assumption (and a fortiori than that of mutual knowledge)" (Sperber and Wilson 1986a: 42). One can only trust that the notion of being manifest is less strict than that of knowledge. However, this does not solve the problems attached to the concept of knowledge; they are simply transferred to the artificial word *manifest*, with which there is another problem, namely, that what it means is anything but manifest to the reader. If we keep in mind the fact that all of our knowledge, and thus our individual competence as well, is of a hypothetical nature, we can safely stick with the concept of collective knowledge in discussing our knowledge of language.[7] Even better, if it is strictly individualistically formulated, any legitimate objections towards holistic collectivism should be taken care of.

Let us consider Hurford's assertion once more: " 'To be familiar with a rule' or 'to know a rule' simply means to be in a certain mental state" (1992: 369). If we compare this with Lewis's definition of convention, the question comes up: in regard to conventions, is anything involved other than individuals' mental states? If not, is Hurford right after all? Yes and no. But this kind of answer, if it is correct, is always a sign of hidden ambiguity. Let us return to Hurford's example of disease, and consider the following inference:

---

[6] It is Esa Itkonen who has most prominently stressed that rules "exist as objects of common knowledge" (1977: 248 ff.).

[7] On the problem addressed by Sperber and Wilson (1986a: 42), that knowledge implies truth ("nothing can be known and false"), see Keller 1975.

(1) To have AIDS means to have blood that is in a certain state.[8]

(2) AIDS is an epidemic.

---

(3) To have this epidemic means to have blood that is in a certain state.

Does 3 follow from 1 and 2? Sentence 3 is ambiguous, and follows from the premises in only *one* reading. To say of the epidemic AIDS that a person has it, is to say that his blood is in a certain state. This is true. To say of someone that he has an epidemic is not to say, however, that his blood is in a certain state. An individual can get AIDS, but a single person cannot get an epidemic. The notion of epidemic implies certain paths of infection and a certain area of dispersal. In other words, performing a blood test on an individual reveals nothing as to whether his sickness is epidemic. A mental test administered to an individual reveals nothing in regard to whether his mental state is knowledge of a *rule*. A single person can have a disease, one that can become epidemic; but what he has is not an epidemic.

From this, it follows that: "To say of a rule R that one knows it is to say that one is in the mental state S." In this reading, Hurford's theory is correct. "To be in the mental state S is to know a rule." In this reading, Hurford's theory is wrong. Hurford's theory is true with the assumption that is already presupposed: that the object of knowledge is a rule. Is the notion of epidemic a holistic-collectivist one, meaning that epidemics "exist outside" the infected individual, as it were? No; but to say of someone that he has an epidemic is an assertion that goes beyond the individual. It says something about the sickness of the individual, and at the same time, something about the disseminatory path and the spread of the sickness within the population. This is why the notion of epidemic cannot be explained exclusively individuo-physiologically. The same goes, mutatis mutandis, for the notion of "rule." If the controlling instance for the correctness of the use a word were solely the individual's memory, Wittgenstein's private-language argument would come to bear: if a rule had conditions of use that, by definition, only I could "know," we could not reasonably speak of knowledge; there would fundamentally

---

[8] My concern here is not the truth value of the claims, but the validity of the inferential process.

be no possibility of distinguishing between knowledge and error. Hence conformity to the rule could not be distinguished from violations of the rule, as there would be no controlling instance whatsoever. In other words, there is no inner event that is itself able to guarantee the correct use of an expression. Hurford explicitly asserts "the private character of rules" (1992: 371); if he means by this what Wittgenstein meant—and he refers to Wittgenstein—his theory is self-contradictory.

What makes communication so risky is, for one, the rules themselves: the fact that they arise, become stable, and change, all in the course of communication. For another, it is risky because of the inferential procedures, which speakers and addressees must perform in different ways. The meaning of the signs of our language is not an algorithm that determines the sense of an utterance. At the most, signs hint at the sense, or suggest it; the rest is a guessing game. "How much guessing can there be?" Hurford critically asks (1992: 368). The answer is that the possibilities range from lottery to certainty. Both extremes, and everything in between, may occur. I would now like to show how the element of guessing comes into play, and why it is a necessary part of the game.

Every communicative act is tied to a series of inferential procedures, and every inferential procedure has, in some form, three elements (or sets of elements): a premise (a set of premises), a rule (a set of rules), and a result. If any two of the three elements are given, we can infer the third. *Interpretation* can virtually be grasped as the inference, from any two elements, of the missing third element. However, these inferred conclusions are usually of an extremely hypothetical nature. Their weakness is due to both contingent, practical reasons (too little knowledge of the facts) and logical reasons. Let's take a closer look at the three possible kinds of conclusions.

I will call the three elements "premise," "rule" and "result," and for simplicity's sake, I will indicate them with numbers (cf. Andersen 1973, Anttila 1989, and Eco 1984: 39 ff.):

premise	rule	result
I	2	3

The three possible kinds of inferential mode, usually called *deduction*, *induction* and *abduction*, are:

1 and 2 → 3 (deduction),
1 and 3 → 2 (induction),
3 and 2 → 1 (abduction).

Consider these three simple examples of inferential modes:

Deduction:
(1) Socrates is human.

(2) All humans are mortal.

(3) Socrates is mortal.

Induction:
(1) Socrates is human.

(3) Socrates is mortal.

(2) All humans are mortal.

Abduction:
(3) Socrates is mortal.

(2) All humans are mortal.

(1) Socrates is human.

Now, as we know, only deductive conclusions are strictly valid. Induction and abduction are not conclusive, and are therefore logically invalid. Our examples make clear how risky inductive and abductive "conclusions" can be. However, they are our usual and, if nothing better is available, completely rational ways of forming hypotheses, and they also play a part in human communication: inductive conclusions lead from individual observations to rule-hypotheses. This is how we come into possession of rules. It can easily lead to over- or undergeneralization, as children's language acquisition demonstrates. Abductive conclusions are diagnostic: "He said *so long*. *So long* serves as a parting greeting. He must have wanted to let me know that he wanted to go." Deductive conclusions are essentially valid, assuming that the rules are strictly valid. In real life, this is normally not the case. We work with so-called practical syllogisms (see Wright 1963, 1972) like the following:

(1) I want to attain *x*.
(2) I assume that doing *y* (usually) leads to *x*.
(3) Therefore, I do *y*.

Let us examine a simplified form of a completely normal communicative situation, from the perspective of both the speaker (S) and the hearer (H).

Speaker S: (1) I want to let H know that *x*.
(2) I assume that, in this place, the utterance *U*, in certain circumstances, serves to let H know *x*, and that H knows this (and also knows that I know it).
(3) Therefore, I utter *U*.

Hearer H: (3) S uttered *U*.
(2) I assume that, in this place, uttering *U* serves, in certain circumstances, to let H know *x*, and that S knows this (and also knows that I know it).
(1) Therefore, S wants to let me know that *x*.

Here, it is clear that the speaker makes, by means of practical syllogism, a deductive inference, while the hearer is forced to make an abductive one. Even with the idyllic conditions assumed here, that speaker and hearer suppose the same rules and judge the situation in the same way, both inferences are extremely unreliable. In real life, conditions are often not quite as ideal as they are assumed to be in this scenario. Hence the "guessing game" is even riskier. Often we even have to inductively infer the rules of use from the speaker's utterances, just in order to be able to use them abductively, in the same breath, as it were. That is, we frequently balance inductive and abductive hypotheses in order to arrive at plausible interpretations.

Our scenario contains yet another abbreviation which absolutely must be revised: the communicative possibilities provided to us by our individual competencies for the realization of a given communicative goal are by no means as few as assumed above (for simplicity's sake). To let someone know *x*, we have, in almost all cases, more than one possibility. There are only a few ritual or existential situations in which there are exact numbers of possible choices: if you are asked in the course of taking marriage vows whether you take *XY* as husband or wife, you should probably answer with *I do* rather than with *of course* or *OK*. If you are in danger of drowning, you should yell *help* and not something like *aid* or *assist*. In most situations, however, we have a number of alternatives available, not only lexical, but also phrasal, syntactical or phonetic. We can pronounce *advertisement* as [əd'vərtáiz'mənt] or [ad'vɜ:rtismənt]. I can choose, among others, either *He's working even though he's sick* or *He's working in spite of being sick*. For a letter addressed to a city official I do not know personally, I can choose the closing greeting *Sincerely* or *With kind regards*, for example. The true number of possibilities is often overwhelming. Let us take a closer look at an example, one to which we shall return later. If I want to let my conversation partner know that the temperature went below the freezing point last night, that the lake is frozen over and that there is a causal relationship between these two occurrences, I can make a choice from among (at least) the following sentences:

(1) *The lake is frozen over because it froze last night.*
(2) *The lake is frozen over, as it froze last night.*
(3) *Since it froze last night, the lake is frozen over.*
(4) *The reason that the lake is frozen over is that it froze last night.*
(5) *The lake is frozen over due to it having frozen last night.*
(6) *It froze last night, and now the lake is frozen over.*
(7) *The lake is frozen over, because last night it got below freezing.*
(8) *It froze last night, because the lake is frozen over.*
(9) *It froze last night, as the lake is frozen over.*
(10) *It froze last night; you see, the lake is frozen over.*
(11) *It froze last night; the lake is frozen over.*
(12) *The lake is frozen over; it froze last night.*

I will end the list here. A brief preliminary glance at these sentences confirms that they have different nuances in meaning and stylistic quality. Sentences (1) through (6) are factual arguments, and sentences (7) through (10) are epistemic arguments (for a detailed description of factual and epistemic arguments, see Chapter 17). Sentences (11) and (12) convey the explanative connection between the arguments, which is not explicitly expressed with the help of a conjunction, but by means of implicatures.[9]

---

[9] On the theory of implicatures, see Chap. 14, as well as Grice 1975.

Thus speakers generally do not have in their practical syllogism just one possibility of a second premise for the realization of their communicative intentions, as assumed above; rather, they find themselves in a decision-making situation: they have a choice among numerous alternatives, all of which work in some way toward the attainment of their goals, but which, however, depending on the framing conditions, are appropriate in varying degrees. Variation (1), for example, is unmarked and hence too dull; (5) is very explicit, but stylistically awkward; (7) is probably a little too colloquial; (11) has the advantage of brevity, but sounds a little stiff; and so on. Speakers must therefore judge their alternatives for action with regard to the goals of their action and their assessment of the circumstances. The criterion for judgment can only be: "Which alternative, under the given framing conditions, gives me the best chance of realizing my communicative goals?" People are capable of ordering alternatives for action according to subjectively expected net benefits, that is, subjectively expected benefits after costs.[10] The ability to make the choice which promises the highest subjective net benefit from among the available alternatives is rational action.[11] Practical syllogism must therefore be expanded with the principles of rational choice,[12] resulting in approximately the following inferential model.

Speaker S: (1) In regard to H, I want to realize the intentions i_1-i_n.[13]

(2.1) I assume that, in this place, the utterance types U_1-U_m serve to realize the intentions i_1-i_n.

(2.2) According to my estimation of the given utterance's situation and of H, U_3 is the best of the available alternatives for realizing the intentions i_1-i_n.

---

(3) Therefore, I utter U_3.

[10] Costs and benefits can be of a purely symbolic nature. "Losing face" is, for example, an important cost factor; see Nozick 1993: 26 ff.

[11] Concerning rationality in regard to belief, see Nozick 1993: chap. 3. On rationality in communication, see Itkonen 1983.

[12] The principles of the so-called rational choice theory in connection with practical inferences are clearly and concisely described (including further references) in Meggle 1977: 415–28.

[13] Generally, we pursue a number of goals with one utterance; see Keller 1994: 96; cf. also Gellner 1988: 43 ff.

The assumption that speakers will make rational choices among the alternatives available to them, that is, that they will attempt to optimize the success of their communicative endeavors, is very important both for theories of language change and for its explanation. I discuss this point in detail in Keller 1994. But this assumption has another crucial consequence. It presupposes that we are able to use language as its own metalanguage. The reason for this is as follows.

Rationality requires the capacity of **semantic representation**. This thought is presented by David Gauthier in his essay "Morality, Rational Choice and Semantic Representation": "What distinguishes human beings from other animals, and provides the basis for rationality, is the capacity for semantic representation. You can, as your dog on the whole cannot, represent a state of affairs to yourself, and consider in particular whether or not it is the case, and whether or not you would want it to be the case. You can represent to yourself the contents of your beliefs, and your desires" (Gauthier 1988: 173ff.). If I decide to go shopping for dinner, I have various options and various criteria: taste, nutrition, availability, the amount of preparation required, and so on. Generally, I will bring the criteria into a hierarchy of priority, and, as far as the options are concerned, into a preferential hierarchy. In order to do this, I must be capable of reflectively considering the criteria and the options. "We order our desires, in relation to decision and action, so that we may choose to maximize our expectation of desire-fulfillment. And in doing so, we show ourselves to be rational agents" (Gauthier 1988: 174). Our options must be at our semantic disposal in order to be at our reflective disposal. "And this reflection, arising also out of the capacity for semantic representation, is an essential dimension of practical reality" (Gauthier 1988: 174).

Before applying these thoughts to the problem of the rational choice of semantic means, I would like to add a thought from Derek Bickerton. Our language, he writes, is a "secondary representational system" (Bickerton 1990: 103). This might be illustrated thus: for a frog to be able to catch a fly, it needs a system of representation. Its brain cells react to the movements of small round objects, and these are directly coupled to its catching reflex. "There is nothing more sophisticated than this inside the frog's brain" (Bickerton 1990: 28). For comparison, Bickerton considers a human reaction:

Suppose that we are alone in a house late at night and hear a sound that we do not immediately identify. Unless we are in an abnormally anxious state we will not immediately respond to it. Rather we will listen intently, and try to identify the sound if it is repeated. In human terms, this means that we will *try to provide a linguistic description* for the sound. Only when we have done this (called it a *creaking shutter*, *cat trying to get out*, *possible burglar*, or whatever) will we take the appropriate action. (Bickerton 1990: 28; emphasis in original)

This means that the choice of appropriate action is based not on sense perception, the primary representational system, but on sense perception classified by linguistic description, the secondary representational system. This theory, too, implies that the capacity of rational choice is tied to the capacity of classification and representation by linguistic signs. To put it simply, rationality requires (for purely practical reasons) language, a language that can be used for classification and representation.

When we apply the idea of rational choice to semantic means, it shows that the capacity to select and employ from among the available alternatives the linguistic means which, under the circumstances, is subjectively viewed to promise the highest degree of success, requires the possibility of representing linguistic means linguistically. How is this done? For nocturnal noises we have, as Bickerton puts it, "linguistic descriptions." How do we represent linguistic signs? We do so by mentioning them.

One of the most characteristic features of natural languages (and one which may well distinguish them, not only from the signalling-systems used by other species, but also from what is commonly referred to as non-verbal communication in human beings . . .) is their capacity for referring to, or describing, themselves. . . . One terminological distinction proposed for this purpose and now quite commonly found in the literature is that of use and mention. (Lyons 1977: 5–6)

In the sentence *Frank has a ball*, *Frank* is used; in the sentence *'Frank' has five letters*, *Frank* is mentioned. The fact that every natural language can be used as its own metalanguage is thus not only a condition of the possibility of using a language to talk about itself; it is also the condition of possibility for the language change that results from optimal choices of action.

Let us return to the question with which we started this chapter: how can I make sure that you will interpret my sentences in the way in which I mean them? How can I make sure that I have understood your sentences in the sense in which you mean them? I have tried to show that the process of mutual influence that we call communication makes downright risky use of inferential procedures, enough so that it is appropriate to turn the question around: what reason have I to hope that you might have understood me? Edmond Wright's answer is correct: "There is no guarantee other than the 'utterer's' and 'hearer's' common satisfaction over their mutual pragmatic success that they are taking their meanings in the same way" (Wright 1976: 519).[14]

[14] See also Sperber and Wilson 1986a: 65.

10

Arbitrariness versus Motivatedness

"In the language of humans, all tones are arbitrarily articulated." Johann Peter Süßmilch knew this as early as the mid-eighteenth century (1766: 15).[1] But languages also often have onomatopoeic words. *Cuckoo* is an example. One could make a game of it: which animal says *gäkol* in Korean? Exactly the animal that Germans think says *quak*! In English-speaking countries people claim that it says *ribbit*. What do *gäkol*, *quak* and *ribbit* have in common? Each is held to be an imitation of the sound that frogs make when they croak.[2] The words *cuckoo* and *ribbit* are symbols in the English language. As we concluded in Chapter 8, symbols are arbitrary. And as we have seen, arbitrariness is often raised to the defining aspect of the symbol. But are onomatopoeic symbols arbitrary, too? In order to answer this question, we must examine the concept of arbitrariness more closely.

The issue of arbitrariness was first discussed by Plato in the dialogue *Cratylus*, as presented in Chapter 3. The question around which the dialogue revolves is whether names have "a truth or correctness in them, which is the same by nature for all," or whether their correctness is based only on that "which men agree to use" (Plato 383b–d). To put it differently, is the criterion for the correctness of words the essence of the things they designate, or is it convention? According to Plato's theory, a thing has its own naturally correct name if the name resembles the thing or represents the thing's essence. Now, if we assume that *cuckoo*

---

[1] Trans. K.D.

[2] A Korean friend expressed to me his conviction that *gäkol* is clearly the best rendering of the frog's croak, though I had always been of the opinion that they "really" say *quak*.

is a symbol, and that the relation of resemblance between the thing and the cry of the animal so named is sufficient to claim the word's natural correctness, it follows that Plato's dichotomy is not an exclusive one. A sign can be thoroughly conventional, and still fulfill the requirements for "natural correctness." *Cuckoo* is both *nomo* and *physei*! Any other answer would be artificial: why shouldn't a relation of resemblance also be conventionally effective?

Now, those who accept what has been said so far will be forced to go one step further, even though it may not be as easy: conventional signs are, as will be demonstrated, necessarily arbitrary. Conventional signs may stand in a relationship of resemblance to the thing designated. The sign *cuckoo* is arbitrary and simulative. Similarity and arbitrariness are not mutually exclusive: "arbitrary" does not imply "dissimilar."

This thesis is not at all common. Hockett uses the term *arbitrary* in contrast to *iconic*, and defines *iconicity* with similarity (1958: 577). Hence, for Hockett, arbitrariness and similarity are mutually exclusive. Lyons writes in a passage concerning symbols that

in contrast [to words like 'tree', 'Baum', and 'arbre'], the words 'cuckoo' in English, 'Kuckuck' in German and 'coucou' in French are, in their spoken form, naturally representative of the characteristic cry of the species of birds that they signify. . . . What is traditionally called onomatopoeia, as illustrated here, is a universally recognized exception to the generality of the Saussurean principle of the arbitrariness of the linguistic sign. (Lyons 1977: 101)

Lyons implies that this principle is excessively generalizing. What does this tell us?

Before I go into more detail on this question, a note on the fundamentals is called for. Saussure's *Cours de linguistique générale* was not written by Ferdinand de Saussure. Rather, it sprang from the pens of Charles Bally and Albert Sechehaye, who based it on notes taken by students attending Saussure's lecture of the same name—though Bally and Sechehaye had themselves not attended the lectures. This daring undertaking practically invites misinterpretation and unintended, perhaps even intentional, distortions. If I refer to the *Cours* in spite of this, fully aware that it does not always faithfully represent Saussure's ideas, I do so for the following reason: it was not Saussure's "authentic" opinions, but this precise work that made a lasting impression on our century's views of linguistic signs. These views will be the object of my critique. Thus

I use the word *Saussure* not to designate a person, but as a name for the *Cours de linguistique générale*.[3]

Saussure expresses himself very cautiously in regard to his principle of the arbitrary nature of the sign: "The bond between the signifier and the signified is arbitrary. Since I mean by sign the whole that results from associating the signifier with the signified, I can simply say: the linguistic sign is arbitrary" (Saussure 1960: 67). This is the locus classicus, as it were, where Saussure introduces the idea of arbitrariness, which is not to say that it is here either explained or even defined. Explanatory remarks can be found scattered in many places throughout the text; we will examine them in synopsis.

The idea of "sister" is not linked by any inner relationship to the succession of sounds *s-ö-r* which serves as its signifier in French. (Saussure 1960: 67)

No one disputes the principle of the arbitrary nature of the sign. (68)

The word *arbitrary* also calls for comment . . . I mean that it [the signifier] is unmotivated, i.e. arbitrary in that it actually has no natural connection with the signified. (68–9)

. . . the choice of a given slice of sound to name a given idea is completely arbitrary. (113)

. . . the bond between the sound and the idea is radically arbitrary. (113)

The fundamental principle of the arbitrariness of the sign does not prevent our singling out in each language what is radically arbitrary, i.e. unmotivated, and what is only relatively arbitrary. Some signs are absolutely arbitrary; in others we note, not its complete absence, but the presence of degrees of arbitrariness: *the sign may be relatively motivated.*

For instance, both *vingt* "twenty" and *dix-neuf* "nineteen" are unmotivated in French, but not in the same degree, for *dix-neuf* suggests its own terms and other terms associated with it. (131)

Saussure's characterizations of arbitrariness are of a mostly negative nature: to say of a sign that it is arbitrary is to say that

    (a) it is not motivated;
    (b) the choice of the *signifiant* for a *signifié* is arbitrary;

---

[3] Ludwig Jäger has put much effort into reconstructing those ideas judged to be "authentically" Saussure's. Good overviews of the debate can be found in Wunderli 1992 and Jäger 1976.

(c) there is no inner relationship linking the *signifiant* and *signifié*;

(d) there is no natural connection between *signifiant* and *signifié*; and

(e) there is a kind of secondary motivatedness.

Finally, Saussure suggests that the arbitrariness of the sign is explained with the fact that "every means of expression used in society is based, in principle, on collective behavior or—which amounts to the same thing —on convention" (Saussure 1960: 68).

Negative characterizations are by nature not very convincing. It would be more interesting to find out in what arbitrariness consists than in what it does not. Even disregarding this deficit, Saussure's characterization, taken as whole, is self-contradictory: if an arbitrary sign is supposed to be, by definition, an unmotivated sign, the choice of a *signifiant* for a *signifié* cannot be "completely arbitrary." After all, the choice of a motivated expression is supposedly impossible. Similarly, the theory that a sign is arbitrary in so far as it is conventional is incompatible with the theory that *arbitrary* means "unmotivated." Nothing prevents a language community from making the use of a motivated sign conventional. *Cuckoo* is motivated and conventional, and thus, according to one principle, it is arbitrary, while according to the other it is not. This inconsistency may have been what motivated Saussure to somewhat half-heartedly ascribe arbitrariness even to clearly motivated signs: "As for authentic onomapoetic words (e.g. *glug-glug*, *tick-tock*, etc.), not only are they limited in number, but also they are chosen somewhat arbitrarily, for they are only approximate and more or less conventional imitations of certain sounds (cf. English *bow-wow* and French *ouaoua*)" (Saussure 1960: 69). Significantly, Saussure refers here to the criterion of conventionality, which favors his argument, and not to the criterion of motivatedness; this alone enables him to bring the theory of arbitrariness into tolerably reasonable agreement with the obvious motivatedness of such onomatopoeia.

Saussure's ideas about relative arbitrariness correspond fairly well to Plato's theory about the "natural correctness" of "secondary" or "derived" words. Transparent word formations are "relatively motivated" in so far as their meaning is compositional. That is, the total meaning can be construed from the meaning of individual components.[4] The meaning of the sign *dix-neuf* results from the combination of *dix* and

---

[4] This is true, of course, for every syntagm; cf. Chap. 15.

neuf. The meaning of this combination is the combination of meanings: here we have a homomorphism, one which Plato, in contrast to Saussure, assumes to be valid down to the level of phonemes. Volker Beeh has attempted clearly and intelligibly to reconstruct the Saussurean concept of arbitrariness (in the sense of unmotivatedness), using the concepts of homomorphism, and of the complexity of description of the meaning of a vocabulary: "A vocabulary V is arbitrary if, and only if, there is no description of V of lower complexity other than V itself" (Beeh 1980: 9). In any case, the description of an entire vocabulary becomes less complex when the meaning of certain of its expressions can be derived from the meanings of their parts. Compositionality makes reduction possible. In other words, Beeh believes that a vocabulary is arbitrary only when there exists no description of all the signs of a vocabulary that is more economical than their enumeration. Beeh's reconstruction of the Saussurean concept of arbitrariness is a good one in the sense of unmotivatedness, but only in so far as this unmotivatedness is grounded in the non-compositionality of the meaning of a sign. This approach does not consider arbitrariness in the sense of a freedom of choice in regard to the signifier (as well as to the signified, an aspect that goes unmentioned in the *Cours*).[5] These are aspects to which we will now turn our attention.

We recall from Chapter 1 what I called the instrumentalist fallacy. Briefly stated, it is the belief that words are tools, and that the specific makeup of a tool is dictated by the purpose it is meant to fulfill. Hence the makeup of a word cannot be arbitrary. Let us examine this fallacy.

Linguistic signs are tools which, in certain circumstances, are suited to certain purposes. Knowing what they mean is knowing to which purposes they are suited, in which circumstances. The meaning of the sign *goodbye* consists, for example, in its being suited to taking leave of another person. A means can be more or less well suited to a particular end. Knowing that a linguistic sign has meaning is knowing that its use in regard to the purpose and situation of use is rule based.

Now, a person might think that an expression *E* is suited to the realization of an intention *I* if *E* has certain properties that make it suitable for this. The expression *goodbye*, for instance, is suitable to be used as a

---

[5] This is an obvious case of a distorting simplification of Saussure's concepts by the authors of the *Cours* (see Jäger 1976: 236ff.).

departing valediction precisely when it has the corresponding meaning. To believe this would be a grave mistake. There are no properties that make a sign suitable (in the sense relevant here). In fact, being suitable is the only decisive property. There is nothing "behind" this fact! The theory espoused here does not claim that the use of a linguistic sign follows from its meaning. Rather, it claims that the meaning of a linguistic sign *is* its use. The answer to the question "Why is an expression used as it is?" reads quite simply: that's just the way it is. What makes the expression *E* suitable for me today it the fact that it has heretofore proven itself to be suitable, and that it has remained suitable—for me, as well as for others, as far as I know. My individual competence is made up of hypotheses about the suitability of means—hypotheses that I continually test, modify and bring up to date (cf. Keller 1994: chapter 6.1). Since the meaning of a linguistic sign consists of nothing other than being suitable for the realization of certain intentions in certain situations, meanings can be identified only by saying which expressions are suitable for which purpose in which situation. And this is to formulate the rule of their use.

Linguistic signs are comparable to tools in many ways, but not in every way. As an example, let us take a switch: switches can be used to whip. Whipping is something intentional. Switches themselves are not intentional. Up to this point, their comparison with linguistic signs is fine. But now it becomes problematic: a switch is suitable for whipping because of the material of which it is made, because it has a certain size and elasticity, and so on. It is the makeup of tools that makes them suitable for their purpose. And it makes the tool suitable for the realization of certain intentions. In contrast, a linguistic symbol is suitable for the realization of a certain intention only because it is common to use it for the realization of this intention. To say of a linguistic sign that it is arbitrary is to say that its suitability is not based on its makeup.

This characterization is in accord with the Saussurean model to the extent that it is nothing but negative. But what is the positive basis of suitability? The answer is *conventionality*. Conventionality and arbitrariness are not identical. But they are inherently connected, in so far as conventionality implies arbitrariness. We would not find certain kinds of behavior conventional if they were not arbitrary. This has been demonstrated by David Lewis. Before I briefly present Lewis's theory of convention, I would like to show the plausibility of the connection by means of example: imagine that there is an African village that has two wells from which its inhabitants can draw water. However, everyone always gets water from just one of the wells. An outside observer might hypothesize that this behavior is conventional. But if it becomes evident that the water in one of the wells is dirtier, or that one of the wells is harder to reach, an intelligent observer will reject the earlier hypothesis of conventionality. No convention is necessary for choosing the better of two alternatives. However, if both wells were really equally suitable, the conventionality hypothesis would be absolutely appropriate. In that case, the same would apply to the oft-used well as to linguistic signs: its use is not based on its makeup.

What is a convention, then? I will attempt to summarize David Lewis's answer. Generally speaking, conventions are solutions to coordination problems (Lewis 1969: chapter 1). A typical and very simple coordination problem is, for example, wanting to meet someone. In order for two people to meet, they have to be at the same place at approximately the same time. If they manage to meet, a *coordination equilibrium* is produced (for a definition of this, see Lewis 1969: 14). A convention is a strategy for producing coordination equilibria. Explicitly arranging to meet is a different strategy. (Maybe the fact that both strategies can lead to the same result is the reason that conventions are often colloquially called "unspoken rules.") How can two people meet without explicitly arranging to do so? In the absence of established conventions, there are two possibilities: either they can meet by coincidence, or by the attempt to anticipate where the other would probably be. Let us assume that a man and a woman see each other in a café at about 4 p.m. on a Tuesday afternoon. Later, the man regrets not having spoken to the woman, and resolves to try and see her again. What can he do? He could fly to New York—there are lots of people there, and maybe she is one of them. Running into her by this means is not logically impossible, but extremely improbable. This would not be a rational choice of action. Since the man knows nothing more about the woman other than that she was in the café where he saw her at a certain time, there is no more rational strategy than to go back to the café at the same time. If we assume that the feeling of regret mentioned above was mutual, the chances are not bad that the two of them will run into each other in the same café the next afternoon at 4 p.m. The strategy of each is to go to the place where he or she thinks the other will go. Each of them makes his or her choice of action according to their expectations of the other's choice of action. This is the only possibility with better chances than coincidence for reaching a coordination equilibrium. Communication is also a coordination problem, and understanding is the targeted coordination equilibrium. The analogous strategy for solving a communicative coordination problem is the following: with you, I choose the linguistic means that I think you would choose if you were in my place. Elsewhere I have called this strategy the "Humboldt maxim" (Keller 1994: 99). In this way, a "system of suitably concordant mutual expectations" can arise (Lewis 1969: 25). Certain kinds of behavior are suitable for reaching the desired coordination equilibrium, as long as such a system of mutually concordant expectations exists.

This somewhat lengthy foreword has prepared us for Lewis's definition of *convention*:

A regularity R in the behavior of members of a population P when they are agents in a recurrent situation S is a *convention* if and only if it is true that, and it is common knowledge in P that, in any instance of S among members of P,

(1) everyone conforms to R;
(2) everyone expects everyone else to conform to R;
(3) everyone has approximately the same preferences regarding all possible combinations of actions;
(4) everyone prefers that everyone conform to R, on condition that at least all but one conform to R;
(5) everyone would prefer that everyone conform to R', on condition that at least all but one conform to R';

where R' is some possible regularity in the behavior of members of P in S, such that no one in any instance of S among members of P could conform to both R' and R. (Lewis 1969: 76)[6]

Simply and colloquially reformulated, this says that similar behavior among the members of a group is called "conventional" if, for every individual, the only reason for choosing exactly this kind of behavior is that each person thinks that the others will do the same. My reason for driving on the right side of the road is nothing more than that I expect others to do the same. If I expected others to drive on the left, I would drive on the left, too.

Condition (5) in Lewis's definition is that of arbitrariness: there has to

---

[6] This is one of Lewis's provisional definitions, but does not differ essentially from the final one (Lewis 1969: 78–80). I have chosen to use the provisional definition because of its greater clarity.

be another possibility, one just as good, for reaching the desired goal. If for logical or practical reasons there were only one possibility of action, that action would not be called a "convention." Hence it is not conventional, for example, that most people use their right hands for throwing: they could not throw just as well with their left hands. "This is why it is redundant to speak of an arbitrary convention. Any convention is arbitrary because there is an alternative regularity that could have been our convention instead" (Lewis 1969: 70). Johann Christoph Adelung expressed a similar thought 200 years ago. He observed in 1782 that "there is nothing in a language of which the opposite could not also occur" (Adelung 1971: I, 113).[7]

Thus we see that the meaning of linguistic signs, if the signs are conventional, is necessarily conventional. But since the meaning not only of a symbol, but also of the expression, is a conventional rule, one might say that the entire symbol is arbitrary. The statement "A conventional sign is arbitrary" is analytically true. The arbitrariness of the symbol is just a special case of the arbitrariness of everything that is conventional. However, not all symbols have a conventional nature in Lewis's sense of the term. Some are ad hoc creations, provided with rules of use by means of definition. Are they arbitrary, too? Even for those that are ruled by definition, it holds that, if there were only a logically or factually possible kind of rule, none at all would be needed. We can generalize again, and say that symbols are arbitrary in so far as their expression and their use is rule based. The arbitrariness of the conventional is a special case of the arbitrariness of that which is rule based.

Up to this point, we may summarize by saying, and keep in mind, that all symbols are arbitrary in so far as they are of conventional nature; and some of them are motivated. The question of the conventionality of a sign is independent of the question of its motivatedness or unmotivatedness. Conventions are arbitrary in the sense that the logical possibility of an alternative that is just as good must exist. If, following common practice, we too call unmotivatedness "arbitrariness," we will be guilty of making an equivocation. Therefore, from now on, we will fastidiously distinguish the words *arbitrary* and *unmotivated*, allowing us to speak of motivated arbitrary signs (*cuckoo*) and unmotivated arbitrary signs (*geac*).[8]

[7] Trans. K.D.

[8] *Geac* is the OE designation for the cuckoo, and it, too, was originally motivated; see Chap. 11.

How did this equivocation become so widespread? There is a certain diachronic connection between conventionality and unmotivatedness, for one thing, and for another, between motivatedness (or semantic transparency) and unconventionality. If, however, an exclusively synchronic perspective is taken, this connection is obscured. It is made up of two aspects:

(1) Communicative attempts with non-conventional means can be successful only if the intended meaning can somehow be determined from the perceptible aspect of the communicative act. That is, the employed means should be semantically transparent. The most prominent form of semantic transparency is primary or secondary motivatedness.

(2) The conventionalization of a means employed for communicative purposes is almost always accompanied by a process of demotivation.

It is primarily Edmond Wright who has made the first aspect a subject of discussion: "One question de Saussure does not seem to have asked himself is how a sign not already dependent on an existing language could come to be made. If signs can only be made within languages, one wonders how our ancestors ever began" (Wright 1976: 512). What Saussure says about signs, values, and arbitrariness, he says about the established signs of language. If we want to take language's genesis into account, "we cannot . . . take *la langue* for granted" (Wright 1976: 514). Rather, we must ask ourselves "how comes it about that a neutral sensory element (seen, heard, felt, or other—for other beings most probably have other sensory modes) is endowed with meaning by an agent?—or, better, how does he come to mean it? . . . How does he become a meaner with a sign he makes himself?" (Wright 1976: 514). Two conditions must be satisfied:

First, there must be *an intentional context*: the agent must be desirous of something. He must also desire to influence another agent . . . in order to further that desire. . . . [Second,] Our speaker is to use a neutral sensory element; he has "to utter" it. It may be a sign he makes with his body; it may be a manipulation of objects around him. . . . The originality of the meaner is to select a neutral sensory element . . . that will indicate what is to be done. And it is at precisely this stage that its neutrality disappears. The "utterer's" meaning must, through some kind of association which the "hearer" can recognize, be indicated in that very sensory element. . . . If de Saussure were right, and transparency were not logically necessary to the transmission of meaning, our presumed first user of a new sign could never use it to communicate at all! His selection cannot be arbitrary in that sense. If there were no transparency whatsoever in the newly-made sign, the communication could not take place. It would be non-sense. (Wright 1976: 514–15)

Wright makes it clear that communicative attempts with nonconventional (or not-yet-conventionalized) means, if they are to have any hope of success, can only be carried out with an iconic method. The iconic method requires the deployment of semantically transparent means. Icons are necessarily motivated. Now let us consider the second aspect.

Under certain conditions, icons become symbols. I will describe this process of sign metamorphosis in the next chapter. For now, a brief reference to it will do: the change from icon to symbol consists of an associative inference being replaced with a rule-based inference. In the course of this process, the aspect of the (old) icon's transparency, which served as an association impulse, loses relevance. When the iconically represented numbers *I*, *II* and *III* are routinely written from right to left by practiced writers, their joined forms, as they are currently written in Arabic, are virtually bound to result: ١, ٢, ٣. In order to interpret these numerals, experienced writers will no longer need to use the number of vertical lines as an impulse for the iconic method of association. Because of the rule of use, they will know that with the sign ٢, the number two is meant. Since iconicity was no longer relevant, the understanding of the Arabic numerals was not at all disadvantaged when Europeans, trained in writing Latin, turned them by 90° to make them easier to write from left to right. So did the motivated icons *II* and *III* become the conventionally demotivated symbols *2* and *3*.

From the fact that icons must necessarily be motivated it does not follow that symbols must necessarily be unmotivated. Only those who definitively equate iconicity with motivatedness find themselves forced to this conclusion. Demotivation is a natural side effect of the process of conventionalization. But it is not necessary, and it must not have been completed by any given state of language. This is why, for every natural language, we must expect motivated, arbitrary signs to be a part of the vocabulary, even if they are only "limited in number" (Saussure 1960: 69).

PART IV

Sign Metamorphosis

11

Iconification and Symbolification

New linguistic signs need some kind of transparency in order to be interpretable at all. "In the beginning was the Word", perhaps, but that word cannot have been unmotivated. There are various ways of communicating transparently. In this chapter, I will show how symbols emerge. My strategy will be to start with symptoms and to show, step by step, how the transitions from symptoms to icons and from icons to symbols are able to occur.

THE ICONIFICATION OF SYMPTOMS

Symptoms are the most primitive kind of signs. They are not there to be used, but are simply put to use. It is their actual use that makes them into symptoms. Blood test results, moving blades of grass, and yawns are examples of possible symptoms. The results of blood tests can be interpreted by a doctor as a symptom of disease (or of health); moving blades of grass can be interpreted as a symptom of wind; yawning can be a symptom of fatigue. The ability to use things and events as symptoms is not restricted to humans. In my experience, dogs in Spain can be chased away by bending down to the ground and making a movement as though to pick up a stone. Spanish dogs evidently interpret this motion as the start of a throwing a stone, and run away. This sort of interpretive ability plays an important part in the evolution of animal communication, as Robert Brandon and Norbert Hornstein write (1986). The signs of animal communication often arise through so-called ritualizations. The process of ritualization begins when "one organism interprets the action, or some part thereof, of another as a sign of that action . . . Typically, the relevant part of the behavioral sequence will be an *initial* part and inference will be a prediction of the subsequent behavior" (Brandon and Hornstein 1986: 172). Thus birds that fly in flocks use typical preflight behavior as a takeoff signal. Ritualizations also have a role in human communication: raising one's hand as if to strike is used as a threatening gesture. The interpreter infers the whole from a part. We have named this method of interpretation the symptomic technique. However, the threatening gesture, as well as the method described above for chasing away Spanish dogs, is no longer a purely symptomatic strategy. As we have noted, symptoms are not used; they are just "there" and undergo interpretation. The gesture of picking up a stone, and of raising one's hand to strike, however, are deliberately employed with the intention of stimulating a particular interpretation. The object of interpretation is not really the start of the action of picking up a stone, or of raising one's hand to strike, but the simulation of the start of the action of picking up a stone or raising one's hand to strike. Brandon and Hornstein's observation applies to this, the first phase of ritualization: "At this stage, the change from behavior to sign takes place purely on the receptor side" (1986: 172). Let's leave the Spanish dogs; for them, the difference between the real and the simulated actions of picking up a stone makes no difference. If I know them, they would not react in the desired way if they saw through the simulation. It's different with human communication. The threatening gesture of "starting to strike" is interpreted as a threatening gesture even if it is recognized as a simulation of starting to strike. This is a significant difference.

With this difference, we have the first step from the ability to interpret to the ability to stimulate interpretation. Because of their knowledge of their species' ability to interpret symptoms, humans are led to imitate symptoms deliberately, namely with the intention that their imitation should be recognized as an imitation by the addressee, and interpreted with the symptomic technique. Interpretive ability is exploited for the purpose of communication.

Let's consider this everyday example: if I want to silently indicate to my companion during the course of a lecture that I find it deadly boring, I can do this by turning to her and simulating a somewhat exaggerated yawn. A slight deviation from an authentic yawn is necessary to make sure that it is not interpreted as a real one. The simulated yawn should be sufficiently salient[1] to cause the addressee to judge it as an attempt at communication and search for an appropriate interpretation. Therefore, the simulated yawn must fulfill two conditions.

(1) It must be recognizable as the simulation of a *yawn*.

(2) It must be recognizable as the *simulation* of a yawn.[2]

Through simulation, the symptom becomes an icon. It undergoes a process of iconification, and this for the following reasons: a real yawn can be a symptom of a shortage of oxygen. A simulated yawn can never be a symptom of a shortage of oxygen. Only real symptoms are symptoms. Imitated symptoms resemble symptoms and are thus icons of symptoms. The addressee of iconified symptoms must perform two successively activated interpretive techniques. Because of the yawn's similarity to a real yawn, as well as its difference from a real yawn, she interprets it as an icon of a yawn; this, in turn, she interprets as an icon of a symptom of boredom, on the basis of her knowledge of the causal connection between yawning, fatigue and boredom.

Here, too, the parallels to the processes of evolution in animal communication are unmistakable. Thus is the behavior that serves pigeons as a starting signal, for instance, "exaggerated beyond what is phylogenetically necessary for flight and beyond what, presumably, was once the preflight pattern" (Brandon and Hornstein 1986: 173). It is typical for the second step in the process of ritualization "that certain features of behavior which function as the (perceptually iconic) sign are exaggerated, stylized, and articulated . . . The function of such exaggeration is to make it less likely that the sign will be missed or misunderstood" (Brandon and Hornstein 1986: 173). Exaggeration provides the degree of salience necessary for the addressee to perceive the sign as an icon, and thus as a communicative attempt, not just as a symptom. The iconified symptom must therefore have two aspects, one that makes it recognizable as a deliberately produced sign (this is accomplished by its salience), and one that makes recognizable what the sign user wants to

---

[1] On the function of salience in the process of the emergence of conventions, see Lewis 1969: 35, 38.

[2] This "trick" played an important part in the story of the apeman Charlie (Keller 1994: 29).

convey with it (this is accomplished by its symptomatic component).[3] The "symptom simulator" must make clear to the addressee both *that* he wishes communicate and *what* he wishes to communicate.

The iconic representation of symptoms is an old and widespread cultural technique, employed as early as in hieroglyphics. It is easy to imagine an iconic character for, say, *amphora*. One might draw a stylized amphora. But what could a character for *beer* look like? You can't draw beer; but what you can draw is, for example, a vessel in which beer is typically brewed or stored: an amphora. The graphic representation of a certain amphora served the Sumerians as the character for beer ("GEOSKOP" 1993: 144), and a representation of bent reeds was the Egyptians' character for wind.[4] The employed inferences are, first, the associative inference, from the graphic representation to the portrayed object, and second, the causal inference, from a part to the whole (from a vessel to its content) or from the effect (the bending of the reeds) to the cause (the wind). In many cases, an iconic-symptomic representation is iconically or symptomically reinterpreted on another level, such as when a character for *beer* is used as a sign for 'drunkenness' or the character for *wind* is used as a sign for 'transitoriness'. We will see that the techniques of the second level of interpretation are very similar to the processes of metonymization (as in the case of 'drunkenness') and of metaphorization (as in the case of 'transitoriness').[5]

Usually, exclamatory expressions, expressions of pain, disgust, etc., still hint at their past as iconified symptoms. Words like *ow* and *phooey* are examples of this. *Ow* came from a simulated expression of pain, and *phooey* imitates the sound of spitting something out in disgust. A fictive, but realistic, instance of the iconification of a symptom of pain would be when, during a playful tussle with my children, I simulate an expression of pain, perhaps with the intention of getting them to leave off. Again, to do this, it is necessary to simulate the symptom of pain in such a way that they see through it. If my expression is mistakenly understood as a real symptom of pain, it would not be understood in the intended sense. For its correct understanding, it is necessary that the communicative

---

[3] These two conditions are analogous to the ones that Sperber and Wilson name (1986a: 54, 153, 163) for so-called ostensive stimuli.

[4] These examples are from a lecture by Raimo Anttila.

[5] Cf. Anttila 1989, § 7.8.

impetus be recognized as such—this happens with the recognition of the simulation—and that what is meant to be conveyed be recognized—which happens with its interpretation as a symptom.

Under certain conditions, the iconification of a symptom can virtually be interpreted as a sign of the absence of the symptom's cause. The following scenario is an example of this, that is, a case in which the iconification of a symptom can itself be interpreted as a symptom. The example is banal, but the analysis it requires is surprisingly complex. A friend makes fun of my new tie; I reply with a tired-sounding *ha-ha-ha*. Formulated as a sentence, my reaction would be something like "I don't find that funny at all." How can I expect my *ha-ha-ha* to be interpreted in the desired way? A slow-motion replay of the reasoning behind my friend's interpretation might look something like this:

> "You say *ha-ha-ha*. This is similar to the sound of laughing. So you're simulating a laugh. But laughing is a spontaneous reaction, the symptom of amusement. The fact that this spontaneous reaction is missing is a symptom of nonamusement. Simulated laughing is not a spontaneous reaction. The simulation itself is thus a symptom for nonamusement. From the fact that you intend me to recognize that your laugh is a simulated one, I infer that you intend to give me to understand that you are in a state of nonamusement. Since your *ha-ha-ha* is a reaction to my comment about your tie, you evidently want to give me to understand that you do not find my comment amusing."

I admit that this is a lot of analytical effort for a *ha-ha-ha*. But the explanation of ironic effects is usually rather complex.[6] However, the fact that even six-year-olds are capable of using and interpreting *ha-ha-ha* in this sense, that is, of performing complex inferential procedures of this sort, is quite enlightening. The ability to interpret, to simulate and thus to iconify symptoms is a fundamental technique of our communicative behavior.

Onomatopoeic linguistic signs are always "former" iconified symptoms when they designate not the sound, but the maker of the sound. One way in which the expression *cock-a-doodle-do* differs from the word *cuckoo* is that *cock-a-doodle-do* does not designate the animal that

---

[6] Cf. Lapp 1992.

makes this sound, while *cuckoo* is the word for the animal that makes the sound *cuckoo*. *Cock-a-doodle-do* designates the sound, *cuckoo* the maker of the sound. The noun *cuckoo* is thus, in the first instance, an iconified symptom of the animal thus designated; however, it is also a symptom that has undergone a process of symbolification. We will examine this process, the symbolification of icons, after discussing the symbolification of symptoms.

THE SYMBOLIFICATION OF SYMPTOMS

As we have seen, symptoms become icons automatically, as it were, when they are simulated. Some symptoms can be consciously staged. This is the process to which we will now turn our attention. Let us begin with a phenomenon known almost the world over: the car as status symbol.

Right now, a certain model of Jaguar costs about £35,000. The possession of such an object is, first of all (under normal conditions), a symptom of a certain level of prosperity. The possession of an unnecessary object of this worth (a car for £10,000 performs most functions equally well) is a sign that the money it costs is not needed for other life-sustaining goods. The possession of any other unnecessary object with the same worth, say, 15 tons of copper, might also be interpreted as a symptom of prosperity. But there is a significant difference between 15 tons of copper and a Jaguar: a Jaguar counts as a status symbol, while 15 tons of copper do not. This is due to the fact that the Jaguar, unlike the copper, is often purchased for the express purpose of making its owner's prosperity visible. This kind of behavior, which just about everyone has experienced in some form or another, I will call the *staging of a symptom*. In the course of time, such staging may have the effect that the interpretive process no longer proceeds by way of causality, by knowing the price of the car, for example, but rather, in a kind of abbreviation, by way of knowledge of a rule. This process of sign metamorphosis may be presented in three steps.

(1) *"A person who has x also has y."*
    Anyone who makes this inference simply interprets *x* as a symptom for *y*: "A person who has 15 tons of copper has too much

money." If the interpreters assume that the "owner" of the symptom is doing some staging, they will proceed rationally to the next interpretive step:

(2) *"A person who shows that he has* x *wants people to know that he has* y."

This kind of inference may very well have presumptive character. The "owner" of the symptom has no chance of dodging such presumptive interpretations. If this model of interpretation becomes, in regard to *x*, a generally accepted one, it becomes "true" of its own accord. If everyone believes that a person who has a Jaguar has it just to show that he's rich, the status of the belief has changed: now the Jaguar really does serve to make its owner's prosperity recognizable. In other words, if interpretation (2) becomes an object of a group's common knowledge, interpretation (3) automatically results:

(3) *"In a group* G, x *serves to make (x has the function of making)* y *recognizable."*

To say that *x* serves to make *y* recognizable in *G* is to say nothing other than that *x* has a meaning which makes *y* recognizable. From now on, *x* has a rule of use and thus a communicative function. With this, *x* has become a symbol.

Thus we observe that the assumption of communicative intent, which must not necessarily be present in every individual act, plus the emergence of common knowledge, makes a symbol of a symptom. Anyone who knows the symbol's value no longer needs the symptomic value for interpretation: a Jaguar can be a sign of prosperity even for someone who does not know its price. Thanks to this mechanism, a used Jaguar for £10,000 is more impressive than a new Mitsubishi for £15,000.

Linguistic symbols can emerge in the same way. The use of Latin and Greek terms is, at the least, a symptom of a certain kind and level of education. Expressions like a priori, in toto and suchlike, as well as other foreign expressions, can very quickly take on symbolic character for the educated classes.

We have now acquainted ourselves with two processes of sign change, the iconification and the symbolification of symptoms. These processes have one principle in common: that symptoms, in order to count as true symptoms, may not be intentionally produced. Consequently, every form of their deliberate production demands reinterpretation. If a symptom is intentionally produced, this in itself is a symptom that it really should not be interpreted as a symptom. There are precisely two ways to produce symptoms intentionally: simulation (which leads to iconification) and staging (which leads to symbolification). There is no alternative. The possibilities for the metamorphosis of symptoms are exhausted with the two processes named here. Let us proceed to icons.

THE SYMBOLIFICATION OF ICONS

We recall that the iconic method is an associative inference on the basis of a relation of similarity, whatever kind it may be. The symbolic technique is rule based. The transition from icon to symbol, that is, from the associative to the rule-based inference, is particularly interesting for linguistic theory, because this process plays a decisive part in what is called *lexicalization*. But we will deal with this topic later.

Consider this fictive example. During a walk through the forest, I want to make my companion aware of a wood pigeon sitting on a branch, but without scaring her away (the pigeon, that is). I could do this by pointing towards the pigeon and imitating its cooing sound. From my pointing gesture and the similarity of the sound I make to that of a pigeon, my companion will infer: "Aha, this guy *probably* wants to show me a pigeon." Let us assume that my communicative attempt is successful, and the situation comes up again the next day. My companion will now infer, on the basis of the successful communicative endeavor of the previous day, "Aha, he *definitely* wants to show me a pigeon." By the fifth time, at the latest, I will not even bother with trying to produce the pigeon's coo with any degree of authenticity. Just the start of an approximate coo will suffice to let my companion know that I want to point out a pigeon. She will no longer need to employ her associative abilities. The basis of her inference will be her knowledge. The moral of the story: anyone repeatedly faced with the same puzzle will not need to guess at its solution; she will know it. Over time, a recurring associative inference *necessarily* becomes a rule-based inference. Recurrence causes icons to become moribund. The mechanism of this metamorphosis is as follows.

Association is a creative process without normativity. You cannot make a mistake while associating. " 'Free association' is really a pleonasm: *association* is inherently free and undisciplined" (Gellner 1988: 57).[7] Undesirable associations go on the sign user's account, not on that of the addressee. Sign users have intended goals, to which they hope, with their iconic attempts, to direct their addressees' associations. The connection between the iconic sign and the associative goal is not an object of common knowledge. However, if an interpreter is *successfully* given an associative problem several times, the process of inference, thanks to the recollection of the precedents, ceases to be an associative one. Very simply, association with a known associative goal just is not association. If the connection between the sign and the "associative goal" has gone on to become an object of common knowledge, a rule of use has arisen, and the icon has become a symbol. That is, through pure repetition, common recollection of precedents, and the assumption of communicative intent, an associative inference becomes a rule-based one. Initially, of course, the symbol will remain onomatopoeically motivated. We have defined iconicity not with motivatedness, but with its capacity to call forth association. But from this point on, the motivatedness of the sign has lost its function as an associative impulse. It may continue to function as an aesthetic or mnemotechnical bonus. However, since it has become obsolete as an associative catalyst, its motivatedness will eventually disappear. The sign user no longer has reason to spend much energy on authenticity. Thus did a drawing of a man become the Chinese character 人 *ren* 'human', the iconic representation of the number three (III) became our number *3*, and the picture of a bull's head 🐂 ultimately became, with some stylization and a 180° turn, our letter *A*. In all three cases, we can comprehend the former iconicity of the sign if we are made aware of it. But it no longer contributes to the current form of interpretation of the sign.

The symbolification of icons results in two advantages for the language user: (a) authenticity loses relevance; now, even bad bird imitators have something to say; and (b) the contextuality of use becomes less strict. A cooing sound uttered at the wrong time has almost no chance as an attempt to say something about pigeons, and even the best representation of a man will not be interpreted as the icon for a men's toilet if it's

---

[7] This applies only to the word *association* in the psychological sense (see Ch. 8 n. 7).

not on a door. A disadvantage of the symbolification of icons is the demotivation that occurs with the process. An icon that has become a linguistic symbol is subject to the normal processes of phonetic change in the respective language. This is probably how, from the original *guk (guk)*, OE *geac*, early modern German *gauch* and Swedish *gök* [jök] developed. What is the disadvantage of this? The answer is that, with the conventionalization of icons and the accompanying demotivation, a process of "bleaching" comes to bear. *Geac* once served to designate the cuckoo. *Cuckoo*, as an icon or symbol whose onomatopoeic character is still evident, is today used to designate the cuckoo. But *cuckoo*, in contrast to *geac*, designates this animal by *showing* something that is characteristic of it. This simultaneous naming and showing is, compared to pure naming, a semantic condensation that can prove to be both practically–communicatively useful and aesthetically appealing. In Chapter 15, I will return to the advantages of semantic condensation and the disadvantages of semantic bleaching.

The process of the symbolification of an icon does not have to occur at the same time for both the speaker and the hearer. What is a symbol for one of them may be an icon for the other. That which one of them interprets associatively can be interpreted on the basis of a rule by a person who has been confronted with this sign many times. The common notions of icon and symbol (cf. Chapter 8), according to which an icon is defined by means of a relation of similarity and a symbol by means of arbitrariness, make it difficult, if not impossible, to imagine how the transition from the iconic to the symbolic might take place in a language community. However, if we view signs as what they actually are, namely, means for letting others know to which inferences we hope to bring them, the transitions do not seem at all contrived.

With the example of the preflight behavior of birds, we saw that even in the biological evolution of animal signs, there are processes analogous to the iconification of symptoms. Natural, functionally necessary preflight behavior becomes, in slightly "exaggerated" form, the iconic takeoff signal for the flock. With the deviation of the exaggerated form from the authentic, the symptom is iconified. Is there anything in the realm of biological evolution that is analogous to the symbolification of icons? The process that biologists call *transference* (Brandon and Hornstein 1986: 173) might be seen as such. It occurs when iconic behavior is transferred to another area, such as ritualized behavior to establish sexual bonds during mating seasons. For example, the male gray crested heron, as a part of courtship ceremonies, routinely performs what is clearly a modified fishing movement (Wilson 1975: 226). Transference results in a reduction of motivatedness in signifying behavior.

The examination of human examples of transference makes even clearer their proximity to processes of icon symbolification. Warriors conveyed their peaceful intentions by opening their hands to show that they concealed no weapons, by opening their helmets to make themselves identifiable, and by kneeling down with bowed heads, a sign of vulnerability and defenselessness. All three elements of this show of peaceful intent, be they symptomic or iconic, have been "transferred," in diminished versions, to our forms of greeting: we hold out our hand to shake, or raise it to wave; we lift our hats or bow slightly. It's the same with these symbols of courtesy as with the number *3*. If we know about their iconic past, we can still recognize it. But this ability plays no part in everyday interpretation of such signs.

We may recapitulate the three processes of sign metamorphosis with which we have thus far become acquainted as follows:

(1) There are three basic interpretive techniques used in communication. They trigger processes of sign emergence.

(2) These processes are not parallel. Symptoms can become icons or symbols. Icons can become symbols. Symptoms change their status by means of exploitative use, icons by means of frequent use.

(3) Various kinds of transition are possible from "bottom" to "top," but there are no regressions. The development is unidirectional.

This can be graphically presented with the floor plan of a three-room apartment, where the doors swing open in only one direction.

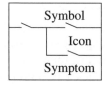

I know of only a single case in which the principle of unidirectionality is violated:

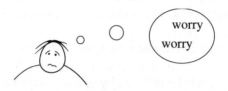

I would like to call this "trick," which can usually be found in comic strips, *pseudo-onomatopoesis*. Usually, onomatopoeic signs emerge when symptomic sounds are imitated in language, thus becoming iconified symptoms. *Sssssssst*, for example, might be used as an icon for the sound produced by tearing a piece of paper. We have seen that, in a second step, iconified symptoms can become symbols. Examples are the words *ribbit* and *cuckoo*. Pseudo-onomatopoesis evidently reckons on the speaker being so familiar with the process that he can apply and understand it even "against the grain." A symbol that is absolutely free of motivatedness is used as though concentrated thought made a symptomic sound, iconically represented with the sound [wʉr'ē]. The technique of pseudo-onomatopoesis acts as though the verb *worry* were a symbolified icon of a symptom. The fact that we are able to interpret this technique, and even to find it amusing (to some degree), confirms that the processes of sign metamorphosis introduced in the previous pages belong to the basic repertoire of our communicative abilities.

Let us return to the "floor plan" of our "three-room apartment." Why do the doors swing open in only one direction? Is there really no way back? We will examine this question step by step.

(1) How do you take a symbol or an icon and turn it back into a symptom? The answer: as soon as a sign is intentionally pro-duced, it cannot be a symptom, because symptoms cannot be produced for the purpose of being symptoms. However, symp-toms do exist on a higher level. The serious use of symbols like *nigger* or *Entjudung* can be interpreted as a symptom of racist tendencies. Here, though, it is not the linguistic signs that become symptoms, but the fact of their use. To put it differently: it's not the symbol that becomes a symptom, but the fact of its use.

(2) How do you turn a symbol back into an icon? The process of the emergence of a symbol from an icon is necessarily bound up with the emergence of common knowledge of its rule of use. Re-iconification would therefore require a loss of knowledge. In order to turn a symbol back into an icon, memory would have to be wiped out. However, as long as a symbol is in use, the knowledge of its rule of use is continually refreshed.[8] A symbol could only become an icon again if it remained unused long enough for the rule of its use to be forgotten. But such a case would not be one of sign metamorphosis in the sense described here; rather, it would be something like a re-initialization of the process. In any case, there is a kind of *use* which results in a symbol returning to the status of an icon. However, icons can occur on another level: there are icons that emerge from symbols. These are metaphors, as we will see. Here, too, it is not a way back through the swinging doors, a retreat in the other direction, but a process that takes place "outside" the three-room apartment—on the next floor, so to speak.

Thus we may summarize: over the course of time, symptoms and icons, if used frequently enough, are doomed to become symbols. The unidirectionality of this development is based in the logic of signs and their use.

---

[8] Linguistic signs can be remotivated by means of popular etymology: hamburgers were originally so called, for example, because they supposedly came from Hamburg, so the morphemic boundary was hamburg + er. Now the boundary is ham + burger, as in *beefburger*, *chickenburger*, *turkeyburger*, etc. This happened although the product was never presumed to contain ham. (Thanks to Jules Levin for this example of remotivation in English.)

However, remotivation is not re-iconification. Re-iconification occurs when the interpretative possibility of the sign follows from its motivatedness. But symbols that have undergone remotivation by popular etymology, such as the examples above, are still interpreted according to rule. The same goes for the remotivation that occurs in word play. For the difference between motivatedness and arbitrariness, see Chap. 10.

12

Metaphorization, Metonymization and Lexicalization

The ability to communicate consists in (among other things) exploiting the interpretive ability of the addressee for one's own ends. Up to this point, we have acquainted ourselves with three forms of the exploitative use of interpretive ability:

(1) I know that you are capable of making causal inferences. I stage a symptom and try in this way to bring you to infer what the symptom is supposed to be a symptom of.

(2) I know that you are capable of making associative inferences. I give you a perceptible expression (a sound, a gesture, a representation, etc.) and try in this way to bring you to an associative inference of what I want you to recognize.

(3) I know that you are capable of making causal and associative inferences. I give you a representation of a symptom (a simulation, for example), and try in this way to bring you to (a) make a causal inference as to what the represented symptom is supposed to be a symptom of, and (b) make an associative inference as to what I might be trying to get you to recognize with it.

As we have seen, the communicative use of these techniques over the course of time results, if they are used with sufficient frequency, in the use of a fourth technique:

(4) I know that you are capable of following rules. I give you a perceptible expression that is used as a rule in our language

community to give others to understand that *p*, and try in this way to bring you to the recognition that my intention is to give you to understand that *p*.

Let's analyze the following case: Bill tells a really corny joke. Bob answers: "Ow, that's *painful!*" I will reconstruct the logic of the genesis of this use of *ow*, step-by-step "from the bottom up."

A person who experiences sudden and unexpected physical pain usually reacts spontaneously with a cry. The cry can be interpreted as a symptom of pain. Such cries can be simulated, giving the addressee to understand, by means of associative inference, "You're hurting me." This is an icon of the symptom of physical pain.

Sufficiently frequent simulation leads to the emergence of a rule of use. *Ow* is an exclamatory expression in the English language, and serves the speaker to indicate to the addressee the sudden occurrence of physical pain. *Ow* is a symbol whose past as an icon and previous life as a symptom are still recognizable.

Now, hearing a corny joke is not usually accompanied by the occurrence of sudden, unexpected physical pain. The utterance of the expression *ow* therefore requires (on the premise that the addressee assumes that the speaker's behavior is rational)[1] a different interpretation than the one that would follow from the rule alone. The inference from the rule would lead, in this context, to the following interpretation: "Bob wants to tell me that I've caused him sudden, unexpected, physical pain." This interpretation must become the basis of a second interpretive step. A causal inference does not suggest itself in this situation. All that's left is an associative inference: "Bob, with his reference to physical pain, wants to associatively let me know that I have caused him mental pain." The interpreter thus applies the iconic technique to the result of the rule-based interpretive technique. The result is metaphor. Our example is a metaphorical use of *ow*. More explicitly, we might say that it is an example of the metaphorical use of a symbol that was once an icon of a symptom of pain.

For the sake of thoroughness, it should be noted that our interpretation is not complete. Bad jokes don't really inflict mental pain, and mental pain does not occur suddenly, unexpectedly and directly. A person suffering from a broken heart does not say "ow." Bob's utterance of *ow* is

---

[1] On the assumption of rationality in communication, see Kasher 1976 and Chap. 14.

therefore insincere. But in a dialogue such as the one above, no secret is made of insincerity. What we have here is an insincere utterance whose insincerity the addressee is meant to notice, if he is perceptive enough to do so. This is exactly what defines irony. "Lying is a simulation of sincerity; irony is a simulation of insincerity," writes Edgar Lapp. Irony is a "staged and transparent lie" (Lapp 1992: 146–7).[2] Bob's utterance of *ow* is thus the *ironic use of the metaphorical use of a symbol that was once an icon of a symptom of pain.*

We will leave the aspect of irony and return to metaphor. The example above is meant to show that we are capable of reapplying the basic methods of sign development and interpretation—in this case, the iconic method—on a higher, symbolic level. This will now be somewhat more systematically explained.

THE SYMBOLIZATION OF SYMPTOMS

With the help of linguistic symbols, everything imaginable can be symbolized, even symptoms, icons and symbols themselves. I will call the process of symbol-making *symbolization*. An archeologist who comes across a keel at an excavation site will take it as a symptom of a buried ship (and continue digging). Now, if an author writes "A thousand keels approached the shore," he indicates a symptom of ships with the linguistic symbol *keel*. This I will call the *symbolization of symptoms*. The archeologist and the reader of the text use analogous interpretive techniques: the archeologist infers, from the obvious existence of a keel, the existence of a ship; the reader infers 'ship' from 'keel'. The inference that the archeologist makes on the level of things is made by the reader on the level of linguistic symbols or concepts. The result of the symbolization of symptoms is metonymy.[3] To interpret an archeological discovery, one must know that the keel is a part of a ship, and infer the whole from the part. To interpret our author's text, the reader must be able successively to employ two interpretive techniques: he must know the rule of use of the word *keel* and infer from this, as well as from the textual

---

[2] Trans. K.D.

[3] A systematic distinction of metonymy and synecdoche seems to me unnecessary for our purposes.

context, that with the use of the word *keels*, keels are meant. Further-more, like the archeologist, he must know that a keel is a part of a ship, and infer from this that with the use of the word *keels*, ships are meant. Because metonyms are symbolized symptoms, both Anttila (1989: 141) and Nerlich and Clarke (1988: 80) call them metasymptoms. The arche-ologist employs the symptomic method of interpretation (see Chapter 8); the author and his readers employ the symptomic technique on the sym-bolic level. I will call this "metasymptomic" technique the *metonymical technique*.

To recapitulate, we will remember that there are three ways in which symptoms can be communicatively used: imitation or simulation makes icons of them; staging leads, over the course of time, to their becoming symbols; and symbolization makes them into metonymies. Next, let's see what happens when icons are symbolized.

THE SYMBOLIZATION OF ICONS

Icons cannot be staged. In contrast to symptoms, they are "always al-ready" communicatively used. The possibility of their simulation is also precluded, as icons do not occur in nature. Of the three possibili-ties named above, only symbolization remains. Here again, let us first consider a rudimentary example. In some cultures, the depiction of an oak can be used as a symbol of steadfastness and dependability. If Bill says of Bob, "He's the oak of our organization," the linguistic symbol *oak* is meant to be interpreted as a metaphor for steadfastness and de-pendability. A person who sees a picture of an oak in an advertisement for life insurance will associatively infer dependability from the picture. A person who hears Bill's comment will, from this use of the symbol *oak*, associatively infer Bob's dependability. In order to interpret Bill's comment, one must again apply two interpretive techniques succes-sively: one must know the meaning, that is, the rule of use of the word *oak*, and then associate which aspect of oaklike-ness could be meant in regard to Bob. The observer of the picture of an oak employs the iconic technique of interpretation; the addressee of Bill's utterance employs the iconic technique on the level of symbols. "Metaphor is a symbolic statement that represents one thing as an icon . . . of something else"

(Haley 1988: 21). I will call this metaiconic technique the *metaphorical technique*.[4]

The metaphorical and metonymical techniques can also be used in combination. For example, if we call a person an *egghead*, we clearly use the word *egghead* first metaphorically, and then proceed to use the metaphor metonymically. Hence it is a *metaphorical metonymy*. When sushi chefs are called "the Green Berets of the culinary world," as they are in a *New York Times* article on sushi (Grimes 1997: B10), a *metonymical metaphor* is employed. These kinds of processes have an important role in historical linguistics. I will demonstrate this with two examples, the etymologies of the words *coach* and luck, respectively.

The person in charge of a sports team is sometimes called the *coach*. This word is related to the German noun *Kutsche* and the English *coach*, that is, a horse carriage.[5] What does one *coach* have to do with the other? In the Hungarian village Kocs, there evidently lived in the fifteenth century someone who made particularly good or attractive horse carriages. The Hungarians called them *kosci szekér* 'wagons from Kocs', which was shortened over time to become *kosci*. The English and the Germans borrowed the Hungarian word and made of it, respectively, *coach* and *Kutsche*. Then the English (but not the Germans) began using the metaphorical technique: *to coach a horse* was to train it to pull a carriage. By way of metonymical transference, *coach* ultimately came to be the word for the person who performed this task. A *coach* was thus a person who trained horses to pull coaches. It is only a small metaphorical step from the name of a horse trainer to that of a sports trainer, or to that of scholastic or academic trainers (tutors). Finally, the English word *coach* became a loanword in German. So ran, approximately, the etymological path from a Hungarian village to a German loanword, used today to designate the person in charge of a sports team.[6] Yet another metaphorical transference occurs when English speakers, or even German speakers,

---

[4] My decision to view metaphors as metaicons is not meant to imply the intention of joining in the discussion of what Peirce tends to view as a metaicons. On metaphor in the light of Peircean semiotics—"through the Peircean telescope" and "under the Peircean microscope"—see Haley's excellent study (1988).

[5] Thanks to Raimo Anttila for drawing my attention to the etymology of *coach* and *Kutsche*.

[6] See the *Barnhart Dictionary of Etymology, The Oxford Dictionary of English Etymology*, and vol. 3 of *The Oxford English Dictionary*.

talk of *coaching* in business consulting. Here, *coaching* means individual problem- or conflict-oriented advising, or the advising of the company's management by (often psychologically competent) consultants.

Our second example, the etymology of the word *luck*, is no less eccentric.[7] *Luck* is etymologically related to, for example, *lock* (both meanings, a lock of hair and a door lock); the German words *Loch* 'hole', *Lücke* 'gap', and *Locke* 'lock of hair'; Swedish *nyckel* 'key', Latin *luxus* 'lush growth', and Greek *lygos* 'young branch'. Where is the connection between the concepts designated by these various words? English *lock* (of hair), German *Locke*, Latin *luxus*, and Greek *lygos* all designate something that grows or sprouts. When one considers that small wooden stakes were once used to close doors, as a sort of deadbolt, it is easy to guess that the designation of such a small piece of wood came to be, through the use of the metonymical technique, a designation for the act of closing. This etymological connection can be found in a number of languages: Swedish *stång* 'pole, stake' to *stänga* 'to close', Latin *clavus* 'nail' to *claudere* 'to close', for example. Evidence of this root, common to *lygos* and *luxus*, could also still be found in Old High German's verb *luhhan* 'to close'. German *Luke* 'hatch' (door) and *Loch* 'hole' designate things that can be closed. The connection between OHG *luhhan*, Eng. *lock* and New High German *Luke* and *Loch* also appears to be a metonymical one—the transition from closing to that which was closed. Old High German had both the word *biluhhan* 'lock' and the word *antluhhan* 'open'. The associative inference from closing something in the concrete sense to abstract, mental closing clearly suggests itself. The metaphorical transference from the process of closing a physical space to the process of closing a mental task had already taken place in Middle High German. Reinbot von Durne wrote in the thirteenth century, in one and the same work, that God *alliu dinc beslozzen* 'determines all things' or 'brings all things to a close' and *alliu dinc belochen* 'closes all things' (Reinbot von Durne, verses 3588 and 3872). With this, we have almost reached the concept of luck. What God has *belochen* is *gelucke*. God's decisions are our fate. At first, *gelucke* designated both positive and the negative twists of fate; then, as the appearance of the word *ungelücke* indicates, *gelucke*

---

[7] Cf. Sanders 1965: 236–61. The following information on the etymology of *luck* (and, analogously, *Glück*) all stems from this volume.

came to be used exclusively for the positive version. Here, we clearly have an entire chain of metonymical and metaphorical processes, leading from the designation of a small stake of wood to the designation of the act of closing, and from there to the designation of godly decisions to the designation of positive fate. And that is the connection between *luck* and *lock*.

THE SYMBOLIZATION OF SYMBOLS

Metonymy is created by the symbolization of symptoms. We create metaphors by symbolizing icons. What results from the symbolization of symbols? Symbols of symbols. But what does that mean? I have alluded to the answer in Chapter 9: we have the ability not only to use the expressions of our language, but also to cite or, as they say, mention them. If we want to talk about an expression, we have to cite it: *and* and *or* are conjunctions. The italicized words in the previous sentence are not just used, but mentioned or cited. Mentioning a symbol is nothing other than using a symbolized symbol. The rule of mention is a rule of use for symbolized symbols. As Freget writes, "We then have signs of signs" (1966*b*: 58). Our ability to use symbols symbolically is decisively important in at least two regards. First, it allows us to talk about our language reflectively, and second, it is the condition of possibility for a certain kind of language change. No small part of language change comes about due to the speakers' choice, from all of the alternatives available to them, of exactly the one that they believe to promise them the most success. If speakers' judgments of the chance of success of a particular linguistic expression undergo a shift in the same direction, language change occurs. But in order to make a choice according to their expectations of success, speakers must be able to call to mind their options. People who want to be able to decide if they should say *goodbye* or *see ya* when taking leave must be able to "visualize" *goodbye* and *see ya* for the purpose of reflective consideration. To have reflective access to these symbols, they must be able to symbolize symbols. Symbols are necessary for making rational choices of action. This has been demonstrated by David Gauthier (1988: 173ff.; see also Chapter 9). Metasymbols are necessary for making rational choices among symbols. This follows from Gauthier's observations. The ability to symbolize symbols is thus nothing less than a condition of possibility for the rational use of semantic means.

The point of these observations, considerations and speculations is the following: We have exactly three techniques at our disposal for the realization of our communicative endeavors. I have called them the symptomic, the iconic and the symbolic techniques. The symptomic and the iconic techniques, following the model of the three-room apartment, "jump" to the level of the symbolic technique without the involvement of plan or intent. These are the processes of symbols' *Urschöpfung*, as it were. The symptomic, the iconic and the symbolic techniques can be reapplied on the symbolic level, creating a new sense with the help of conventional means: metonymies, metaphors and the mention of symbols. If we want to communicate in a foreign language without access to the appropriate symbols, or when the symbols available to us in our mother tongue seem ill-fitting, we have the competence to remedy the situation—a kind of creative programming that allows us to revert to symptoms and/or icons, or to build metasymptoms or metaicons. And this is exactly what we do. We talk either "with our hands" or with metonymies and metaphors. Metaphorically, we might say that gesticulating with one's hands is to talk iconically, while talking metaphorically is to "gesticulate" with symbols. Both are techniques for the innovative generation of sense.

New linguistic signs need some kind of transparency in order to be interpretable at all (cf. Chapter 10). Symptoms and icons are directly transparent; they are motivated by causal and associative relations, respectively. Metonymies and metaphors are indirect and relatively motivated. Anyone who knows German and knows that UN soldiers' helmets are blue stands a good chance of understanding what is meant when he hears, in an appropriate context, the metonymy *Blauhelm* for the first time. Anyone who knows English and knows that the oak is a stable, long-lived, hardwood tree has a good chance of understanding what is meant when a person is called an oak. Often, *relative motivatedness* is understood, following the Saussurean tradition, to mean only rule-based relative motivatedness: anyone who knows that Turkish *on* means 'ten' and *dört* 'four', and also knows the rules of Turkish word formation, can "figure out" what *ondört* means. This is the relative motivatedness of *meaning*: the meaning of the elements' connection is the connection of the elements' meaning. Rule-based relative motivatedness concerns *langue*. With the causally based motivatedness of metonymy and the associatively based motivatedness of metaphor, we are dealing with, first, the relative motivatedness of the sense of the sign use. This concerns *parole*. In other contexts, *Blauhelm* and *oak* can be meant and understood in completely different senses than the ones named here.

Like the categories of symptoms and icons, those of metonymy and metaphor are here defined according to the techniques of inference employed in producing and/or interpreting them. Just as icons are not defined by their motivatedness (nor symbols by their unmotivatedness), metaphor is not defined by its imagery. The verb *grasp* may, in some sense, conjure up an image; but it is not metaphorical in the sense suggested here. For in order to interpret the utterance "She grasped the problem," it is not associative inferences that are needed, but rule-based ones.[8] Just as icons and symptoms can become symbols, so can metaphors and metonymies. The word *grasp*, once a metaphor, is now a new symbol, one whose metaphorical past can still be seen. The processes by which metaphors and metonymies become new symbols are usually brought together in the term *lexicalization*. We will now examine these processes in detail.

THE LEXICALIZATION OF METAPHORS AND METONYMIES

With sufficiently frequent use, nonliteral meaning becomes literal, if rule-based inferences replace causal or associative inference over time. I will call this process *lexicalization*. Breaking with the pattern I have followed so far, I will begin with the consideration of metaphors. Metaphors are metaicons, and they behave like icons.[9] Frequent metaphors necessarily become lexicalized, and the reasons for this are as follows: In order to interpret a metaphorical utterance as a metaphor, the addressee must perform two inferences, one rule-based and one associative. The reasoning behind the interpretation of the metaphorical utterance "Bill is a parrot" might read like this: "*Parrot* serves to designate a

---

[8] I. A. Richards's comment, "Thinking is radically metaphorical" (1938: 48), applies only when there is no distinction made between metaphors and former metaphors. This comment emphasizes the fact that symbols cannot have been originally unmotivated.

[9] On the conventionalization of metaphors, see, above all, Traugott 1985.

parrot, or to attribute to something the quality of being parrot-like. Parrots are exotic birds with colorful feathers. Since Bill is a person, the predicate *parrot* cannot have been used to subsume him under the class of parrots. So the predicate *parrot* was probably used in this case to refer to Bill's colorful clothing." Associative inferences which occur sufficiently frequently must necessarily become rule-based inferences, by the path described above, so that both successively activated inferences merge to form one rule, such as in the case of the former metaphor *fox*. Back when the expression "Bill is a fox" was still truly metaphorical, it was interpreted something like this: "*Fox* serves to designate a fox. In many animal fables, the fox is especially crafty. So *fox* is probably used here to attribute particular craftiness to Bill." Since then, these two inferences can be said to have merged to become a single rule: "*Fox* is used to attribute craftiness to people." This is the process of the lexicalization of a metaphor. Sense that was once created by pragmatic means becomes the rule, and a semantic meaning of the word *fox*.

In the previous chapter, we saw that it is very possible that one person interprets a sign as an icon, while the conversation partner interprets it as a symbol. What one infers associatively, the other can infer according to the rule, based on greater familiarity with the sign. The same is true on the level of metaphor. What may (still) be a metaphor for one person, can (already) be lexicalized for another. This is a normal state in language acquisition. Learners must get along associatively, while more knowledgeable people use rules. The first time I heard the word *abierta* 'open' used in reference to light by a Spanish electrician (*Está abierta, la luz?* 'Is the light open?'), I understood it on the basis of my associative ability and not, like the electrician, due to knowledge of the rule. In other words, learners understand a use with which they are as yet unfamiliar as a metaphor. As David Rumelhart has pointed out, child language acquisition cannot function otherwise. "Thus, the child's language acquisition process should not be construed, as it often seems to be, as a process of first learning literal language and then, after that is thoroughly mastered, moving on into nonliteral language. . . . The processes involved in the comprehension of nonliteral speech are part of our language production and comprehension equipment from the very start" (Rumelhart 1979: 80ff.). Processes of transformation to rules, analogous to those of lexicalization, take place in the individual competence during language acquisition. The process of transformation into a rule is accompanied by a process that is usually expressed in the metaphor of bleaching. In the next chapter, we will go into this topic in more detail.

When the process of the lexicalization of a former metaphor is completed, the resulting symbol can become the object of a metaphorical technique yet again. Consider, for instance, the following short story: "I have five hens. One of them is really nutty. Every time it's butchering day, it acts like it's dead. This hen is a real fox." Calling a hen a fox is a true metaphor. For the hen is viewed not only as another animal, a fox, but also as a crafty person. The hen is anthropomorphized. That is, the metaphor makes use of the rule with which *fox* is used to ascribe people with particular craftiness. From a formerly metaphorical sense, a new meaning has arisen, one with which new metaphors can be created. The possibility of the formation of new, creative metaphors can virtually be seen as a test of the completed conventionalization of former metaphors.

Frequently occurring metasymptoms, that is, metonymies, also become lexicalized. In many languages, the symbol for "language" itself arose through the use of the metonymic technique in regard to the body part with which the language is spoken: Lat. *lingua* 'tongue', 'language'; Gr. *glossa* 'tongue', 'language'; Turk. *dil* 'tongue', 'language'. However, metonymies can escape lexicalization, as metaphors cannot. The metonymy *Green Beret*, for example, in spite of the frequency of its use, stands a good chance of remaining a metonymy, that is, of being interpreted by means of inferring the whole from a part. The reason for this difference between metaphors and metonymies is the following: associative inferences automatically become rule-based inferences if common knowledge arises concerning the associative goal. Causal inferences, however, do not necessarily change their character when they have become the object of common knowledge. Causal inferences are already based on knowledge. The only thing that distinguishes them from an inference by rule is the kind of knowledge employed. The causal inference uses knowledge of natural facts, the rule-based inference that of institutional facts. In regard to causal connections, which are the basis of causal inferences, there need be no common knowledge; but nothing is lost if there is. If metonymies undergo lexicalization, it occurs simply through the fusion of the rule-based inference with the causal one. The reasoning behind a metonymical interpretation of the utterance "I'm going to have a bite to eat" runs something like this: "The word *bite* serves to designate a mouthful of food. A mouthful of food is part of a

whole meal. Therefore, *bite* is here probably used to designate a meal."
Such an inferential sequence can fuse to become one rule: "*Bite* serves
to designate a meal."

To summarize the above observations, we will remember that:

(1) The symptomic and the iconic techniques can be newly applied on
the level of symbols. The results of this are called, respectively,
metonymy and metaphor.

(2) Frequently used metaphors must become new, lexicalized
symbols, and frequently used metonymies may do so. This development is unidirectional.

In other words, in the long run, everything becomes a symbol sooner or
later. There is no way back. For lexicalization always goes hand in hand
with the emergence of common knowledge. A reversal would require a
kind of use resulting in common amnesia—an unlikely scenario.

13

Literal and Metaphorical Sense

"The metaphorical use of a word changes its meaning. The literal meaning is transferred to the metaphorical one." This theory is as widespread as it is inadequate. I will try to show why it cannot be correct.*

Let us consider an example. If I were to read the sentence, *The face of his new car smiled at him contentedly*, I would, under normal circumstances, interpret it as a metaphorical utterance. What does it mean to interpret an utterance as metaphorical? We discussed this question in detail in the last chapter. It means that two interpretive techniques must be used in succession: one must know the rules of use of the employed words, including syntax, and then, on the basis of one's knowledge of the sentence meaning, associatively infer what it could mean to relate the idea of a contentedly smiling face to a car. However, in order to do this, the words *face*, *smiled*, etc. must be understood with their normal meanings. If the interpreter assumed that, in this sentence, *face* "really" means *grille*, the metaphor would be destroyed. For the metaphoricity of the utterance consists precisely in the invitation to see the car as having a contentedly smiling face. For this, it must be assumed that the words *face*, *smiled*, etc. have their normal meaning. "[I]n a genuine metaphorical utterance it is only because the expressions have not changed their meaning that there is a metaphorical expression at all" (Searle 1979: 100). The awareness of the metaphoricity of the meaning of the utterance requires awareness of the normal meaning of the sentence. "If

*Thanks to Frank Liedtke for his helpful and critical comments on this and the following chapter.

knowledge of the nonliteralness dies, so does the metaphor" (Keller-Bauer 1984: 65).[1]

Let us consider another, real-life example. Some time ago, one of the Westdeutsche Rundfunk's radio announcers opened a midday news program ("Das Mittagsmagazin") with a greeting that has since become classic: "Guten Tag meine Damen und Herren, guten Morgen liebe Studenten." There's no doubt what he meant to express with this teasing comment: students have the tendency not to roll out of bed until noon. The announcer used the expression *guten Morgen* metaphorically. The listeners are invited to associatively infer what might be meant when students are greeted at noon with the expression *guten Morgen*. We, too, will ask: does *guten Morgen* have a different meaning from usual in this sentence? No, of course not! The effect of the wisecrack practically demands that the listeners grasp the expression *guten Morgen* in its normal meaning, that they proceed from the assumption that *guten Morgen* is used to greet people before noon. The listeners use this knowledge, and the knowledge that it is noon, as the basis for an associative inference. If the announcer had said something like "Guten Morgen meine Damen und Herren; Studenten stehen um diese Tageszeit gerade auf" ("Good morning, ladies and gentlemen; students are just getting up at this time of day"), the humor would be lost precisely because the listeners would not need an associative inference to reach the appropriate interpretation. The humor is created by the knowledge of the conventional meaning and the resulting discovery of the limited violation of the rule. If the sentence meaning had changed, the listeners need not have interpreted it metaphorically; they could just as well have interpreted it literally.

The same goes for metonymies. The *deployment of Green Berets* does not mean that soldiers are using green berets in combat, but that soldiers with green berets, that is, an elite company of the US Army, are in action. The claim that, in this metonymy, a part is used to mean the whole, requires that *Green Beret* designate a part (namely, a green beret) and not the whole soldier. If *green beret* meant 'specialized US Army soldier', it would not be a case of metonymy, but of the ambiguity of the words *green beret*. This situation occurs at just that point when the metonymy becomes lexicalized in the way described in the last chapter. (We will not

---

[1] Trans. K.D. Cf. also Davidson 1978.

decide whether, with *Green Beret*, this is already the case.) A linguistic sign simply has the meaning that it has. A meaning, that is, a rule of use, is something relatively stable. Frequently broken or stretched rules can have rule change as a long-term consequence. But rules cannot be changed ad hoc, unless by explicit agreement: "I will now use the word *face* in the way that the word *grille* is usually used: my car has a dented face." However, such a bizarre procedure would be an example not of metaphorical use, but of an agreement to use a secret code.

The upshot of the discussion is that the assumption that a linguistic sign is the object of metaphorical interpretation requires that the linguistic sign in question have its usual meaning. If *face* already had the meaning 'grille', it would have to be interpreted literally.

What does it mean to mean or interpret an utterance literally? There is much talk of the literal (or nonliteral) meaning of linguistic expressions. With the manner of speech proposed here, the question of literalness in regard to the meaning of linguistic expressions does not come up. The meaning of a symbol is the rule of its use, and to say of a rule that it is literal or nonliteral makes no sense. The literal or nonliteral interpretation[2] of a particular utterance of a linguistic sign can be desired by the speaker or attempted by the hearer. We have called this the sense of the utterance. In the proposed terminology, only the sense of an utterance can be said to be literal or nonliteral. Before explaining in what the literal sense of an utterance consists, I would like to introduce what is probably the most elaborate current representational theory of the concept of literal meaning. Manfred Bierwisch presents this theory in his well-known 1979 essay "Literal meaning—a pragmatic *Gretchenfrage*."[3] I will first attempt a congenial presentation of Bierwisch's theory, and then, in a second step, critically compare it with my own views.[4]

Bierwisch differentiates, as is common and sensible, between the linguistic sign, for example the sentence, and its use. The linguistic sign is called the *expression* (*Ausdruck*), and abbreviated as A. A use of A is called a *specimen utterance* (*Äußerungsexemplar*) and is abbreviated as t. Every expression A has a "linguistically determined meaning" (Bierwisch 1979: 123), called the $B(A)$. The meaning of an expression is

---

[2] The term *interpretation* is act–object ambiguous; the word may designate the act or the object. The question of literalness arises only in the object-reading.

[3] All subsequent quotations from Bierwisch's essay are my translations (K.D.).

[4] For another critique of Bierwisch, see Feilke 1994: 315 ff.

conceived as the "logical form of *A*" (130), which can be "specified" as "a combinative structure of basic semantic elements that represents the logical form of *A*" (136). A specimen utterance *t* has an utterance meaning *M(t)* and a communicative sense *CS(t)*. A meaning of an utterance *M(t)* can be, depending on the circumstances, "literal meaning" *LM(t)* (123) or "nonliteral meaning" *NM(t)* (130).

Bierwisch thus suggests a three-tiered model:

(1) Linguistic meaning *B(A)*.

(2) Utterance meaning *M(t)*:
    (2.1) Literal utterance meaning *LM(t)*;
    (2.2) Nonliteral utterance meaning *NM(t)*.

(3) Communicative sense *CS(t)*.

He explains the connection between these three levels as follows:

For every *A* in *L* [the language], linguistic knowledge . . . determines the logical form of *A*, which I designate with *B(A)*. Together with general knowledge of the circumstances, to which the specimen utterance *t* of *A* is related, *B(A)* determines the literal meaning *LM(t)*. Under certain conditions, general knowledge further determines a nonliteral meaning *NM(t)*, which differs from *LM(t)*. The utterance meaning *M(t)* is then either *LM(t)* or *NM(t)*. Finally, *M(t)* determines, along with general knowledge of the interactive conditions, the communicative sense *CS(t)*, dependent on the communicative situation. (Bierwisch 1979: 130)

The speaker thus has three sources of knowledge: linguistic knowledge, situational knowledge and interactive knowledge. Starting with *A*, a determinative chain arises and continues through *CS(t)*, triggered by the intervention of the next highest level of knowledge:

[[*A* + linguistic knowledge → *B(A)*] + situational knowledge → *M(t)*] + interactive knowledge → *CS(t)*.

Bierwisch illustrates this theory with a number of examples. An analogous example in English,[5] somewhat shortened, is as follows:

---

[5] Bierwisch's German example (1) is the sentence *Das habe ich nur mit der linken Hand gemacht* (*I made that with my left hand only*). In German, to do something *mit links* (*with the left hand*) means to do it easily, quickly or carelessly. Since this colloquialism does not exist in English, I have provided what I hope is an analogous example for this translation—K.D.

(1)   *I'm out in left field today.*

(2)   *Today I will be playing baseball in the left part of the outfield.*

(3)   *I'm having a bad day and making lots of mistakes.*

(1b) *I'm playing in the left part of the baseball outfield today.*

(1c) *I am mistaken.*

With the use of sentence (1), the speaker can mean either (1b) or (1c), depending on the context. (1b) and (1c) are paraphrases of possible communicative sense. If the speaker has expressed, with the utterance of (1), the communicative sense (1b), the specimen utterance (1) had the utterance meaning (2). However, if he meant (1c) with the utterance (1), the utterance had the utterance meaning (3). In other words, in the first case, the utterance meaning $M(t)$ is the literal meaning $LM(t)$, and in the second case, the nonliteral meaning $NM(t)$. "In borderline cases," writes Bierwisch, "$LM(t)$ can coincide with $M(E)$, but in most cases this identity does not occur" (1979: 140). I will end my description of Bierwisch's theory here, and begin with my critique of it.

The meaning of an expression, according to this theory, is not a rule of use, but a logical form that can be "specified" with a set of so-called semantic features. The "linguistically determined meaning" $B(A)$ of the expression *bachelor* is "UNMARRIED ADULT MALE PERSON" (Bierwisch 1979: 139). The capital letters, in words that are uninterrupted by commas, are supposed to indicate that these are not normal English words, but so-called semantic features. But how do speaker and hearer know which "logical form," as "specified" by these features, "designate" the expression *bachelor*? And thanks to which feature is the expression able to "designate" exactly this form? The answer to the second question is the secret of all representational approaches. The answer to the first question, I think, is that speaker and hearer know that *bachelor* represents the above semantic features—if they know it at all—because they have learned to use the word *bachelor* to refer to unmarried, adult, male persons, or to say of adult men that they are unmarried. But if we assume that this is what they know, it obviously means that we assume that they are familiar with a rule of use. Now, we might be tempted to say that the words designated as the set of semantic features are just another formulation of a rule of use. However, this is not compatible with the thesis that an expression represents its meaning *B(A)*. For an expression does not represent its rule of use; it follows it.

According to Bierwisch's theory, the meaning of an expression and the meaning of an utterance can coincide. From this, it follows that the the meaning of an utterance is conceived as a set of features. Usually, claims Bierwisch's theory, the utterance specimen does not represent exactly the set of features that the expression does. However, it is not impossible "in borderline cases." The literal meaning *LM(t)* of a specimen utterance *t* of the expression *E* occurs, according to Bierwisch, at exactly that point when the linguistically determined meaning *M(E)* does not conflict with the context of the utterance (1979: 140).

This model completely neglects to take into account speakers who try to realize communicative intentions and addressees who try to decipher those intentions. Inferential techniques which are in large part "guessing games" (cf. Chapter 9) are reified as determinative chains. This is not per se inadequate. Descriptive requirements may call for the invention of "semantic features" and an impersonalized, quasi-algorithmic conception of the communicative process. In that case, though, what we have is not an unwillingly accepted abbreviation, but a mistake. Bierwisch—along with most representational semanticists—believes that basing meaning on the communicative praxis of language users is misguided. He obviously has a hard time grasping the basic idea of such an approach, and evidently believes that its agenda consists in "deriving" the meaning of an expression from the sense of its uses; countering this idea, he writes that "in this sense, my thesis is that language meaning enters into language behavior as a separate determinative structure, and cannot be reduced to such by the assignment of abstraction. (The laws of flow and gravity, too, which determine the path of a falling leaf, are not practicable abstractions, but determinative systems.)" (Bierwisch 1979: 120). The addition of the parenthetical comment allows us to pinpoint the mistake. Bierwisch fails to see the aspect of genesis that lies at the action-theoretical foundation of sign theory. Language meaning can be said, of course, to be a "determinative structure"; certainly, the meaning of a sentence cannot be "derived" from the sense of its uses. If meaning is supposed to make interpretation possible, it cannot have interpretation as a prerequisite (see Chapter 4). Nevertheless, it is because of communicative praxis that the expression *bachelor* has meaning. In Bierwisch's language, one might say that the currently valid determinative structure is the result of the conventionalization of past communicative praxis. But this categorically distinguishes meanings from the laws of flow and gravity! The meaning of the word *bachelor* is the praxis of communicating people become custom. Gravity, in contrast, is not the praxis of falling apples become custom. The existence of the determinative structure "gravity" is not due to the fact that leaves and apples tended to fall in the past. But the existence of the current meaning of a word is due exclusively to the fact that speakers and hearers tended to use that word in a certain way, and still do. It is in exactly this sense that today's meanings are functions of past communicative acts. This thesis is very different from the wild idea that meaning is an abstraction of linguistic behavior.

As we saw, the three levels in Bierwisch's model are motivated by the assumption of three sources of knowledge. The application of linguistic knowledge leads to linguistically determined meaning; the additional application of general knowledge leads to literal or nonliteral utterance meaning; finally, the application of knowledge of interactive conditions leads to communicative sense. I find it sensible to postulate three steps of this kind, but would like to try to prove their motivation by different kinds of interpretive inferences. First, let us compare the sentence example (1) with a similar sentence (1′):

(1)   *I'm out in left field today.*

(1′)   *I'm out in right field today.*

We'll assume that with (1′), the speaker wants to express that he is having a good day. The difference between (1) and (1′) is clear: a reading of (1) as 'I'm having a bad day and making lots of mistakes', which Bierwisch's theory would denote as the nonliteral meaning, is provided for by the rule of use of the expression *out in left field*, while a reading of (1′) as 'I'm having a good day and enjoying many successes' is one that requires, besides a rule-based inference, an associative one. In other words, our reading of (1′) is metaphorical, while that of (1) is not. (If (1) or (1′) is uttered by someone who is a well-known left fielder, a metaphorical reading would suggest itself in both cases!) The expression *out in left field* is clearly a former metaphor which has in the meantime become lexicalized, that is, a linguistic sign whose metaphorical past is still evident. As long as the earlier meaning is not lost, the lexicalization of metaphors leads to ambiguous expressions.[6] As Nelson Goodman writes, ". . . the metaphor freezes, or rather evaporates, and the residue is a pair of literal uses—mere ambiguity instead of metaphor" (1968: 71).

In the sentence

(1″)   *They got themselves a new coach.*

would we take the reading "a horse carriage" as the nonliteral meaning in Bierwisch's sense, and the reading "a sports trainer" as the literal meaning? No, and the reason for this is that *coach*, like *out in left field*, is (in certain readings) a lexicalized metaphor, but in the case of *coach*, the lexicalization occurred longer ago, so that its former metaphoricity is not as transparent as in the case of *out in left field*. If this is true, though, the following conclusion results: the expression *coach* is ambiguous and has two linguistically determined meanings $B(A)$; the utterance (1″) has two utterance meanings $M(t)$, and both are literal meanings $LM(t)$ (cf. Bierwisch 1979: 138 ff.). The expression *out in left field* also has two linguistically determined meanings $M(E)$, but one of the two utterance meanings of the utterance (1) has the nonliteral meaning $NM(t)$. From this, it follows that the differentiation of literal and nonliteral utterance meaning is historically motivated. This is not Bierwisch's preferred solution, of course. The alternative is to assume that the expression *out in left field* is not a lexicalized metaphor, but a true one.[7] For this situation, Bierwisch has earmarked a "transfer function MET" (1979: 142). He assumes that "the development of the transferred meaning is determined by a function of metaphor formation, belonging to the knowledge system and operating not only on linguistic structures" (1979: 142). Naturally, Bierwisch is confident of the fact that "the simple postulation of the transfer function MET does not clarify, of course, with which criteria $LM(t)$ and $NM(t)$ may be distinguished" (1979: 142). With the help of the transfer function MET, there is only a "connection produced" within the stock of everyday knowledge "if t is used with nonliteral meaning" (1979: 142).

The framework that I propose also provides for levels which correspond to Bierwisch's $A(B)$, $M(t)$, $LM(t)$, and $NM(t)$. Let's say that a man known for his long standing as a left fielder on the local baseball team utters the sentence:

---

[6]   Cf. Nieraad 1977: 45 ff.

[7]   I hold this assumption to be inadequate. However, this does not affect my understanding of Bierwisch's theory.

(1′)   *I'm out in right field today.*

in the middle of winter.

The addressee and interpreter of the sentence will complete the following interpretive steps: The meaning of the uttered sentence results from the rules of use of the words and from morphological and syntactical rules. Thanks to their knowledge of the English language, the speaker and the hearer are familiar with these rules. The meaning of the sentence consists in being capable of letting the addressee know that the speaker is (or will be) playing a position on the right side of the baseball outfield. We reach the literal or nonliteral sense when we complete no interpretive steps other than rule-based inferences, except those necessary for reference fixation, and perhaps those which serve to dispel ambiguity (cf. Chapter 5). In our example, there is no need to dispel ambiguity, but reference fixation is required. The knowledge of language rules is usually not sufficient to make even a literal interpretation of an utterance. If someone says *Come on over here*, my linguistic knowledge alone does not allow me to infer that I am meant! Normally, I reach this conclusion by virtue of eye contact, because I am the only one in the room besides the speaker, because of the fact that I am on familiar terms with the speaker, or something similar. That is, I take these "attendant circumstances" as symptoms of the fact that the speaker means me. Sperber and Wilson call this construction of literal sense from the language material, the fixation of reference as well as the elimination of ambiguity, "the *development* of a logical form" (1986a: 181). Echoing Grice's use of the term implicature, they call the result of such a development an explicature (Sperber and Wilson 1986a: 182).[8]

Thus, the person meant by *I* in the above sentence cannot be determined by the rules of language. The rules of a language permit only the recognition that the speaker refers to himself. The hearer must infer who is meant by *I* by some other method. There are two alternatives: either he sees who the speaker is, recognizes his voice, or—in the case of a written utterance—he knows its author, or can determine who is meant by *I* by means of contextual information.

When the interpreter has completed these steps, those that are based on the rules of the respective language and those necessary for reference fixation, he has interpreted the literal sense of the utterance.

---

[8] On the concept of implicature, see Chap. 14.

Now, our utterance scenario includes the information that the speaker is a well-known left fielder. Under the right circumstances, this will lead the hearer to assume that the speaker wants his utterance to be metaphorically understood. To interpret an utterance metaphorically is to make the literal interpretation the basis of one or more associative inferences. Such an associative inference might look something like this: "He said that he will be playing in right field. I know that he usually plays in left field, and that he knows that I know this. I know that the expression *out in left field* can be understood as 'being mistaken'. He (presumably) wants me to associate, on the basis of my knowledge of his position in the game of baseball and of the rule of use of the expression *out in left field*, what it could mean for a left fielder to say that he is in right field, namely that he 'is having a bad day and making a lot of mistakes'." But what kind of inference leads the hearer to the metaphorical technique? The ability to use the metaphorical technique is one thing. Recognizing that the use of this technique is called for is another.[9] To explain this, I will have to backtrack a little.

First, let us examine the simplest expression imaginable, and assume that it is not meant to be interpreted metaphorically:

(2) *I have a headache.*

Thanks to his knowledge of the meaning of this sentence, the addressee to whom this utterance is directed is able to infer that the speaker intends to let him know that the speaker has a headache. In English, this sentence is an appropriate way, by virtue of convention, to let someone know this. Under normal circumstances, the hearer will believe, after interpreting this utterance, that the speaker has a headache. But what makes him believe this? It can't be a rule of language. No linguistic rule in the world can make me believe everything I read! Another step is required. That step is the inference from the means to the end, along with the consideration of the given conditions: "I see that the speaker is using a means which I know serves, thanks to the conventions of English-speaking countries, to let someone know that you have a headache. The fact that the speaker is using this means with me is a symptom of his desire to make me believe he has a headache. Since I hold him to be an honest person, and see nothing that would indicate the opposite, I judge the fact that he uttered this sentence to be a symptom that he does, in fact, have a headache."

[9] Keller-Bauer (1984) differentiates systematically between the interpretation of metaphor and the recognition of metaphor.

To put it differently: on the one hand, we interpret sentences, and on the other, we interpret the fact that they are uttered under certain circumstances. We interpret the sentences themselves on the basis of the language rules we know, and which we assume that the speaker knows, too. The interpretive technique is that of rule-based inference. This interpretive step leads us (if things go well) to the recognition of what the speaker wants to let us know—or, casually put, of what he wants to tell us. We interpret the fact that he uttered this sentence by means of the symptomic technique. The interpretation of the state of affairs as a symptom leads us (if things go well) to the recognition of the end to which this means was used—simply put, to what the speaker wants us to do or believe.

To illustrate this, let's take a look at a non-linguistic example: I see a man sitting on the shore of an artificial lake, holding a fishing line in the water. Under normal circumstances, I would assume that he is fishing. What leads me to this assumption? It is the inference from the means to the end: "I know that what he's doing is what you do to catch fish. He's doing it, so he probably wants to catch some fish." This inference is not conclusive! What justifies my assumption, on the basis of my familiarity with the means-to-end relationship, that the man is using this means to the usual end? It could be that he wants to catch UFOs. Sperber and Wilson would say that the justification is the assumption of relevance: what a person does should be relevant. But doing something relevant is nothing more than a special case of rational action.[10] It is the assumption of rationality that justifies my assumption that the fisherman means to catch fish. In Nozick's formulation, it reads like this: "Interpret or translate what the person says and does so as to make the person as *rational* as possible" (1993: 153). What we have here is a default assumption, an "as-long-as-there's-no-reason-not-to" assumption (as Dorothea Franck (1980: 43) calls it),[11] which we make in dealing with our species, at all times and in all places, until there seems reason not to. It is a tenacious assumption, one that we cling to as long as possible.[12]

We will broaden our scenario somewhat, and further assume that I know that there is not a single live fish in this artificial lake, and that

[10] On the connection between rationality and relevance, see Chap. 14.

[11] Trans. K.D.

[12] This is true regardless of the fact that different (sub-)cultures have different judgments as to what aims are worth pursuing, how those aims are to be reached, and which factors are to be seen as costs and benefits.

everybody around here knows it. I know that the man lives in the area and assume that he knows that there are no fish in the lake. On the basis of these assumptions, I am left with two interpretive options.

First, I can infer that the man is crazy. Second, I can infer that he really doesn't want to catch fish; he's just acting as if he does. (He's a detective and wants to quietly keep an eye on the area around the lake shore.) Usually, we reserve the first option until there is really no other choice. This is not an unfair interpretation of a fellow human's actions, but a refusal to interpret. Assuming that the man is crazy is accepting the uninterpretability of his actions. But this also means accepting one's own inability to interpret, to understand the action. So in saying that we cling to the assumption of rationality as long as we possibly can, it means that we try to make interpretations as long as we possibly can. If I choose the second option, I try to interpret the observed event as a rational means for what seems, under certain circumstances, a plausible end. From the observed means, I try to infer an end to the actions that accords with the knowledge I bring with me and the assumption that the man's actions are rational. This means that I assume, from the man's perspective and on the basis of the possibilities subjectively available to him, that his means optimally fulfill his end. To me, the means is a symptom of the end. If I am able to make a symptomic inference from the means to the end, I have the satisfaction of having understood what the man on the lake shore is doing. Now let us return to metaphorical utterances.

A well-known left fielder who utters the sentence *I'm out in right field today* on a winter day in the office uses a means that, by virtue of convention, serves an end of which it would be implausible to assume, under the given conditions, that the speaker aims to realize. Telling someone in winter the position one will be playing in a (highly improbable) baseball game would not usually count as a "worthwhile undertaking," as long as there is no intention of giving the hearer to understand something beyond the words. An irrelevant communication is not worth the effort it takes to make it. It results in a negative net benefit and thus in a suboptimal means-to-end relation. In other words, the assumption that I should assume, in regard to the speaker, *only this* means-to-end relation, is not in tune with the assumption of rationality. The employed means *must* serve another end. The implausibility of the assumption that the prima facie interpretation is the desired one, as well as the implausibility of the assumption that the literal interpretation of the utterance reveals its purpose, is for the addressee a symptom that he should undertake further interpretive steps. However, the interpretive steps grounded in his *linguistic* knowledge are exhausted. He is left with association on the basis of literal sense and the other knowledge he brings to the situation, knowledge which the utterance has activated. The addressee reinterprets the linguistic means as a metaphor in order to relate it to a plausible end, enabling him to keep the assumption of rationality intact. When we assume that the addressee is aware of the metaphoricity of his interpretation, we must also assume that he still has the prima facie interpretation in mind. For the recognition of metaphoricity stems exclusively from the realization that the interpretation requires *two* inferences.

To summarize our thoughts up to this point:

(1) The addressee must always interpret two things: the uttered sentence and the fact that it was uttered under the given circumstances. Simply put: in order to understand an utterance, the addressee must find answers to the questions "What did he say?" and "Why did he say it?"

(2) The interpretation of the uttered sentence ("What did he say?") leads to literal sense; its interpretation takes place with the help of the symbolic technique. If the elimination of ambiguity or fixation of reference is necessary, which is usually the case, the symptomic technique must also be employed. That is, linguistic knowledge alone is usually not enough to reach a literal interpretation of an utterance.[13] If one restricts linguistic studies to the study of purely linguistic knowledge, as Bierwisch suggests (1979: 130), it follows that even what he calls literal meaning has no place in linguistics.

(3) The interpretation of the fact that exactly this utterance was spoken under the given conditions ("Why did he say it?") may lead the addressee to make further interpretive efforts, proceeding from the basis of the literal sense of the utterance. Anyone who interprets the fact that the utterance was made, infers the end from the means, and views the use of the means as a symptom for the intention to reach a certain end. If, on the basis of the literal

[13] Cf. Rumelhart 1979: 83 ff.

interpretation and the assumption of rationality, a plausible end to the speaker's actions cannot be discerned, this fact is itself a sufficiently clear symptom that the utterances must be put to another interpretation besides the literal one. Literally interpreted, a metaphorical utterance is an irrational act. If a literally interpreted metaphor represents "a semantically irregular predication" (Köller 1975: 335);[14] if it is irrelevant, contradictory, or sortally incorrect (Keller 1975)—it is in every case a form of irrational action. Briefly stated: metaphors, taken literally, are irrational.

Therefore, in the case of metaphor, the result of the symbolic interpretation of an uttered sentence is a symptom of the need for iconic interpretation. However, if the attempt to interpret the literal sense as a symptom of a plausible end is successful, this is a symptom to stop at the literal interpretation.

The interpretation of the purpose of the utterance is thus always implicative. It is this thesis to which we will turn our attention in the next chapter.

[14] Trans. K.D.

14

Rationality and Implicatures

In the previous chapter, we saw that the hearer, in order to understand an utterance, must always undertake two inferential procedures. He must interpret the utterance on the basis of his knowledge of linguistic rules (which in most cases must be supplemented with non-linguistic knowledge), and view the result of this interpretation as a symptom of the end meant to be reached with the utterance. In other words, he must employ the result of use of the symbolic strategy to reconstruct the means-to-end relation with the symptomic strategy. The semantic interpretation must be followed by a pragmatic means-to-end judgment.

Though the above is formulated from the perspective of the addressee, it does not mean that our theory is biased in favor of the hearer. But the presentation can be simplified by choosing one of the two perspectives. I continually proceed from the assumption that the inferences made by the hearer are exactly those that the speaker has in mind with the making of an utterance; that is, I continually assume completely successful communication.

The symptomic inference from the means to the end leads hearers to the understanding of that to which the speaker wants to bring them, to what the speaker wants to make them do or believe. There is a grave oversimplification hidden in this manner of speaking, one which I noted in Chapter 9: the inference of the end from the means is abductive. The means-to-end relation is not unambiguous. Consequently, there is no sure strategy for hearers to identify a given utterance U as the employment of the means M. For the identification of U as M, hearers first need hypotheses about the pursued end. They need prejudices,[1] 'r schemata,[2] or

---

[1] Cf. Gadamer 1975: 238 ff.   [2] Cf. Rumelhart 1980.

whatever one might want to call them. Hearers often find themselves in a kind of hermeneutical dilemma, from which they are able to escape only through an alternating comparison of hypothetically assumed means and hypothetically assumed ends. But for the purposes of my description, I will continue as if the inference from means to end were a purely linear, unidirectional process.

At this point I would like to turn to the thesis presented at the end of the previous chapter, that the sense of an utterance is always implicative —not only in those cases in which the utterance is interpreted in the nonliteral sense.

In the 1970s, Herbert Paul Grice developed a theory[3] that has two explanative goals. First, how is it possible to mean something other than what one says? Second, furthermore, how can speakers be fairly sure of being interpreted by hearers in the way they, the speakers, intend? There must be a reasonably systematic strategy for getting from the literally said to the nonliterally meant. Otherwise, the relatively high degree of reliability of communication would be nothing less than a miracle. Grice's proposal is generally called the theory of conversational implicatures. In spite of its explanatory strength, it has certain internal weaknesses. It is my intention to remedy these flaws. Before I do this, though, let me briefly present the theory.

In communicating, we use all kinds of indirect means to give the hearer to understand something. To the question "Was John F. Kennedy Catholic or Protestant?" I could answer "He was Irish!" To the question "Is Paul still home?" I could answer "There's a yellow VW in front of the house." What justifies my assumption that my exchange partner will even interpret these statements as answers? Why should they not assume that I want to abruptly change the subject? Grice's answer to this is the following:

Our talk exchanges do not normally consist of a succession of disconnected remarks, and would not be rational if they did. They are characteristically, to some degree at least, cooperative efforts; and each participant recognizes in them, to some extent, a common purpose or set of purposes, or at least a mutually accepted direction. . . . We might then formulate a rough general principle which participants will be expected (ceteris paribus) to observe, namely: Make your conversational contribution such as is required, at the stage at which it

---

[3] Grice 1975. This essay was in circulation long before its official publication as an unofficial "samizdat" publication.

occurs, by the accepted purpose or direction of the talk exchange in which you are engaged. (Grice 1975: 45)

This is called the cooperative principle. Thus, according to Gricean theory, the exchange partners in both fictive dialogues above will not interpret the replies as a change of topic, because they will assume of the speaker that he or she heed the cooperative principle. Grice supplements this general principle with four "maxims," which he calls, following Kant, the maxims of *quantity*, *quality*, *relation*, and *manner* (1975: 45–6). They read as follows:

Maxims of quantity

(1) Make your contribution as informative as is required (for the current purposes of the exchange).
(2) Do not make your contribution more informative than is required.

Maxims of quality

(1) Try to make your contribution one that is true.
    (1.1) Do not say what you believe to be false.
    (1.2) Do not say that for which you lack adequate evidence.

Maxims of relation

Be relevant.

Maxims of manner

(1) Avoid obscurity of expression.
(2) Avoid ambiguity.
(3) Be brief (avoid unnecessary prolixity).
(4) Be orderly.

"And one might need others" (Grice 1975: 46).

Before I go into the mechanism of the implicature, it would be wise to issue a caution against a possible misinterpretation. Sperber and Wilson formulate it with great clarity: Grice's principle and maxims are norms which communicators and audience must know in order to communicate adequately (1986*a*: 162). This is absolutely not the case, in my opinion. Grice's maxims are in the form of imperatives solely for the purpose of presentation. General kinds of behavior can be very economically described, as in the Kantian manner, if they are seen as the fulfillment of requests. Grice does not want to convince anyone to practice, or force anyone into, particular communicative behavior; rather, he wants to describe general principles of behavior. His theory is completely misunderstood if its maxims are seen as idealistic suggestions for idyllic togetherness. He formulates neither a communicative utopia that would "practically require freedom from any regulation" (Braunroth, Seyfert *et al.* 1975: 184),[4] nor a set of norms with which every exchange participant must be familiar, but principles that every person involved in communication assumes are fulfilled in communication until there is reason to believe otherwise.

The basic idea of this thesis is the following: speakers may expect that hearers essentially proceed on the belief that they, the speakers, will act according to these principles. Thus, speakers can expect hearers to infer that, if the literal interpretation cannot be brought into accord with the assumption that the speakers are acting according to these principles, the hearers must undertake to find a further or a different interpretation, one that is compatible with the assumption that these principles are observed. Hearers "tell themselves" something like this (a somewhat simplified version): "At first glance, it seems that you have not followed the principles! Since what shouldn't be can't be, I will have to give up my prima facie interpretation. I will have to look for an interpretation that somehow relates to the prima facie interpretation, but which allows me to keep your utterance in accord with my assumption that you have followed the cooperative principle and the maxims."

Applied to the fictive dialogues above, this means, for example: "The fact that there is a yellow VW in front of the house is, in regard to my question, whether Paul is still home, an uncooperative change of subject and an irrelevant observation. The assumption that the speaker is generally uncooperative and, in this case, that his remark is irrelevant, is not admissible. Therefore, the speaker wants me to look for another interpretation on the basis of my prima facie interpretation. Since he knows that I know that Paul drives a yellow VW (etc.), he probably wants to let me

[4] Trans. K.D.

know that he thinks that Paul is still at home. In other words, the answer 'There's a yellow VW in front of the house' implicates that the speaker assumes that Paul is still at home."

The words *implicature* and *implicate* are artificial words that Grice "invented" in order to suggest that what we have here is similar to implication and implying, but that it should not be identified with the logical relation of implication. Grice introduces the following general model of implicative inference:

He has said that *p*; there is no reason to suppose that he is not observing the maxims, or at least the CP [cooperative principle]; he could not be doing this unless he thought that *q*; he knows (and knows that I know that he knows) that I can see that the supposition that he thinks that *q* is required; he has done nothing to stop me thinking that *q*; he intends me to think, or is at least willing to allow me to think, that *q*; and so he has implicated that *q*.[5] (1975: 50)

With this, I will end my description of Grice's theory and begin with its critical examination. The theory is, in my understanding, a *theory of symptomatics*. The general model of the implicative inference runs like this:

First, the fact that what the speaker said (namely, that *p*) is not compatible with the assumption that he has observed the cooperative principle and the maxims is a symptom of his desire that I search for another interpretation. Second, the fact that he said that *p* is a symptom of his desire that the interpretation that I am looking for somehow relate to *p*.

The maxims of quantity, quality, relation and manner thus indicate something of which they should be viewed as a symptom—namely, the prima facie violation of at least one of them—a symptom for the fact that an interpretation must be found that goes beyond the literal sense.

Generally stated, we may say that (a) the prima facie interpretation *I* of the statement that *p* necessarily leads to the inadmissible assumption that the cooperative principle and/or at least one of the maxims has not been observed. This is a symptom that *I* is not the interpretation that the speaker desires be made; and (b) the choice of statement "that *p*" is a symptom that the desired interpretation should somehow relate to *p*.

[5] Grice's formulation "that *p*" makes it clear that he has exclusively assertive utterances in mind. I will retain this manner of speech for the sake of simplicity. A generalization of the theory to include all kinds of speech acts is certainly possible.

Grice's theory leaves three questions open (or unexplained):

(1) To what extent is cooperativity a necessary aspect of communication?

(2) In what relation do the four maxims stand to the cooperative principle?

(3) What leads the speaker to choose the indirect path when a direct one is also available?

While the first two questions definitely belong to the explanatory expectations of Grice's theory, the third question lies beyond its explanatory goals.

Let's start with the first question. Why is it inadmissible to assume that someone has not observed the cooperative principle? Why must a conversation have "a common purpose or set of purposes, or at least a mutually accepted direction" (Grice 1975: 45)? Being cooperative may be virtuous, but is it also necessary? Consider these two unspectacular examples:

(1) A woman approaches me on the street and asks, "Say, isn't there a single phone booth in this town?" My answer: "Right around the corner!" Admittedly, my answer was cooperative, but did the question already exhibit a "common purpose" or a "mutually accepted" direction? Since I have never seen this person before, she cannot know my purposes; the question of the mutually accepted direction does not come up, since the direction is only established with the sudden start of the exchange.[6] The first move of a new game, by definition, cannot be cooperative. Nevertheless, I have interpreted the woman's question not literally, but implicatively.

(2) At a small gathering, someone asks an indiscreet question about a colleague. The questioned party ignores the question with "meaningful" silence. Does this silence follow a common purpose or a mutually accepted direction? Surely not. But every person at the gathering would be capable, in certain conditions, of implicatively interpreting the refusal to answer, even without assuming that the "silent one" has observed the cooperative principle.

---

[6] On the question of cooperativity at the start of conversations, see Keller 1987: 11 ff.

The second example adheres to the observations of Asa Kasher (1976: 213). Every communication is cooperative in the trivial sense that everyone must choose the linguistic signs which they believe their exchange partners will understand. In this sense, even violent disagreements, verbal abuse, and insults are cooperative (Keller 1987: 11). But as Kasher correctly points out, such general aims are "not sufficiently specific to have them serve as assayers of the contributions to the conversation, as is required by the cooperation principle" (1976: 202).[7] Even if we were to assume that humans are always cooperative in communicating, this would not have to mean that they have common goals. Mutually dependent goals are sufficient: "I have my goals, and you have yours. Our goals are different. But I can only reach my goals if you reach yours, and vice versa." Not even the mutual dependence of goals is required to explain implicative inferences. In other words, successful communication, as well as the ability or the possibility to make implicative inferences, does not require that the speakers behave cooperatively, except in the trivial sense that they try to speak "each other's language." Kasher's laconic comment is: "The cooperation principle is regarded as wrong and needless" (1976: 210).

The second question left open by Grice's theory is that of the relation in which the four maxims stand to the cooperative principle.[8] Are they related to it as the specific is to the general? Do they represent an explication of the cooperative principle? Grice's formulation is significantly vague in exactly the place where an explanation might be expected: "On the assumption that some such general principle as this [the cooperative principle] is acceptable, one may perhaps distinguish four categories" (Grice 1975: 45). Grice neither demonstrates nor establishes a systematic connection between cooperativity and the maxims.[9]

The third unanswered question is: what leads the speaker to choose the indirect path when a direct one is also available? As noted, Gricean theory does not pretend to want to answer this question. Since the direct path, if there is one, is by definition as cooperative as the indirect path, the choice of the indirect path cannot be deduced from or explained by the cooperative principle.

[7] Similar objections are raised by Sperber and Wilson (1986a: 162ff.).
[8] See also Sperber and Wilson's critique (1986a: 36ff.).
[9] Here, too, see Sperber and Wilson's critical comments (1986a: 36).

Our provisional summary is that the assumption of a generally valid cooperative principle is implausible, the relation of such a principle to the four maxims is unexplained, and the choice of the indirect over the direct path remains unmotivated.

I think that the solution to these problems lies in giving up the idea of the cooperative principle and, as Kasher suggests, replacing it with a principle of rationality. In anticipation of this, I have applied the rationality principle in the previous chapters. Very generally, one might formulate this principle as follows:

> Consider the conversational contributions of your exchange partner to be rational actions.

What does it mean to say of an action that it is rational? To act rationally is, for the attainment of the goal of the action, to choose and apply, from among the subjectively available alternatives for action, the one which promises the highest subjectively expected net benefits.[10] The restriction to subjectively expected net benefits is needed because speakers may not be conscious or aware of the possibilities which are objectively available to them. Net benefits are gross benefits minus costs. Though a cost-benefit calculation of available linguistic means is not quantifiable, this does not mean that they are incalculable. We are fully capable of weighing the articulatorily thrifty *bye* against the somewhat more costly *farewell* to determine which of the two yields higher net benefits in a given situation, that is, to decide which of the two is the better choice. Grice himself refers to rationality in two places. His aim, he writes, "is to see talking as a special case or variety of purposive, indeed rational, behavior" (1975: 47); in the aforementioned passage, where the cooperative principle is introduced, he implies that uncooperativity is irrational. But the connection is nowhere described. It could be that in many, or even in most cases, it is rational to cooperate. But our examples make clear that

[10] Sometimes the objection is raised that this is a theory of egoism (see, for example, Prechtl 1991: 178). This is not the case. If one equates self-interested behavior with egoistic behavior, one is forced to distinguish between altruistic egoism and egoistic egoism. Even those who wish to lead virtuous lives and go to heaven will choose from among their alternatives for action those which they expect to enable the realization of their goals. In this sense, even altruistic behavior would be egoistic. Altruistic behavior is action performed with no expectation of praise from others. Egoistic behavior, on the other hand, is characterized by the fact that the costs that it creates for others are not calculated in the cost–benefit balance. On the theory of rational behavior, see Nozick 1993.

this does not have to be the case. An indirectly formulated conversational start is implicatively interpretable precisely because the one who starts the conversation is assumed to be acting rationally. Significant silence can be interpreted as "meaningful" because it is assumed to be rational. Refusing to cooperate can be a completely rational choice.

Kasher formulates the principle of rationality as follows: "Given a desired end, one is to choose that action which most effectively, and at least cost, attains that end, ceteris paribus" (1976: 205). Rational action is thus, simply put, the optimization of the means-to-end relation. The only dimension in which it can be optimized is the economy of the means-to-end relation.

In their well-known work *Relevance*, Dan Sperber and Deirdre Wilson suggest that Grice's cooperative principle be replaced by a principle of relevance. This principle reads: "Every act of ostensive communication communicates the presumption of its optimal relevance" (Sperber and Wilson 1986a: 158). In very abbreviated form, the basic idea of this theory is that the addressee and interpreter of an utterance assumes that the speaker wishes to communicate exactly that proposition that is of optimal relevance for the addressee. According to Sperber and Wilson's definition, relevance is not an absolute measure, but a matter of degree. The content of an utterance can be more or less relevant from one conversational situation to another. The degree of relevance of an uttered proposition is defined by the strength of the so-called contextual effect that it has in the given context, and the processing effort that the utterance requires of the addressee. The larger the contextual effect and the smaller the required cognitive effort, the more relevant the uttered proposition in the given context (Sperber and Wilson 1986a: 122ff.). For the interpreter, the context of an utterance consists of background assumptions and encyclopedic knowledge, together with all their implications. "In real life, contexts are not fixed in advance, but are chosen partly in function of the proposition being processed" (Sperber and Wilson 1986b: 252). For the interpreters of an utterance, this means that "according to relevance theory, the correct interpretation of an ostensive stimulus is the first accessible interpretation consistent with the principle of relevance" (Sperber and Wilson 1986a: 178). The interpretive task of the addressees thus consists of choosing the interpretation that has for them the highest degree of relevance. Much of this theory is questionable. How can the context be reduced to what is relevant for the calculation of relevance?

Is this concept circular, as Levinson claims?[11] What follows from the thesis "that every act of ostensive communication *communicates* a presumption of relevance" (Sperber and Wilson 1986a: 162; my italics, R.K.)? If communication requires the inference of intentions, and those intentions are inferred from the assumption of relevance, one would think that the assumption of relevance itself cannot be communicated. I will not go into detail on the internal questions of the theory, but return to the central line of our argument and weigh the following questions:

(1) Is the principle of relevance an appropriate replacement for Grice's cooperative principle?

(2) How do the principle of relevance and the principle of rationality relate to each other?

In one passage, Sperber and Wilson note that the addressee must assume of the speaker that she is behaving rationally:

In trying to identify this informative intention, the addressee must assume that the communicator is communicating rationally. . . . This applies not just to the identification of informative intentions, but to the inferential identification of intentions in general. Intentions are identified by assuming that the agent is rational, and by trying to find a rational interpretation of her actions. (Sperber and Wilson 1986a: 165)

This insight seems to have no prominent role in their theory. It is not brought into systematic relation with the principle of relevance. (Rationality is not even to be found in an otherwise extensive index.) Could it be that rational action is the same as relevance as defined by Sperber and Wilson? Communicating rationally means optimizing the means-to-end relation. The communicated proposition is optimally relevant when there is maximum contextual effect with minimal processing effort. With this, first of all, different perspectives are assumed. The principle of rationality claims that *speakers* act rationally. The principle of relevance claims that *addressees* choose the interpretation that is optimally relevant *for them*. The principle of rationality is primarily one of action, while the principle of relevance is primarily one of interpretation. Now, one might say that they both add up to the same thing. The theory based on the principle of rationality proceeds on the assumption that addressees

[11] "R [relevance] thus controls the basis for assessing R; this is one of a number of apparent circularities" (Levinson 1989: 459).

assume that speakers will observe the principle of rationality, and arrange their interpretation accordingly. The theory based on the principle of relevance proceeds on the assumption that speakers assume that addressees will make their interpretation according to the principle of relevance, and arrange their utterances accordingly. However, it can be easily demonstrated that these two principles, of rationality and of relevance, operate on different levels and cannot replace each other.

Let us assume that a constant goal of communication is to achieve, in regard to the addressee, maximum contextual effects with minimal processing efforts. If we say that acting rationally is choosing the means that promises to optimally achieve this goal, it follows that speakers will choose from among their linguistic alternatives the one that, with a certain addressee, achieves maximum contextual effect and minimal processing efforts. But this means only that speakers must make a rational choice in the creation of utterances to express propositions with optimal relevance. Consequently, the principle of rationality concerns the relation of the means to its end or goal. In contrast, the principle of relevance concerns the goal. The principle of rationality is not unnecessary for the principle of relevance; it is downright essential. (Maybe this is what Sperber and Wilson are trying to say in the above passage.) The principle of rationality has logical priority over the principle of relevance. Therefore, the principle of relevance is also not an appropriate candidate for assuming the role that Grice intended for the cooperative principle. At best, it is an explication of the relation of the Gricean maxim "Be relevant."

Thus, to our initial question regarding Grice's theory, whether cooperativity is a necessary characteristic of communication, we must give a negative answer. Other than in the trivial sense that the communicator must choose a language that the addressee understands, cooperativity is not binding. The principle of relevance proves itself to be a poor substitute for the cooperative principle. In contrast, however, rationality is a logical necessity. This is why a demand like "Make an irrational utterance!" is paradoxical,[12] and thus, by definition, cannot be met. In order to meet it, one would have to choose the means that best fulfill the required purpose. This would be, by definition, a rational choice. The replacement of the cooperative principle with the principle of rationality also has the advantage that it makes the theory more general. It includes

---

[12] On paradoxes in communication, see Watzlawick, Weakland, and Fisch 1974: 62 ff.

all forms of linguistic communication, and furthermore, makes clear that linguistic communication, as Grice himself writes (and Sperber and Wilson intimate) is a special case of rational behavior.

The second question left open by Grice's theory concerns the connection between the cooperative principle and the maxims. I would like to approach this question in a revised version: in what does the connection between the cooperative principle and the maxims consist? The answer is: the principle of rationality concerns the choice of means in regard to a given end or goal; the maxims concern the identification of the goal. Let me try to explain this. In Chapter 9, we saw that the addressee is faced with an entirely different inferential problem than the speaker. Speakers have (in simplified form) goals, and search for the means in their repertoire that promises the most success in reaching their goals. Addressees receive the means, and have to reconstruct the speaker's intended ends. The means-to-end relation, however, is far from being completely unambiguous (see Chapter 9). That is, addressees and interpreters must choose, from among a number of possible goals (themselves made conceivable by the given means), the one that is most plausible. It is precisely for this that they need the maxims. Consider the aforementioned dialogue. Question: "Is Paul still at home?" Answer: "There's a yellow VW in front of the house." The process of the interpretation of this answer might be traced as follows:

(1) The speaker uttered the sentence *There's a yellow VW in front of the house*. This sentence is an appropriate means, according to the rules of our language, to let someone know that a yellow car of "VW" make is parked in front of the house.

(2) The assumption that the speaker wants to let me know this and only this is indeed compatible with his chosen means of doing so, but it is implausible. An utterance that is supposed to be an answer to my question should stand in some sort of relevant relation to the content of the question. The assumption thus violates the maxims of relation.

(3) I can avoid the assumption of a maxim violation if I assume that, first, the speaker knows that I know that Paul drives a yellow VW, and second, that he wants me to use the information about the VW and my knowledge in regard to Paul to infer that Paul is still home.

(4) But why didn't he just say "Yes"? Evidently the speaker has no better evidence available for the assumption that Paul is still home than the fact that there is a yellow VW parked in front of the house. If he had said "Yes," he would have violated the maxim of quality, which requires, among other things, that you should not say anything for which you lack adequate evidence.

(5) So the speaker evidently is pursuing the end of letting me know that he is of the opinion that Paul is still home, that he is not sure of this because he lacks adequate evidence, and that he is not prepared to take responsibility for what he has said.

This kind of "slow motion replay" always costs more effort than cognitive reality itself. Here is the structure of the reasoning behind the interpretation: the assumption of rationality serves the interpreter, by means of an essentially rule-based inference, to make (1) a prima facie interpretation. The recognition that this prima facie interpretation would mean assuming of the speaker that he has violated the maxim of relevance is (2) used by the addressee as a symptom that he must search for (3) another interpretation. The second interpretation is in fact quite close to the final one, but is not compatible with the assumption that the speaker has observed (4) the maxims of manner. This is for the addressee a symptom that he must search for (5) yet a third interpretation, at which, depending on the situation, he may leave things.

This analysis should make clear how the addressee manages, by means of the assumption that the speaker has violated none of the maxims, to filter out the most plausible of the possible goals. Or, to put it differently: the prima facie violation of one of the maxims is seen by the addressee as a symptom that he must come up with a further interpretation. Maxims are needed because the means-to-end relation does not deliver unequivocal results. With the use of languages in which the end can be unequivocally inferred from the means, such as algebra, maxims are superfluous.

A directly related question is that of the justification of the kind and number of Grice's proposed maxims. "Are there just the nine maxims [classified in four categories: R.K.] Grice mentioned, or might others be needed, as he suggested himself?" as Sperber and Wilson correctly ask (1986*a*: 36). In other words, are the number and kind of Grice's proposed maxims ad hoc? If it is true that the maxims serve to identify the goal, the number and kind of maxims should be derived from a classification of possible communicative goals. This is indeed the case.

Elsewhere (Keller 1994: 122) I have suggested a classification of the factors that are taken into account in our calculations of costs and benefits regarding the choice of linguistic means. The classification diagram looks like this:

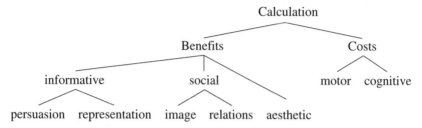

This diagram is to be interpreted as follows: the calculation of choice of linguistic means takes into account both costs and benefits. The speaker's costs are motor and cognitive in nature.[13] That is, communication costs mental and articulatory effort, which we try to minimize. On the benefits side, we can hope for informative, social and aesthetic benefits. (I want to tell you something, and at the same time, cultivate our relationship; also, I try to express myself eloquently.) The informative benefits may consist of a persuasive aspect and a representative one. (I want you to believe me, or I want to convince you; and I want to make clear what I am trying to tell you.) The social aspect may consist of an image aspect, that is, the aspect of self-representation, and a relational aspect. (I want you to find me intelligent, modest and nice, and I want us to remain friends.) I will leave out the aspect of cost minimization here,[14] and restrict my discussion to the goals of benefit maximization. For this, we may concentrate on the last line of the diagram. If we reformulate these goals, in the manner of Grice's maxims, as imperatives, approximately the following maxims result:

---

[13] Additionally, speakers must add the costs that their contribution will bring the addressee. Listening takes time and mental effort; it should be weighed with an eye to the value of what is conveyed (information, affection, etc.). The resulting costs/benefits balance for the addressee, as it should be taken into consideration by the speaker, will not be discussed here.

[14] Certainly, significantly careless articulation, that is, significant minimization of articulatory costs, can generate implicatures, under certain conditions.

Persuasion	Make your contribution believable (convincing, emphatic, etc.).
Representation	Make clear what you want to say.
Image	Present yourself in a positive way.
Relation	Be polite (dominant, deferential, etc.).
Aesthetic	Express yourself eloquently (wittily, sophisticatedly, etc.).

Now, Grice himself writes that he only wants to consider a partial aspect of communication: "There are, of course, all sorts of other maxims (aesthetic, social, or moral in character), such as 'Be polite', that are also normally observed by participants in talk exchanges, and these may also generate nonconventional implicatures. . . . I have stated my maxims as if this purpose [that talk (and so, talk exchange) is adapted to serve] were a maximally effective exchange of information" (Grice 1975: 47). This means that Grice's maxims concern only the first two lines of the above diagram, the aspect of informative benefits, and that he had only assertive speech acts in mind. What must speakers do if they want to choose linguistic means that make them believable and convincing, and that make clear what they want to say? The answer is that they should be as informative as necessary, but not more informative than is necessary; they should say nothing which they themselves do not believe, or for which they do not have adequate evidence; they should say nothing irrelevant; and they should express themselves clearly, unambiguously, concisely and in an organized fashion. These, precisely, are the Gricean maxims.

If this classification of the factors that can play a part in the rational choice of linguistic means is exhaustive (which I assume it is), it follows that the kinds of possible maxims are not ad hoc. However, it must be admitted that the number of sentences into which the maxims are formulated is variable and indeterminate.

Our third question, which the Gricean theory must leave unanswered, is: what leads the speaker to choose the indirect path when there is a direct one? Due to the fact that, in considering the dimension of cooperativity, there is no principal difference between the direct and the indirect paths, a theory based on the cooperative principle cannot provide an answer to this question. But against the backdrop of the principle of rationality, this question has a completely natural answer: speakers choose the indirect path precisely when they judge it to be the one with the best prospects. If we assume that speakers hope to optimize the means-to-end relation, that is, to make a rational choice from among the means available to them, we have an explanatory model for both, the speakers' choice of indirect means and the interpreters' choice of implicative interpretive techniques. In many cases, the choice of the direct path would be judged as suboptimal. The directly formulated utterance is indeed generally easy to understand but, communicatively, often holds less promise of success. A directly formulated request or demand would probably have, in some situations, less chances of being granted than an indirectly, implicatively formulated one. Both aspects, the path of the hearers' interpretation as well as the speakers' choice of means, are brought into inherent connection by the assumption of the principle of rationality. The interpretive steps of hearers are motivated precisely by the assumption of the rationality of speakers' choice of means. Or, to express it from the complementary perspective, the speakers' belief that their utterances will be interpreted in their sense, even if they choose nonliteral means, is based precisely on their belief that hearers will assume the rationality of their choice. The same goes for the belief of speakers that they will not be indirectly interpreted when what they say is literally meant.

In the next chapter, using examples of metaphorical and metonymical expressions, I will illustrate the advantages and disadvantages that nonliteral alternatives have in comparison to literal ones.

PART V

The Diachronic Dimension

15

Costs and Benefits of the Metaphorical Technique

In the long run, all signs become symbols, as we have seen. With sufficiently frequent occurrence, sense once created with pragmatic means
becomes semanticized, that is, rule based. The process of semanticization
is a one-way street. It is true that, under certain conditions, the possibility
exists to "re-literalize" metaphors ad hoc, such as in the headline "Don't
Get Scalped" for an article dealing with balding treatments (*Men's
Health*, July/August 1997, p. 82). But I know of no case in which a re-
literalization itself has become lexicalized. If the evolutionary trend
necessarily moves towards semanticization and lexicalization,[1] the question arises as to why we haven't been communicating exclusively with
lexicalized symbols for a long time already. The rash answer is that new
situations demand ever new, creative, linguistic means, such as the aforementioned *Green Berets* as the designation for a certain kind of military
company. But what seems plausible at first glance proves upon closer
examination to be an overgeneralization. We could just as well have called
this military group a *US Army Special Force*. On the other hand, age-old
phenomena only become really "catchy" when they have acquired a new

[1] I employ the expression *semanticization* to denote the process of the regulation of
sense which previously had been created with pragmatic means. When metaphorical
sense becomes literal sense, semanticization occurs. *Lexicalization* is the name for the
process whereby linguistic expressions become a part of the lexicon. The expression *pea
green* is lexicalized, for example, while the ad hoc formation *John Deere green* is not.
Nevertheless, the use of the expression *John Deere green* is interpretable only with the
help of knowledge of linguistic rules (and some knowledge of farm machinery).

designation.[2] In other words, the advent of new phenomena in the world is neither necessary nor sufficient for the introduction of new designatory forms. The truth is that the metaphorical and metonymical techniques (along with loanwords) suggest themselves for the interpretable, that is, semantically transparent, designation of new things. On the other hand, people often choose a metaphorical or metonymical technique even though the purely symbolic technique is also available. Since there is clearly nothing that forces them to do this, we are forced to ask: Where do the speakers see the advantage that justifies their choice? We will have to weigh the advantages and disadvantages of the symbolic and metaphorical techniques and determine which of them, under given conditions, promises to deliver higher net benefits.

The advantages of direct, clear and literal expressions are undeniable. Anyone who wants nothing more than to be understood should choose this route. However, this would mean adopting a diminished view of the purpose of communication, in which speakers desire nothing other than that their words be understood. The purpose of a communicative act does not consist in saying what one has to say, but in reaching what one wants to attain. The "saying" is in the service of the "reaching." Communication is a form of influence. Let us discuss the advantages and disadvantages of a pair of examples, whereby we will assume that the intended sense of (1) is contained in that of (2).

(1) *Ernest likes to wear colorful clothing.*
(2) *Ernest is a parrot.*

First, it is evident that the utterance (1) is considerably more likely be interpreted in the intended sense than is utterance (2). To put it differently, the danger of misinterpretation is considerably larger with (2) than with (1). In order for the speaker to even hope that (2) will generate the desired association, very specific conditions must be fulfilled. Different utterances of the sentence (2) could lead to very different associations. It could mean to say that Ernest repeats everything he hears, that he has a screechy voice, that he uses his "beak" for climbing, and so on.

The rule-based inference thus has three distinct advantages compared with the associative inference: it is shorter, safer and less contextually dependent. This is why metaphorical expressions are often discouraged in scientific texts, for instance.

[2] See *channel surfing*, Chap. 5, n. 10.

"If there are two ways to reach your goal, and one of them is shorter and safer, that is the one you should choose." This seems to be a reasonable maxim, one that we often follow. But if all speakers always followed this maxim, metaphors, at least, would have long since disappeared from our everyday language. This is clearly not the case. There is a continual coming and going. New metaphors are formed, establish themselves, become de-metaphorized, turn into conventional metaphors, only to finally eke out a miserable, mousy existence as completely inconspicuous members of the vocabulary. It doesn't occur to most English speakers that the word *dashboard*, now used to designate the instrument panel of a car, was originally the word for the panel that protected the coachman from the flying mud of the horses hooves (Keller 1994: 5). German speakers don't usually consider that *Angst* is etymologically related to *Enge* 'narrowness' and was once a spatial metaphor. Why do speakers persist in choosing the metaphorical technique? There are essentially two answers. First, not every goal can be reached by a short and safe path. Second, short and safe is not always tempting, and not necessarily optimally adequate to the goal. I will try to explain these metaphorical answers in a nonmetaphorical way.

In considering the vocabulary of a language, it becomes evident that lexicalized metaphors from the realm of the inner and the abstract occur in great number. Consider the vocabulary for our cognitive abilities, for example. When we *get the picture*, we have *grasped* something, *fathomed*, *discerned*, or *dug* it. We often feel a need to *get to the bottom* of something, and to do this, we *plumb*, *probe*, or *unravel* it. If we don't *see through* it, we might *swallow* it. These are just a few examples in which former metaphoricity is still apparent. *I see* means 'I have understood'; the German *ich weiß* ('I know'), a former past-tense form that now has present-tense meaning, the so-called preterite present, is analogously metaphorical. It is easy to see how its development proceeded when one considers that the verb infinitive *wissen* is etymologically related to the Indo-European root **ueid* or **uid* (cf. med.L *video* 'I see'). Thus, *ich weiß* once had the meaning 'I have seen', and what I have seen, I know. The meaning of *to hear/to have heard* is currently undergoing a similar change. When I ask someone, "Did you hear that the Steelers won?", I would be surprised if he answered "No! I read it in the paper." When someone says "I heard that . . .," it does not have to mean that they have acquired this piece of knowledge by acoustic means. *To have heard* something means (in a certain reading) to have *discovered* something, to have *got wind of it* or *come upon* it. In earlier times—to continue with the etymology—a person *came upon* something while journeying through the country, when he *dis-covered* something, that is, something from which he removed the cover. There's just no getting away from language's imag(e)inative nature!

Anyone who wants to talk about inner or abstract things is principally able to do so by means of analogy only. In order to communicate something to which only they have access, speakers must offer to hearers something accessible to them both, and by this means, bring them to the desired inference. That is, they must choose the iconic technique. It is seldom the case that something concrete is designated with the metaphorical use of an expression whose literal sense is abstract: lately, many German young people colloquially use the verb *meinen* 'to mean' in the sense of *said*, as an introduction to verbatim reporting of speech: "Ich sag zu ihm: 'Kannste nicht endlich damit aufhören?' Da *meint* er: 'Du hast doch damit angefangen'" ("I say to him 'Can't you finally just stop it?' Then he *means*: 'You're the one who started it'"). Lakoff and Johnson note that metaphor is frequently systematically structured. Bodily metaphors are one instance. Putting the above example into service once more, we observe that for cognitive activities, we systematically use the analogy of bodily ingestion: we can *assimilate, swallow, drink in, devour, absorb* or *relish* an idea, a book, a theory, etc. It's the same in many other areas. When something really impresses us, we say, for example, that it's *out of sight, out of this world, real gone, fantastic, unreal,* or a *trip*. German employs adjectives of mental derangement to express this: something really great is *toll, wahnsinnig, verrückt* or *irre*. This is exactly where the advantage of systematic metaphoricity lies: the association is led in the right direction. Even a creative metaphor such as "That film was positively *otherworldly*" stands a good chance of being interpreted in the sense in which it is meant. Thus, bodily metaphors are doubly useful: everybody has a body, and it's easy to refer to its parts, so that they can continually and unproblematically be used as starting points for associative inferences. The strategy of the speaker is "If I'm not going to fall back on a rule of use, at least I can make use of image systematicity." If I ask someone, "So, have you finally inhaled that theory?" I will be understood because the hearer is familiar with this kind of iconicity. The risk of creative innovation is reduced by second-order regularity. The regularity of the imagery replaces the regularity of rule-based use. The metaphor cited above,

(2) *Ernest is a parrot.*

is, I assume, a creative metaphor. But it is considerably more conventional than the metaphor

(2′) *Ernest is a flowerbed.*

Utterance (2) has better chances of being interpreted as intended, even though parrots and flowerbeds can be equally brightly colored. The reason for the impression that (2′) is less conventional than (2) is in the systematicity of the conceptualization. The interpretation of (2) can make use of a tradition of animal metaphors, while the interpretation of (2′) has to start from square one, so to speak, and is completely on its own. This is not to say that (2′) is uninterpretable. It means only that its framing conditions must be much more specific.

Up to this point we have mostly emphasized the advantages of non-metaphorical expressions, and said that speakers, if they want to talk about something inner or abstract, often have no choice but the metaphorical technique. This makes it sound as if metaphor is a kind of necessary evil, made tolerable by conceptual systematicity. Such an impression would be false. A downright lusty use of metaphor can be found in the editorial section of almost any daily newspaper. The metaphorical technique not only has disadvantages; it also has its benefits. Metaphors are, as they say, colorful and vibrant. They fade in the course of their lexicalization, and are frequently replaced with new, more colorful ones. "As hieroglyphs preceded letters in writing, in the speech metaphor . . . was the earlier word which slowly had to fade into denotative expression" (1973: 131). This is Jean Paul's early nineteenth century description of the process that in the meantime has come to be called *semantic bleaching*. What is it that makes metaphors seem more vivid than literal expressions?

The deciding factor is metaphor's quality of expressivity. The expressivity of the metaphorical technique is a function of four closely connected characteristics.

(1) The metaphorical technique implies the request to see something as something else.

(2) Every metaphor is a miniature epistemological model.

(3) Metaphor has predicative structure.

(4) The metaphorical technique is a game of surprise.

We will examine these characteristics in succession.

THE "SEEING-AS" PROCESS

Metaphors are often compared to comparisons. But they are not comparisons; not even abbreviated ones.[3] Taking our previous example, we might compare the sentences

(2) *Ernest is a parrot.*

(3) *Ernest is like a parrot.*

The decisive difference is that in (3), Ernest remains what he is, and is compared to a parrot. In (2), however, he is transformed into a parrot! Sentence (3) basically says "Take a look at Ernest, and take a look at a parrot, and compare the two of them." Sentence (2), on the other hand, says "See Ernest as a parrot! View him under the aspect of parrot-ness." As Nerlich and Clarke write, it is "the 'seeing-as' process which is essential for metaphor" (1988: 84). Seeing something as something is something other than comparing something to something. If I see a cloud as a face, I see a face. If I compare a cloud with a face, I must regard the cloud as a cloud. Otherwise I wouldn't be able to make the comparison. It is the seeing-as aspect of the metaphorical technique that produces what is perceived as richness of imagery. Humans are known to be visual creatures. Metaphors are pictures painted with linguistic symbols.

MINIATURE EPISTIMOLOGICAL MODELS

A metaphor is not a comparison, but a conceptual model. It's a pair of eyeglasses through which we see things that we would never see without them (as we might metaphorically say). Sentence (2) also says, "Try to comprehend Ernest by seeing him under the aspect of parrot-ness." In cases in which there is no possibility of direct perception, such as in

---

[3] The idea that a metaphor is an abbreviated comparison can be traced back to Quintilian (*Institutio oratoria* 8.6.8).

inner and abstract matters, metaphor is, as long as no lexicalized means has developed, the only possible epistemological model. *I have a tinny taste in my mouth.* How else could I express this, if not with the help of the metaphorical technique? In cases where an alternative epistemological model is available (such as Ernest's preference for colorful clothing), the impression might arise that metaphors can be explicitly and completely nonmetaphorically paraphrased. This idea is similar to the theory that you can tell a joke in such a way that it's no longer funny. Paraphrasing a metaphor nonmetaphorically is declining to use a specific epistemological model. Admittedly, it is possible to arrive at one and the same recognition by different routes.[4] The metaphorical technique isn't a kind of witty method to say things in an unconventional way, but a method of arriving at or conveying knowledge with the help of a witty, unconventional method. The usefulness of metaphor is not primarily in its surprise-and-amusement quotient, but in its cognitive quotient. Its ability to surprise and amuse is a result of the ability to convey knowledge. Mary Hesse (1980) explains the analogy between metaphors and explanative theories, or between metaphoricity and explanativity. Metaphor and explanative theories have in common that concepts from a primary system, as she calls it, are viewed in light of the concepts of a secondary system. The evolutionary theory, as an example of an explanative theory, derives its explanative power from the fact that the process of change (= primary-system concepts) is seen in the light of the reproductive probability of individuals of certain types (= secondary-system concepts). In our example above, the parrot metaphor, a person is seen in light of a secondary system, namely that of a parrot. Applied to a person, the parrot model evokes richer, more specific cognizance than conforming to the rule of use for the expression *colorful clothing* would.

PREDICATIVE STRUCTURE

Since metaphor is always an invitation to see something as something else, it always has predicative structure. Even metaphorical names contain implicit predication.[5] Anyone who names things with metaphor names them with iconic characterization. This is the basis of the epistemological

---

[4] Cf. Köller 1975: 188.   [5] See Köller 1975: 170 ff.

function. I assume that a metaphorical name relates to a nonmetaphorical name as a definite description does to a name, such as *the author of the Canterbury Tales* to *Chaucer*. As long as the word *companion* (from the med.L *companio* 'one who eats bread with another', 'messmate') was still metaphorically understood, the utterance "My companion is sick" meant as much as "The one with whom I eat is sick." In the course of lexicalization, metaphorically descriptive references become labels. With this, the informational content of the utterance is diminished. With sufficiently frequent use, even nonmetaphorical descriptions become labels. Just consider the name *El Pueblo de Nuestra Señora La Reina de los Angeles de Porciuncola* 'The Village of our Lady, the Queen of the Angels of Porciuncola', reduced to the fully unmotivated *Los Angeles* and finally to *L.A.* Or the *Hotel del Coronado* 'hotel of Coronado' on the peninsula of the same name: for insiders, it's simply *The Del* 'the of'! These are processes of demotivation, as discussed in Chapter 10. Descriptions are "relatively motivated" in precisely the Saussurean sense that *fourteen* is relatively motivated. The principle of compositionality holds: the meaning of the combination of signs is the combination of the meaning of the signs. (In this sense, every syntagm is a relatively motivated sign.) Through frequent referential use, the relationship to the referent short-circuits, so to speak, and is no longer produced through an understanding of the description. As a result, the compositionality of the meaning becomes obsolete. The expression can be reduced to what is necessary for the identification of the sign. When, in 1709, the Florentine instrument maker Bartolommeo Cristofori built a stringed instrument that made the strings resound by means of a hammer mechanism, thus enabling an increase in volume with an increase in the applied force of the hammers, he gave his invention the descriptive name *Gravecembalo col piano e forte*. In the meantime, it has become the completely unmotivated *piano*. Analogously, *Colonia Claudia Ara Grippinensis* finally became Colonia (Cologne) and *Surfer's Paradise*, the name of an Australian city south of Brisbane, is on the way to becoming simply *Surfers*.

A GAME OF SURPRISE

The metaphorical technique, as we have seen, consists in using linguistic symbols to give an impulse, one that should generate an associative inference. Association is a game of surprise. Following rules, by definition, is not. Of course, there is a continuum between creative association and the following of rules. It corresponds to the continuum from creative, new metaphors (*the sun weeps*) to clichés (*the sun smiles*), all the way to fully lexicalized metaphors (*the sun sets*).[6]

What we perceive as the vividness of the metaphorical technique, as opposed to the symbolic technique, is the function of a new way of seeing (the seeing-as effect), the epistemological model, the predicative character and the surprise effects. During the process of lexicalization, that is, the process of the gradual transition from an associative to a rule-based inference, these qualities necessarily are lost. That is, a process of information loss always accompanies the process of lexicalization.[7] The more strictly regulated the use of a linguistic means, the less informative it is. This is most clearly evident when a former metaphor is not only lexicalized, but also grammaticalized. Morphological units are perceived to be less meaningful than lexical units. There is also a continuum from metaphor to morpheme, as the study of grammaticalization has proved. A development such as the Catalonian noun *cap* 'head' having become a component of the combinatorial preposition *cap a* 'to' (*Vés cap a casa!* 'Go home!') is a clear example of the grammaticalization of a former metaphor. The Catalonian preposition *cap a* 'to' was once apparently used in the sense of 'with one's head in the direction of'.

The answer to the question with which we started this chapter— what advantages does the metaphorical technique have in comparison to the symbolic one?—is that the metaphorical technique provides an imaginative epistemological model with surprise effects and minimal accuracy. In this sense, metaphor is more colorful than literal alternatives. Depending on the prevailing framing conditions and the speaker's communicative goals, the speaker should opt for one of these techniques. The calculation of costs and benefits should be ideal with the use of "semi-lexicalized" metaphors—from a literary perspective, clichés. They combine the essential advantages of both techniques: they are explanative, imaginative, predicative, accurate, and highly independent of context, though they do lose a few points in the area of surprise

---

[6] Cf. Kurz 1982: 19.

[7] This loss of information is presumably what is meant by the word *desemanticization*. See, for example, König and Traugott 1988: 121.

effects. Recall Plato's theory: "the most perfect state of language" (435c) is when similarity joins conventionality.

A glance at any random issue of a news magazine confirms this prognosis. In a July 21, 1997 *Newsweek* article about the Martian rover Sojourner, we read that while on the Pathfinder mission, *she* arrived on Mars and *paid courtesy calls*, naturally *showing the exemplary manners expected of any ambassador*. After a *10-hour handshake* with the rock *Barnacle Bill*, she set off on her *next visit*, to *Yogi*. Due to a *fender bender*, she was *hung up* on Yogi's *face* for two days. Inexpensively built, Sojourner proved that the *right stuff* can be bought for a *supersaver fare*. It helped the *bottom line* to let well-paid, long-serving *space jocks* retire and *make way* for *kids* happy to work long hours. Not only that, the Pathfinder mission *pumped up* public, media and presidential interest in the space program. CNN seemed to be *gunning* for the position of "official Martian network," and President Bill Clinton couldn't stop himself from *channel surfing* to see Pathfinder from Warsaw. Of these metaphors —which can all be found in little more than one column of a single article—a good number are semi-lexicalized. Through the use of such just-barely-still metaphors, the rule-based inference is supported and enriched, as it were. This creates a kind of information compression. However, the appeal of "semi-lexicalization" has a self-destructive effect: it raises the frequency of use, thus speeding the process of complete lexicalization. When this stage is reached, the expressions have become unsuitable for the purpose of information compression, and new semi-lexicalized metaphors arise to take their place.

16

The Metaphorical Use of Modal Verbs

Image systematicity increases the interpretability of the metaphorical technique. However, there also exist systematic relations which are not motivated by the speaker's attempt to make things easier for the addressee, for the purpose of ensuring his, the speaker's, communicative success. Similar problems often lead to similar solutions. Let us consider a simple example. The feeling that chili peppers create on the tongue is called *hot* in English, *scharf* in German, and in Spanish, *picante* (the present participle of *picar* 'prick'). Chili *is hot and burns, ist scharf und brennt, es picante y pica.* Though these three languages use different images, there is one thing they all have in common. All use the concept of physical wounds: burns, cuts and pricks. (Interestingly, German—in contrast to English and Spanish—combines two different sorts of conceptual images: "sharp" things "burn" the tongue, rather than "cutting" it (*schneiden*).) With burning, cutting and pricking, the external phenomena suitable to be used as associative impulses for the metaphorical denotation of the internal taste sensation in question are, I think, pretty much exhausted. Some languages, as a means of drawing comparison, use a word such as *chili-like* to designate the sensation of tasting spicy-hot things. Chinese makes use of this method, for example. The Chinese word for *hot* is *la* 辣 and can be etymologically translated as *pepper-like*.[1] But in languages in which the metaphorical technique is employed for such sensations, the occurrence of wounding images is highly probable.[2] As noted above, similar problems lead to similar solu-

---

[1] Thanks to Professor Ma Wentao of Peking University's German Department for providing this information.

[2] In Turkish, 'spicy hot' is *yakıcı* (from *yakmak* 'burn'); the Japanese Kanji sign for 'hot' 辛 (*karai*) can also mean 'painful' (*tsurai*).

tions.

Usually, when we think of the metaphorical technique, we think of metaphorically employed adjectives, adverbs, verbs and nouns. But if the metaphorical technique consists in triggering associative inferences (from the perspective of the speaker) or in drawing such inferences (from the perspective of the addressee), there is no reason why it should fundamentally be restricted to these four types of word. In recent years, metaphorical formations have in fact been discovered and described in spheres of language where they traditionally were not expected: many uses of conjunctions, modal verbs and prepositions were formerly metaphorical and in the meantime have become lexicalized; in these cases, the metaphorical technique is still productive. Anyone who says, for example, that he is working *under* a new boss, is clearly using a former metaphor—namely, a spatial preposition—for the characterization of a social relation. Space is visibly external. Prepositions that indicate spatial relations, or spatial particles such as *where*, *back*, and so on, are perfect for expressing temporal relations, and thus for composing more abstract concepts: *go three steps back—way back when*; *the place where the maple tree stood—the case where some are weak and others must shoulder the burden*; *the week before last—generals come before colonels*. True, constructions like *way back when* or *a case where I didn't know what to do* may be viewed as stylistically clumsy, but colloquially they are in wide use.

Modal verbs, conjunctions and prepositions are often subject to the process of so-called epistemization. Epistemization is a special case of the process of subjectification. Subjectification and epistemization are usually generated with the help of the metaphorical technique. In the following paragraphs, I would like to introduce and explain these various processes.

An example may provide a first intuitive impression of the makeup of the subjectification process. The conjunction *while* currently has two uses, one of them temporal and the other adversative. Between the two, transitional elements can be found. Consider these three utterances:

(1) *While you mowed the lawn, I did the dishes.*

(2) *While you lay in the sun, I did the dishes.*

(3) *While Virginia belonged to the Confederacy, West Virginia opted*

to join the Union.

In sentence (1), the temporal reading is clearly required: 'During the time that you were mowing the lawn, I was doing the dishes'. The described circumstances are compared with regard to elapsed time. In the third sentence, *while* is purely adversatively used, in the sense of 'in contrast to'. The political positions of the two US states are contrasted. The second sentence is an example of transition. Here, as in sentence (1), it is asserted that the two named occurrences took place at the same time. But this sentence also expresses a reproach. The temporal and the adversative readings coexist. According to Webster's, adversative conjunctions serve to express "opposition or antithesis." Now, in what regard are lying in the sun and doing the dishes antithetical? The antithesis is not in the factual, but in its valuation: while I was working, you were lazing around. Utterance (2) can be paraphrased approximately thus: "During the time that you were lying in the sun, I was doing the dishes. I disapprove of this, because lying in the sun is pleasant and unnecessary, in contrast to doing the dishes, a necessary and unpleasant activity." Industriousness and laziness are contrasted. The condition of use for *while* as it is employed in utterance (1) is exclusively the external factor of simultaneity. In sentence (2), internal factors, namely, differing valuations, are made into conditions of use. Elizabeth Traugott characterizes the general trend towards subjectification as follows: "Meanings tend to become increasingly based in the speaker's subjective belief state/attitude toward the proposition" (1989: 35).[3] The change of meaning that the German adjective *nett* underwent, from 'clean, pure' to its current meaning 'friendly, lovable' is an example of such a process. The process of subjectification occurs precisely when the speaker's beliefs, attitudes, valuations, etc. become conditions for the use of an expression. When, as in many languages, verbs of motion become tense or aspect markers, this, too, is a process of subjectification. Well-known examples of this are the emergence of the periphrastic future forms in English and most Romance languages.[4] Engl. *I'm going to eat*, Span. *voy a comer*, Fr. *je vais manger*

---

[3] Traugott 1989 is the most significant reference on the concept of subjectification as it is meant here. It should be noted that Ronald Langacker (1990) uses the expression *subjectification* in a completely different sense.

[4] On the development of the English future form *going*, see Traugott 1993; on this aspect of Romance languages, see Fleischman 1982.

all mean (among other things) 'I will eat'. (Catalan is an exception: *jo vaig menjar* 'I have eaten'.)[5] The absolute distance from the aspect of motion is clear in sentences in which the subject refers to immovable things: *it's going to rain, va a llover, il va pleuvoir* 'it will rain'. In English, the verbs *come* and *go* are also used as aspect markers: *Then I went and wrote the whole chapter again. Then you go and take a piece of paper and lay it underneath. After we'd been arguing for 20 minutes, he comes and says he loaned 20 dollars.* The verbs *come* and *go* are not used here to indicate physical motion, but a kind of "mental motion" of decision or beginning, a metaphorical "coming" and "going" with an inchoative aspect.

The process of subjectification plays a large part in the so-called epistemic use of modal verbs.[6] I would like to describe this usage in detail, and show to what extent epistemization is an application of the metaphorical technique. Consider the following dialogues:

(1) Fritz: *Has he finished everything?* Paul: *He may go home now.*

(1′) Fritz: *How long is the drive?* Paul: *He may be home now.*

What's the difference between these two uses of *may*? Webster's describes the meaning of *may*, as it is used in (1), as 'to be permitted to', and as used in (1′), as 'expressing possibility'. Before I go into more depth, I would like to present another example:

(2) Fritz: *What's he doing with that?* Paul: *He must drink it.*

(2′) Fritz: *Do you know where he is?* Paul: *He must be home now.*

Webster's describes the meaning of *must* in (2) as 'to be obliged or required or compelled to' and in (2′) as 'to be certain, likely or probable to'. In view of Webster's above definitions of 'possibility' (for *may*) or 'certainty, likelihood, probability' (for *must*), might one conclude that the sentences *He must be home* and *He may be home* express similar things? Of the meaning of *should*, too, in sentences such as *He should be home now*, Webster's states that it is used 'to express probability'. Although it must be admitted that all of these sentences can be used to express an assumption on the part of the speaker, we still intuit that these

---

[5] To my knowledge, there is as yet no explanation for this unusual exception, where a periphrastic form with a verb that means 'to go' has past tense meaning.

[6] Cf. Lyons 1977: 682, 787 ff., Traugott 1989, and Sweetser 1990.

sentences have differing meanings.

I will call the meaning of modal verbs as they occur in sentences (1) and (2) *factual meaning,*[7] and their meaning in (1′) and (2′) *epistemic meaning.* The difference between the epistemic meanings of various modal verbs can be clearly demonstrated when they are contrasted with the respective factual meanings. Eve Sweetser has successfully under-taken such an analysis of English—namely, within the framework of cognitive semantics—in the 1990 book *From Etymology to Pragmatics* (Sweetser 1990: 49–73). Disregarding our criticism of the cognitivistic superstructure (cf. Chapter 5), Sweetser's observations are extremely insightful, and in principle, also applicable to German modal verbs. Sweetser is able to demonstrate plausible connections between the fac-tual and epistemic readings of modal verbs (as well as between those of other expressions). That such connections exist is by no means a part of common linguistic knowledge. Peter Eisenberg, for example, in his 1989 *Grundriß der Deutschen Grammatik*, writes that "The meaning of *dürfen* in [*Er dürfte das gemerkt haben*] has little to do with the meaning of *dürfen* as 'having permission' in [*Er dürfte das behalten*]. The same is true for the other [modal verbs]" (1989: 102).[8] Following Sweetser, I would like to show that these two uses are in fact closely related.

First we will consider the German verbs *dürfen, können, mögen, müssen* and *sollen* in their factual readings. As we will see, the verb *wollen* is an exception. Let us assume that *dürfen* serves to express permission. In that case, *Du darfst schwimmen* can be approximately paraphrased as *Someone or something permits you to swim.* We can para-phrase the remaining German modal verbs after the same pattern, with the exception of *wollen. Können* serves to express ability, *mögen* to express desire, *müssen* a compulsion and *sollen* an obligation. On the premise that these assumptions are relatively accurate, we may formulate the following paraphrases:

(1) *Er darf schwimmen.* *Someone/something permits him to swim.*

(2) *Er kann nach Hause gehen.* *Someone/something enables him to go home.*

(3) *Sie mag Kakao trinken.* *She has the desire to drink cocoa.*

[7] Sweetser calls it *root meaning,* while others have named it *deontic meaning.* On terminology, see Heine 1992: n. 2. [8] Trans. K.D.

(4) *Er muß nach Hause gehen.*   *Someone/something compels him to go home.*

(5) *Er soll seine Suppe essen.*   *Someone/something obligates him to eat his soup.*

Now, what does the epistemic reading of these modal verbs have to do with the factual reading assumed here? Can their epistemic readings be analogously paraphrased? We recall what the metaphorical technique is usually capable of doing: it allows us to name inner or abstract phenomena by means of an associative inference, one which has as its point of departure an outer, concrete phenomenon. What is the inner correlate of the permission or compulsion to do something? It is the permission or compulsion to believe or to assume something: epistemic permission or epistemic compulsion. *Something requires you to X*, for example, becomes *Something compels me to assume that you are X-ing.* To exemplify the epistemic reading, let us examine five analogous sentences. If, in paraphrasing the respective modalities (permission, ability, desire, compulsion, obligation), we transpose the factual sphere to the epistemic sphere, we arrive at exactly the paraphrases corresponding to the meanings of modal verbs in the epistemic readings.[9]

(1) *Er dürfte der Täter sein.*   *Something permits me to assume that he is the culprit.*

(2) *Er kann jetzt zu Hause sein.*   *Something enables me to assume that he is home now.*

(3) *Sie mag recht haben.*   *I desire to assume that she is right.*

(4) *Sie muß jetzt zu Hause sein.*   *Something compels me to assume that she is home now.*

(5) *Sollten ihre Augen lügen?*   *Is there something that obligates me to assume that her eyes lie?*

Here, we see what might have motivated the authors of the Duden grammar to ascribe the aspect of 'Vermutung' ('presumption') to all of these epistemic uses (*Duden Grammatik* 1984: §§130–62), as well as the reasons that point to an assumption of intuitive meaning difference.

---

[9] On contextual conditions that call for an epistemic reading, see Heine 1992.

When I say Peter *dürfte/kann/mag/muß/sollte jetzt zu Hause sein*, I express the fact that the evidence available to me is such that my presumption that Peter is home is *permitted/enabled/desired*, or that I am *compelled* or *obligated* to presume that he is home. To express this always means to utter a presumption. This also applies in first-person uses: I will utter the sentence *Ich muß jetzt zu Hause sein* when I want to say that evidence compels me to the conclusion that I am at home. If I know that I am at home, and simply want to say this, I cannot use the sentence *Ich muß jetzt zu Hause sein*, but simply *Ich bin zu Hause*. The various modal verbs differ on the basis of the respective presumptions that they express. Feeling compelled to make an assumption is different from feeling permitted to presume something. This is precisely the difference between *Peter muß jetzt zu Hause sein* and *Peter dürfte jetzt zu Hause sein*. The nuances in meaning that result from alternating between indicative and subjunctive modal verbs can also be identified thus.[10] Anyone who wants to express that the evidence is such that he feels himself compelled to presume that Peter is home should choose the indicative variation: *Peter muß jetzt zu Hause sein* ('Peter must be home now'). However, if he wants to express the fact that the evidence is such that he *may* see himself compelled to assume that Peter is home, he should choose the subjunctive variation: *Peter müßte jetzt zu Hause sein* ('Peter would have to be home now'). The degree to which the epistemic reading of German modal verbs has asserted itself becomes clear in sentences in which, for example, the subject of the sentence makes a factual reading impossible: "Die feuchtkalte Luft, die vom Meer kommen *mochte*, verlieh der Atmosphäre etwas Ländliches" ('The cold, moist air, which may have come from the sea, lent the atmosphere something rural'; Nooteboom 1993: 1. My emphasis, R.K.).[11]

As noted above, the verb *wollen* is an exception. If *wollen* behaved like the other modal verbs, the following paraphrases would be correct:

(6) *Fritz will sie sehen.*　　　Fritz has the desire/intention
　　　　　　　　　　　　　　　　to see her.

(6′) *Fritz will sie gesehen haben.*　*I have the desire/intention to
　　　　　　　　　　　　　　　　　presume that Fritz saw her

---

[10] *Sollen* and *dürfen* have no indicative forms with epistemic readings.
[11] Trans. K.D.

When we attempt mechanically to paraphrase an epistemic reading of the verb *wollen* after the pattern established by other modal verbs, a sentence such as the one above* results. This sentence could in fact be used to express a possible epistemic modality, but it is not the modality of the epistemic use of *wollen*. In other words, the marked sentence (6′) is not a paraphrase of the sentence that precedes it. Can this use of *wollen* justifiably be called epistemic anyway? In order to decide this, we must analyze the meaning of the sentence *Fritz will sie gesehen haben* in more detail. The Duden grammar describes the meaning of this use of *wollen* as 'assertion', giving the following explanation: "In this variation, the speaker/writer expresses with *wollen* that someone asserts something that should not necessarily be held to be true" (*Duden Grammatik* 1984: §154).[12]

The correct paraphrase of sentence (6′) above is:

(6′) *Fritz will sie gesehen haben.*   *Fritz asserted (implicitly or explicitly) that he saw her; I, the speaker, hold this assertion to be implausible.*

How can a meaning that ascribes intent become a meaning that ascribes implausibility? It is not a metaphorical technique that is involved here, but the exploitation of a pragmatic inference: when someone says *Er will sie sehen* ('He wants to see her'), that person (usually) wants to get across that, at the time of the utterance, he does not see her. In other words, *He wants to see her* usually implicates *He does not see her*. (This is not a logical implication, however, for it is not contradictory to say *I see her and want to see her*.) Analogously, the present perfect form *Er will sie gesehen haben* (literally, *He wants to have seen her*) implicates that he has not seen her. An interpretation indicating the ascription of intent is blocked, as it were, by the conditions imposed by tense. You can't have intentions in hindsight. The remaining possible interpretation is the implicature above. If we include implicatures in our paraphrases, the mechanism becomes clearer:

(6) *Fritz will sie sehen.*   *Fritz has the intention to see her, and he does not see her now.*

(6′) *Fritz will sie gesehen haben.*   *Fritz has the intention to have seen her, and he didn't see her.*

---

[12] Trans. K.D.

The first part of the paraphrase of (6′) is logically impossible; what is left is the second part. In sum: the use of *wollen* in (6′) is epistemic. This is because one of the conditions of use is the speaker's belief that an untruth has been asserted. However, epistemization does not occur through the use of the metaphorical technique, as it does in the cases of the other German modal verbs, but through the semanticization of a formerly pragmatic inference.

In conclusion, and for the sake of thoroughness, another auxiliary verb should be mentioned. Seen under the aspect of epistemization, the German auxiliary verb *werden* has much in common with the modal verbs above. *Werden* can have future and epistemic readings, as illustrated in the sentences below:

(7) Fritz: *Was hast du morgen vor?* Paul: *Ich werde das Auto reparieren.*

(7′) Fritz: *Weißt du, wo Erwin ist?* Paul: *Er wird zu Hause sein.*

In (7), *werden* (along with the infinitive) serves to say of a state of affairs that it will occur in the future. In (7′), *werden* is used to say of a state of affairs that its current existence is presumed. What do the future tense and presumption have in common? The fact that the speaker, at the time of the utterance, does not know the truth value of the proposition in question. The future-tense sentence, like the presumption, can only be confirmed in the future.[13] In the first case, the event is to be confirmed; in the second, the belief or conviction. The Duden grammar comments on the meaning of *werden* in uses such as (7′) as follows: "[The speaker] allows himself to be led by the expectation that his assertion will be confirmed as true" (*Duden Grammatik* 1984: §232).[14] Thus we may observe that here, too, a linguistic means is transferred from the external world to the inner one. Linguistic means that serve to say of an event that it will be confirmed in the future are now used to say of an assumption that it will be confirmed in the future. The following paraphrases make clear the metaphorical connection between the factual and the epistemic readings of *werden*:

(8) *Ich werde das Auto reparieren.*   *The fact of my repairing the car will be confirmed in the future.*

---

[13] See Fourquet 1970: 160 and Ulvestad 1984: 276. As Ulvestad has demonstrated (74 ff.), Brugmann had noted this as early as 1918.   [14] Trans. K.D.

(8′) *Er wird zu Hause sein.*   *My assumption that he is home will be confirmed in the future.*

Using German modal verbs as an example, I have attempted to show that the metaphorical technique, one of the basic techniques of sign formation, is also employed in areas of language where this was not previously recognized. The metaphorical technique is part of our creative programming. This can be proved with countless other examples. The English conjunction *before*, for example, can be metaphorically transferred from the expression of temporal sequence to the expression of preference:[15]

(9) *I'll wash my hands before I sit down at the table.* (temporal sequence)

(10) *I'll enter the convent before I marry George.* (preference)

In German, the conjunction *aber* has become, through the use of the metaphorical technique, an expression not only of opposition but one of surprise:[16]

(11) *Er is stark, aber feige* 'He's strong, but cowardly.' (opposition)

(12) *Der ist aber stark!* 'Is he ever strong!' (surprise)

The use of German's subjunctive II has become, rather than an indicator of the non-factual, an indicator of the unexpected:

(13) *Hätte ich Geld, so würde ich nach Indien reisen.* ('If I had money, I would take a trip to India'. The fact is that I have no money.)

(14) *Jetzt hätten wir das Haus gefunden.* ('We'll have found the house.' We had expected that we would not be able to find it.)

In the next chapter, I would like to illustrate the processes of metaphorization and the accompanying epistemization with the example of the German conjunction *weil*, and attempt an explanation of the process of meaning change currently under way in regard to this word.

[15] Cf. König and Traugott 1988.
[16] "*Aber* ... indicates that a statement is based on perceptual evidence, but is in contrast to possible inferences from the context" (König and Requardt 1991: 74).

17

The Epistemic *Weil*

"Save the Causal Clause" is the name of an action group in Hamburg, Germany, whose members have taken upon themselves to prevent adult speakers of German from uttering sentences like this: "Ich muß noch einkaufen, weil wir bekommen heute abend Besuch" ('I still have to go shopping, because we're having guests tonight').[1] The background of the problem is as follows. In German main clauses or coordinate clauses, the finite verb is always in second position: *Er hat ein Auto* 'He has a car'. However, in subordinate clauses, the finite verb comes last: *Ich weiß, daß er ein Auto hat* 'I know that he a car has'. In colloquial German, *weil* 'because' is undergoing a process of change from a subordinating to a coordinating conjunction. "Normal" speakers notice only the resulting "incorrect" word order, often interpreted as evidence for the decay of the German language. The change of the conjunction *weil* will be the subject of this chapter. I will try to show that it has less to do with syntax decay than with semantic enrichment. This enrichment is created with the application of the metaphorical technique to the causal conjunction *weil*.

Henning Venske, an author of children's books, has written a story for beginning schoolchildren: "Schultüte für Berni." In the story, the narrator—"I'm five, and I'm big, and my name is Berni"—utters sentences like these:

"[Mein großer Bruder] der macht nächstes Jahr Abitur, weil, der ist schon alt."
'[My big brother], next year he's doing his exams, 'cause he's already old.'

---

[1] In reply to this undertaking, Peter Eisenberg has written a gloss (1993) with the title "Der Kausalsatz ist nicht zu retten" ("The causal clause can't be saved").

"Aber das is gar nicht wahr, weil, ich kann schon alleine über den Zebrastreifen gehen bei Grün, ganz ohne gelbe Mütze."
'But that's not true at all, 'cause I can walk over the pedestrian crossing all by myself when the light is green, even without a yellow cap.'

"Und da war Mama noch viel mehr beleidigt, weil, sie kann gar nichts dafür, aber Max ist schuld, weil, der kommt immer, wenn man ihn gar nicht gebrauchen kann."
'And then Mama was even more insulted, 'cause she can't do anything about it, but it's Max's fault, 'cause he always comes along when you have no use for him.'

"Und da hat die Mama den Kopf zu mir gedreht und gesagt, so was darf man nicht sagen, weil, der Papa ist dann nicht tot, sondern nur Rentner."
'And then Mama looked at me and said, don't you say that kind of thing, 'cause Papa won't be dead then, just retired.' (Venske 1993)

The author tries to emulate the somewhat worldly tone of a five-year-old, and one of his ways of doing so is the use of *weil* without subject–verb inversion. In fact, in spoken language, it is not only children who currently prefer this usage.[2] Anyone who learns contemporary spoken German learns *weil* with main-clause word order. Is this an incorrect usage? No; rather, it is a systematic form of usage that is not tolerated in standard language. But toleration of it is only a matter of time, because the systematic "mistakes" of today are the imminent changes of tomorrow. Right now, this use of *weil*, with the verb in second position, is ignored by most grammar books and criticized by most speakers (see Wegener 1993: 291). All the famous personalities "caught in the act" by the "Save the Causal Clause" action group solemnly pledged to change their errant ways (Eisenberg 1993: 10). An indignant student told me that she would never utter such a sentence, and immediately added her reason, apparently unwittingly formulated with the verb in second position, that is, "incorrectly": "weil das find' ich fürchterlich" ('because I think it's just awful').

The systematicity of this paratactic use of *weil* can be found in other, complementary places, so to speak. A glance in the notebooks of lower-grade pupils shows that currently a certain mistake occurs frequently which could not have occurred so systematically twenty years ago.

---

[2] Wegener proves that this use of *weil* is widespread in all social classes and all German-speaking regions.

Mistakes, as we all know, are the windows to children's souls (Wiese 1987). For linguists, they are windows to their language competence; and they also allow a glimpse into the historical–linguistic future. The following sentences were found in fifth-grade essays:[3] "Sie möchte aber auch immer nett und beliebt bei anderen sein, weil sie sich vorgenommen hat, bei Familie Gast alles schön zu finden." "Sie hat auch Mut, weil ich mich das nicht getraut hätte." "Außerdem ist sie dankbar, weil sie sich bei Anton dafür bedankt, daß . . ."

Where are the mistakes here? At first glance, the answer is simple: *weil* should be replaced with *denn*, after which the inflected verb (indicated below with boldface type) normally comes in second position. That is, (1') or (2'), for example, should replace (1) or (2).

(1) *Sie hat auch Mut, WEIL ich mich das nicht getraut*
    She has also pluck, because I [myself] that not dared
    hätte.
    would have.
    'She's plucky, too, because I wouldn't have dared to do that.'

(1') *Sie hat auch Mut, DENN ich hätte mich das*
    She has also pluck, because I **would have** [myself] that
    nicht getraut.
    not dared.
    'She's plucky, too, because I wouldn't have dared to do that.'

(2) *Außerdem ist sie dankbar, WEIL sie sich bei Anton*
    Besides is she grateful because she [herself] with Anton
    dafür bedankt, daß . . .
    for thanked, that . . .
    'And she's grateful besides, because she thanked Anton for . . .'

(2') *Außerdem ist sie dankbar, DENN sie bedankt sich bei*
    Besides is she grateful, because she **thanks** [herself] with
    Anton dafür, daß . . .
    Anton for, that . . .
    'And she's grateful besides, because she thanked Anton for . . .'

---

[3] Some of these sentences have been abbreviated, and freed of mistakes that are irrelevant here.

But the error of children who make such mistakes is probably a different one. According to the practiced competence of these children, if they wrote the way they speak, they would choose (1″) or (2″):

(1″) *Sie hat auch Mut, WEIL ich hätte   mich   das*
  She has also pluck, because I **would have** [myself] that
  nicht getraut.
  not dared.
    'She's plucky, too, because I wouldn't have dared to do
    that.'

(2″) *Außerdem ist sie dankbar, WEIL sie bedankt sich   bei*
  Besides   is she grateful, because she **thanks** [herself] with
  Anton dafür, daß . . .
  Anton for,   that . . .
    'And she's grateful besides, because she thanked Anton
    for . . .'

In spoken language, these schoolchildren would have used *weil* with main-clause word order. And with this, we're back to Berni. Schoolchildren are probably corrected when they put the verb in second position after *weil*: "Not *Er ist nach Hause gegangen, weil er hatte Kopfweh*, but *Er ist nach Hause gegangen, weil er Kopfweh hatte*." If they mechanically follow these directions, they will come up with sentences like the ones above. Could it be that the correction is inappropriate? Yes—*weil* it is too across-the-board. It does not take into consideration that two uses of *weil* have established themselves, uses which have much in common with those of the modal verbs examined in the previous chapter. There is an epistemic *weil* that is used as a substitute for the conjunction *denn* in colloquial spoken German, after which, as with *denn*, the verb comes in second position. And there is the good, old factual *weil* that requires that the verb come last.[4] Not only do these two variations of *weil* follow different syntactic rules; they also have different meanings. The mistake made by the young authors of the above sentences (1) and (2) is that they have used the epistemic *weil*, which the logic of the sentences requires, with the word order appropriate to the factual *weil*.

The thesis which I will now argue is that, in current German usage,

---

[4] The action group mentioned above therefore cannot really want to save "the causal clause," for the causal clause is not in danger. What its members actually want to do, as will shortly become clear, is to prevent the rise of the epistemic explanative clause.

there exists a factual *weil* and an epistemic *weil*. The factual *weil* clause usually answers the question "Why is that?", while the epistemic *weil* clause usually answers the question "How do you know that?"[5] Thanks to the use of the metaphorical technique, the epistemic *weil* grew from the factual *weil*, and is in the process of becoming lexicalized.

Consider the following two sentences:

(1) *Peter ist nach Hause gegangen, weil   er Kopfweh* **hatte**.
    Peter is to   home gone   because he headache had.
    Peter went home because he had a headache.'

(2) *Peter ist nach Hause gegangen, weil   er* **hatte** *Kopfweh*.
    Peter is to   home gone   because he had   headache.
    Peter went home, because he had a headache.'

The naive reader might think that the sentences (1) and (2) are synonymous, and that they differ only stylistically or in the degree of their colloquiality. Their English counterparts differ only in punctuation and/ or intonation. But there's more to it than that,[6] and this can easily be demonstrated with an analysis of the presuppositions.[7] First, though, let me explain what this involves.

Most assertions are made on the basis of unspoken assumptions, which the speaker presumes he and the hearer unquestioningly share. These assumptions are called presuppositions. An assertion can be judged to be true or false only if its presuppositions are considered to have been fulfilled.[8] Presuppositions are unquestioningly respected, unspoken assumptions. When I make the assertion "My two children are well," for example, I normally assume that my exchange partner shares with me the knowledge that I have two children. If I do not have two children, the assertion that my two children are well is neither true nor false—due to a lack of quantity, so to speak. When I assert "My two children are

---

[5] In recent years, the epistemic use of *weil* has become a popular object of linguistic reflection. See Eroms 1980, Gaumann 1983, Küper 1984 and 1991, Günthner 1993, Eisenberg 1993, Wegener 1993, Keller 1993 and 1995, Feilke 1996, and Willems 1994. For English, cf. Sweetser 1990 and Schleppegrell 1991.

[6] Gaumann (1983: 126ff.) believes them to be "semantically equivalent."

[7] Sweetser (1990: 83ff.) also considers the aspect of presupposition, as opposed to assertion, in factual and epistemic conjunctions in English usage.

[8] This goes, mutatis mutandis, for other illocutionary acts as well. For the sake of brevity, I will deal here only with acts of assertion.

well," I have not *asserted* that I have two children, I have *presupposed*[9] it. The presuppositions of a sentence can be determined by means of a negation test. Namely, the sentence's presuppositions are not negated by the negation of the sentence. Whatever is negated therefore cannot be presupposed, but must be asserted. Both the above assertion "My two children are well" and its negation "My two children are not well" presuppose that I have two children.[10] Let's apply this test to sentences (1) and (2), respectively, to determine what is asserted in each case and what is presupposed.

(1) *Peter ist nach Hause gegangen, weil er Kopfweh hatte.*
'Peter went home because he had a headache.'

(1′) *Peter ist nicht nach Hause gegangen, weil er Kopfweh hatte.*
'Peter didn't go home because he had a headache.'

What is asserted in (1′), and what is presupposed? The difficulties of quickly ascertaining this are due to the fact that (1′) is ambiguous. This ambiguity becomes more evident when we choose a formulation of the negation in which the negator comes first:

(1″) *Es ist nicht der Fall, daß Peter nach Hause gegangen ist, weil er Kopfweh hatte.*
'It's not the case that Peter went home because he had a headache.'

The two readings of (1′) or of (1″) are:

(i) 'Peter went home, and he had a headache, but his headache was not the reason that he went home.'

(ii) 'Peter did not go home, and he had a headache, and his headache is the reason that he did not go home.'

According to reading (i), only the *weil* relation is negated: 'Peter's headache was not the reason that he went home'. According to reading (ii), only the first clause is negated: 'Peter's headache was his reason not to go home'. If we assume that (i) is really the reading that represents a complete negation of sentence (1), we may conclude that anyone who asserts sentence (1) presupposes both that Peter went home and that he

---

[9] Of course, presuppositions can be communicatively exploited to convey something implicitly to the addressee.

[10] On the theory of presupposition, see Keller 1974.

had a headache. Only the causal *weil* relation is asserted. Now let's take a look at the unorthodox alternative, with the verb in second position, as well as its negation:

(2) *Peter ist nach Hause gegangen, weil er hatte Kopfweh.*
     'Peter went home, because he had a headache.'

(2′) *Peter ist nicht nach Hause gegangen, weil er hatte Kopfweh.*
      'Peter did not go home, because he had a headache.'

(2″) *Es ist nicht der Fall, daß Peter nach Hause gegangen ist, weil er hatte Kopfweh.*
      'It is not the case that Peter went home, because he had a headache.'

First of all, it is interesting that (2′) and (2″) each have only one reading. For neither (2′) nor (2″) is the reading possible that a headache was *not* the reason that Peter went home. Only the clause preceding the *weil* clause is negated. This might lead to the assumption that the proposition that Peter had a headache is presupposed, including the *weil* relation. But it is easy to show that this cannot be the case. This is because the negator's range does not include the final clause. Sentence (1′) has the form:

(1′) ¬ [*er ist nach Hause gegangen, weil er Kopfweh hatte*],

while (2′) has the form

(2′) ¬ [*er ist nach Hause gegangen*], *weil er hatte Kopfweh.*

The difference in scope also becomes clear if we put the sentence through an operation other than negation:[11]

(3) *Ich vermute, daß Peter nach Hause gegangen ist, weil er Kopfweh hatte.*
     'I assume that Peter went home because he had a headache.'

(4) *Ich vermute, daß Peter nach Hause gegangen ist, weil er hatte Kopfweh.*
     'I assume that Peter went home, because he had a headache.'

In (3), the whole sentence is the object of the assumption, but in (4), only the first clause is. The proposition expressed in the final clause is not a part of the assumption, but gives the reason for the assumption. In (3),

---

[11] Cf. Wegener 1993: 294.

the argument is assumed; in (4) the assumption is justified. If, in sentence (2'), the final clause is beyond the negator's range, the final clause cannot be presupposed.

We may therefore keep in mind the following result of our presupposition analysis: sentences (1) and (2) are not logically equivalent. In (1), the proposition that Peter had a headache is presupposed, and in (2) it is asserted. If two sentences are not logically equivalent, they are also not synonymous, that is, their meanings are not identical. No matter how meaning-identity is defined, the very least of its requirements is usually logical equivalence.

The different presupposition relations are part of the differing meanings of (1) and (2): anyone who wants to assert that they had a headache, and who does not assume that the hearer already knows this, should choose sentence (2) rather than (1). To put it differently, if my exchange partner, after an exchange concerning Peter's headache, were to ask "Where is he now, anyway?", I could not answer with sentence (2), "Der ist nach Hause gegangen, weil er hatte Kopfweh" ('He went home, because he had a headache'). But this is only one of the variations in meaning of the two kinds of *weil*. Another is the epistemic quality of the argument relations in *weil*-sentences with the verb in second position. This can be most easily illustrated with sentences in which its opposite, the version of *weil* with the verb in final position, does not allow a plausible interpretation. Compare sentences (5) and (6):

(5) *Fritz ist nach Hause gegangen, weil ich seinen Mantel nicht mehr an der Garderobe **sehe**.*
'Fritz went home because I don't see his coat in the cloakroom anymore.'

(6) *Fritz ist nach Hause gegangen, weil ich **sehe** seinen Mantel nicht mehr an der Garderobe.*
'Fritz went home, because I don't see his coat in the cloakroom anymore.'

Note that both sentences are semantically correct. However, rather strange circumstances are needed for sentence (5) to be uttered and make any sense.[12] A fitting scenario would be, for example, a party attended

---

[12] A sentence like (6) is not absurd, as Heide Wegener seems to believe, but simply a rarity.

by Fritz, John and Mary. Fritz and John are in the cloakroom, and John is so drunk he can't see Fritz's coat. Fritz says to John, "If you're so drunk that you can't even see my coat hanging in the cloakroom, I'm going to leave right now." (Fritz leaves.) A few minutes later, Mary asks John, "Where's that Fritz got to?" John answers (babbling), with sentence (5), "He went home because I don't see his coat in the cloakroom anymore" ('Er ist nach Hause gegangen, weil ich seinen Mantel nicht mehr an der Garderobe sehe'). This is, of course, the orthodox use of *weil*. It is considerably easier to come up with scenarios for the use of sentence (6), the unorthodox version. A paraphrase of John's drunken response (5) reads thus:

(5′) 'The fact that I don't see Fritz's coat hanging in the cloakroom was his reason for going home.'

The paraphrase of John's response (6) is:

(6′) 'From the fact that I don't see Fritz's coat hanging in the cloakroom, I conclude that he went home.'

The final *weil*-clause in (5) names Fritz's reason for going home, but the final *weil*-clause in (6) names the *speaker's*, that is John's, reason for the assumption that Fritz went home. Sentence (5) contains a factual argument, (6) an epistemic one. The factual argument answers the question "Why is that the case?" The epistemic argument answers the question "What makes you think so?"

Let us return to the kinds of *weil*-clause in which both variations are possible, and test whether this thesis can be generalized. Compare:

(7) *Peter wird nach Hause gegangen sein, weil er Kopfweh **hatte**.*
    'Peter will have gone home because he had a headache.'

(8) *Peter wird nach Hause gegangen sein, weil er **hatte** Kopfweh.*
    'Peter will have gone home, because he had a headache.'

Here, too, the different logical structures of both complete sentences, as well as the different meaning contribution of the *weil*-clauses, is very clear. In (7), the presumption concerns the whole sentence, while in (8), it concerns only the first clause. The subordinate *weil*-clause in (7) names the presumed reason for Peter's having gone home, or the reason for his presumably having gone home. The final clause in (8), in contrast, names the reason for the presumption. Therefore, it is also true that the factual *weil* names a reason or a cause for a state of affairs, while the epistemic *weil* names the reason for an epistemic state. Now we will re-examine the pair of sentences with which we started our analysis:

(1) *Peter ist nach Hause gegangen, weil er Kopfweh **hatte**.*
'Peter went home because he had a headache.'

(2) *Peter ist nach Hause gegangen, weil er **hatte** Kopfweh.*
'Peter went home, because he had a headache.'

It may seem that, in this simple example, there is nothing that indicates that we are dealing with anything but a stylistic variation. However, one such indication to the contrary is the fact that the adverbs *deshalb* and *deswegen* ('therefore') may be added to (1), but not to (2). The sentence **Er ist deshalb nach Hause gegangen, weil er hatte Kopfweh* is ungrammatical because *deshalb* correlates exclusively with a factual argument, and not with an epistemic one.[13] Here again, the final clause of (1) names the factual reason for Peter's going home, while the speaker of (2) names with the final clause his argument for the occurrence described in the first clause. The final clause of (2) has epistemic weight. In the final clause (1), the speaker is talking about Peter's headache, and in (2), about her *knowledge* of the headache. Basically, the speaker says "Peter has gone home. I know why and I'll tell you why: he had a headache." Anyone who utters (1) describes a state of affairs; anyone who utters (2) supplies a reason. But reasons cannot be conveyed by way of presuppositions. They must be explicitly asserted. If the first clause is supposed to contain the thesis, and the final clause the reasons for the thesis, the first clause and the final clause must be situated on the same logical level. That is, the final clause may not be embedded in the main clause, nor may the proposition that it expresses be presupposed. Like the first clause, the final clause must have main-clause structure. In other words, putting the verb in second position after the epistemic *weil* is not colloquial sloppiness in the service of reducing processing effort,[14] but the linguistically logical and proper consequence of the change of meaning.

Since the epistemic *weil* serves not as a factual argument for a state of affairs, but as an argument for an epistemic state, its use is consequently not restricted to assertive sentences. Just as people can argue their reasons for knowing something, they can argue their reasons for wanting to

---

[13] Cf. Wegener 1993: 293; Günthner 1993: 52 ff.
[14] Cf. Gaumann 1983: 135, 140.

know something, wanting to have done something, wanting to keep someone from doing something, and so on. In other words, the epistemic *weil*, but not the factual one, is also usable in connection with speech acts other than assertive ones, as the following examples demonstrate.

Question: *Hast du noch was zu trinken? Weil ich **hab** riesigen Durst.*
                     'Do you still have something to drink? Because I'm really thirsty.'

Imperative: *Mach die Tür zu! Weil wir **haben** hier geheizt.*
                     'Close the door! Because we have the heater on.'

Warning: *Beiß da lieber nicht hinein! Weil das **ist** unheimlich scharf.*
                     'Better not bite into that! Because it's really hot.'

Threat: *Sieh bloß zu, daß das beim nächsten Mal klappt. Weil ich **kann** das nicht mehr mit ansehen.*
                     'Just make sure it works the next time. Because I can't watch that happen again.'

Promise: *Bis morgen haben Sie Ihr Geld. Weil ich **will** endlich wieder in Ruhe schlafen können.*
                     'You'll have your money by tomorrow. Because I want to be able to finally sleep in peace again.'

A further consequence of the change of meaning of *weil* is its applicability in so-called replicative inferences, which naturally—by definition—stand in diametrical opposition to causal arguments. In such cases, the factual *weil* would stand the logic on its head. The epistemic *weil* in these two sentences avoids this problem:

(1) *Es hat heute Nacht gestürmt, weil die Bäume sind umgeknickt.*
     'There was a storm last night, because the trees are bent over.'

(2) *Er ist ins Wasser gefallen, weil er ist völlig durchnäßt.*
     'He fell in the water, because he's totally wet.'

Let us go back to our point of departure, the matter of the action group "Save the Causal Clause." Our argumentation has confirmed that the causal clause is not in need of being saved. It is not in any danger whatsoever. For anyone who wants to deliver a causal argument, German offers a multitude of possibilities. One of them is the conjunction *weil* with subordinate-clause word order. Such word order is also not endangered. "German has approximately forty subordinate conjunctions, but only in the cases of two of them, namely, *weil* and *obwohl*, is there a tendency to main-clause word order. With all the others, it is impossible" (Eisenberg 1993: 10).[15] Those who claim they want to save something old evidently want (presumably without being fully aware of it) to put a stop to something new. They want to prevent German speakers from applying their semiotic knowledge of the metaphorical technique to causal conjunctions, which makes them appropriate for the expression of epistemic arguments. "*Weil*-clauses with the verb in second position are concerned not with a form of a certain capacity, but ultimately with a communicative intent. Are there really people who want to tell others not only how they should talk, but even what they should say?" (Eisenberg 1993: 11).[16]

In conclusion, I would like to pose the question of a possible explanation. Explaining a phenomenon of language change means showing that the change—generally neither intended nor noticed—is a consequence of the choices of action made by the individuals in a language community. The choice of the individual speaker is normally not directed towards the change or the conservation of the language, but towards the success of individual communicative endeavors. If choices are similarly directed, because of similar preferences on the parts of individual speakers, cumulative effects emerge which we perceive, *post festum*, as language change. I have presented this thesis in detail elsewhere (Keller 1994), and so will confine myself to these brief remarks. For our purposes, only one thing is important: if we assume that people tend to act rationally in the sense that they choose, from the means available to them, the one that they think promises the highest degree of success, we may say: a choice of action is explained when it can be shown that it is a rational choice. A phenomenon of language change is explained when it can be shown that it is the macrostructural consequence (that is, the consequence on the level of language) of individuals' rational choices of action.

What exactly is the aspect of epistemization that requires explanation? There are two questions. When German speakers want to make an epistemic argument, the conjunction *denn* ('because, since') is an option. Thus

---

[15] Trans. K.D.   [16] Trans. K.D.

the first question to be answered is as follows: why do German speakers, at least in spoken language, choose *weil* over *denn*? The second problem: contemporary speakers have a strong tendency to opt for an epistemic argument even in cases where a factual one would also be possible.[17] The question is therefore: what do speakers see as the advantage of the epistemic argument, as opposed to the factual one?

We'll begin with the first question. What justifies the choice of *weil* over *denn*? Susanne Günthner points out that in her entire collection of data of spoken material, *denn* as a conjunction[18] occurs only once, spoken by a radio host. "*Denn* as a conjunction seems to be unpopular in spontaneous everyday language, and to function more as a mark of 'official' language use" (Günthner 1993: 54).[19] Helmut Feilke has identified a plausible reason for this unpopularity (which the conjunction *da* also suffers). Because only *weil* can be dialogically used, *weil* is becoming a "prototypical causal conjunction" (Feilke 1996: 48):[20]

Fritz: *Warum kommst du nicht mit?*
        'Why don't you come along?'
John: *Weil ich müde bin. *Da ich müde bin. *Denn ich bin müde.*
        'Because I'm tired. *As/since I'm tired. *Since I'm tired.'

Of these three conjunctions, children learn *weil* first and "at the beginning, it has every function" (Feilke 1996: 48). In spoken, dialogically oriented language, *weil* is the causal conjunction par excellence. The use of *da* and *denn* requires that the propositions to be argued be named by the speaker him- or herself. This does, in fact, seem to me to be a plausible reason for speakers' judgment of *da* and *denn* as belonging more to the written language; even as adults, by which time *da* and *denn* have become a part of their repertoire, they avoid them in spoken communication for reasons having to do with the adequate choice of register. Since a sentence cannot start with *denn*, not even in elliptical speech, the use of *denn* is completely out of the question for the justification of epistemic views in non-assertive speech acts.

(11)   *Hast du was zu trinken? Denn ich hab unheimlichen Durst.*
      *'Do you have something to drink? Since I'm really thirsty.'

---

[17] Cf. Feilke 1996: 46.
[18] *Denn* is often used in German colloquial speech as a modal particle, or as a means of emphasis.   [19] Trans. K.D.   [20] Trans. K.D.

Additionally, there are two further arguments which show that the use of *weil*, as opposed to *da* and *denn*, lowers the costs of processing effort.

THE REPLACEMENT-FUNCTION ARGUMENT

Weil is capable of fulfilling the functions of both *da* and *denn*. This is illustrated by sentences in which both conjunctions occur.

(12) *Carol ist nach Hause gegangen, DA die Geschäfte gleich zu-machen, DENN sie bekommt heute abend Besuch.*
   'Carol went home, as/since the shops are closing soon, since she's having guests tonight.'

(13) *Carol ist nach Hause gegangen, WEIL die Geschäfte gleich zu-machen, WEIL sie bekommt heute abend Besuch.*
   'Carol went home because the shops are closing soon, because she's having guests tonight.'

THE REDUNDANCY ARGUMENT

In the case of *weil*, factuality and epistemology are sufficiently marked by the differing word order.[21] If *denn* is used instead of *weil*, word-order marking is joined by lexeme marking. Epistemic quality is thus twice marked when *denn* is used. The epistemic use of *weil* is therefore less costly than the use of *denn*. Now let us consider the second question. Why do speakers choose the epistemic argument over the factual one even when the latter is just as possible and as appropriate? To this question, there is a whole array of answers which speak for the increased communicative benefits accompanying the choice of the epistemic argument over the factual one.

THE PRESUPPOSITION ARGUMENT

When the speaker wants to convey the justifying circumstances to the

---

[21] The redundancy argument is presented by Heide Wegener (1993: 303).

addressee, a sentence in which the circumstances are asserted is better than one in which they are presupposed.

THE EXPANDED EXPRESSIVE POSSIBILITIES

The epistemic *weil*, in contrast to the factual one, allows the topicalization of an object and the infinite part of the predicate, as well as the shift of the subject to the left and its repetition in an anaphoric clause.[22] The construction with the epistemic *weil* thus gives the speaker more possibilities for emphasis. The sentences marked with asterisks, that is, those with the factual *weil* and the verb in final position, would be identified by any speaker of German as ungrammatical:

(13) *Und was gibt's außer* Casablanca*? Weil DEN **hab** ich schon gesehen./ *Weil DEN ich schon gesehen **hab**.*
    'And what's playing besides *Casablanca*? Because THAT I've already seen.'

(14) *Ich nehm nur was zu trinken, weil GEGESSEN **hab** ich schon./ *Ich nehm nur was zu trinken, weil gegessen ich schon **habe**.*
    'I'll just have something to drink, because I've EATEN already.'

(15) *Da gehen wir nicht hin, weil MEINE SCHWESTER, die **mag** keinen Fisch./*Da gehen wir nicht hin, weil meine Schwester, die keinen Fisch **mag**.*
    'We're not going, because MY SISTER, she doesn't like fish.'

EPISTEMIC WEIGHT

The epistemic *weil* is a part of modern German speakers' show-off repertoire. An epistemic argument makes a more "imposing" intellectual impression, even when the argument is actually trivial, as the following sentences confirm.

---

[22] The expanded expressive argument and sample sentence (13) are from Heide Wegener (1993: 302).

(16) *Er hat die Wahl gewonnen, weil er **konnte** die Mehrheit der Stimmen auf sich vereinen.*

> 'He won the election, because he was able to collect the most votes.'

(17) *Er hat die Wahl gewonnen, weil er die Mehrheit der Stimmen auf sich vereinen **konnte**.*

> 'He won the election because he was able to collect the most votes.'

THE INCONTESTABILITY ARGUMENT

Epistemic arguments are harder to attack than factual ones. To say how I came upon an idea is less binding than to say why something is the case:

(17) *Peter ist nach Hause gegangen, weil er Kopfweh **hatte**.—Nein, nicht weil er Kopfweh hatte, sondern weil er keine Lust mehr **hatte**.*

> 'Peter went home because he had a headache.—No, not because he had a headache, but because he lost the desire to stay.'

(17′) *Peter ist nach Hause gegangen, weil er **hatte** Kopfweh.—Nein, nicht weil er Kopfweh hatte, sondern weil er **hatte** keine Lust mehr.*

> 'Peter went home, because he had a headache.—No, not because he had a headache, but because he lost the desire to stay.'

(17″) *Peter ist nach Hause gegangen, weil ich **sehe** seinen Mantel nicht mehr an der Garderobe.—Nein, nicht weil du **siehst** seinen Mantel nicht mehr an der Garderobe, sondern weil sein Auto **steht** nicht mehr im Hof.*

> 'Peter went home, because I don't see his coat in the cloakroom anymore.— No, not because you don't see his coat in the cloakroom anymore, but because his car's not in the parking lot anymore.'

THE ARGUMENT OF COMPLEXITY

In complex sentences, putting the verb in second position is easier than putting it at the end. Cognitive costs are thus lowered. See sentence (18), with the epistemic *weil*:

(18)   *Ich muß jetzt gehen, weil, wenn ich noch hier bleibe, **kriege** ich den Bus nicht mehr.*

(18′)   *Ich muß jetzt gehen, weil ich, wenn ich noch hier bleibe, den Bus nicht mehr **kriege**.*

It is plain to see that the balance of the seven arguments above is extremely positive. The use of the epistemic *weil* lowers cognitive costs and raises communicative benefits. If it is possible to increase benefits and simultaneously lower costs, that is what one should do. Every other choice would be irrational. Currently, the costs of violating written-language norms is evidently so highly rated that negative net benefits are expected with the written use of the epistemic *weil*. But this will change, because worse alternatives, which are in use only because "That's the way it's always been," don't last long.

SUMMARY

Humans are interpretive creatures. Like most other animals, they are capable of making inferences from perceptions, and of using those inferences to influence the natural course of things to their own advantage. But this alone does not set humans apart from animals. What distinguishes humans is their ability to exploit the interpretive ability of others for the purpose of influencing their feelings, thoughts or behavior. Animals use their perceptual ability to interpret; humans further use their interpretive ability to communicate. Humans go yet a step further, using their communicative ability for the creation of cognitive worlds.[1] Thus we are dealing with a hierarchy of abilities, in which the one below is used to reach the one above. Perceptual ability is used for interpretation, interpretive ability is used for communication, and communicative ability is used for the creation of cognitive worlds. Communication is doing something with the intention of bringing others to make interpretive inferences, inferences which allow their recognition of how one intends to influence them. The ability to communicate is an exploitative use of the ability to interpret. In the course of the exploitative use of the interpretive abilities of others, signs emerge. These are the assumptions upon which the theory of linguistic signs presented in the previous pages rests.

These fundamental assumptions suggest a certain terminological use of the word *meaning*. There are essentially two choices: one may call a sign's meaning that which the sign represents (whatever it may be), or that which enables its interpretation. If the aspect of reference is to be emphasized, the first option should be chosen. This view is introduced and explained by means of Frege's and Aristotle's theories, and termed the representational notion of signs. I have opted for the second choice, the goal of which is to derive the emergence and functioning of signs

---

[1] This thought is Petra Radtke's.

from their functions. This is called the instrumental notion of signs, introduced and explained with the thought of Plato and Wittgenstein. The question of how signs function is very different from that of what they stand for. We think in concepts, concepts that we form and learn through the rules of use of words. The types of conceptual categories correspond to the types of rules of use of linguistic signs. As above, the primary function of signs is to be interpreted. All types of sign have this characteristic in common.

We are capable of making exactly three types of interpretive inference: causal, associative and rule-based inferences. Following a common terminology, their modes of employment are here called the symptomic, the iconic and the symbolic techniques. The three types of sign—symptoms, icons and symbols—are defined by the technique that is chosen for their interpretation. When we classify signs according to interpretive technique, we are able to describe and explain how signs of a certain type become signs of another type. It is completely possible—and common—that a sign functions for one speaker as an icon, and for the other as a symbol. In this way, and over the course of time, one interpretive technique may be replaced by another within a language community. Consequently, symptoms may become icons; symptoms and icons may become symbols. Such a change in sign type is here called sign metamorphosis. Sign metamorphosis is generally the unintended result of the communicative use of signs. The great majority of signs are therefore invisible-hand phenomena.

The three basic interpretive techniques can be newly applied on the level of symbols. When symptoms are symbolized, metonymies arise; the symbolization of icons results in metaphor. Metonymies are thus metasymptoms; metaphors are metaicons. The mechanism of sign metamorphosis, by means of which symptoms and icons may become symbols, also occurs on the level of metasymptoms and metaicons. This is precisely the process called lexicalization. In lexicalization, nonliteral sense becomes rule-based, and literal, that is, iconic and symptomic interpretive techniques are succeeded by rule-based techniques.

The point of all these observations is the following: there are precisely three techniques for using perceptual data as signs, or for putting them to use as signs. These three techniques are employed on different levels and in different combinations for the purpose of realizing communicative goals. Every conceivable process of sign formation and sign interpretation can be described on the basis of these three techniques. If we view signs as techniques that serve to bring the addressee to certain inferences, we are able to explain processes such as metaphorization and lexicalization, or the phenomena of imag(e)inative richness and semantic bleaching, in a nonmetaphorical way.

Whoever wants to understand the behavior of another person must assume that person's rationality. Whoever wants to understand *what* others do, and *why*, must assume that the others believe, within the framework of the given circumstances and possibilities, that their behavior is optimally suited for the realization of their goals. Rational action is the choice of optimal means under subjectively given conditions. To interpret an action is thus the attempt to understand it in its rationality. That is, it is searching for answers to the questions "What is he/she doing?" and "What does he/she hope to achieve with this action?" This applies to every kind of action, and thus also to communicative actions. In regard to communicative actions, the questions are "What did he/she say?" and "What did he/she mean?" The addressee uses the answer to the first question, from the means employed by the speaker, to infer the speaker's goals. The addressee interprets the utterance as a symptom of that which is meant. Grice, with his theory of conversational implicatures, presents a respected theory whose goal is to explicate the logic of inferring the meant from the said in those cases where the speaker means what is said nonliterally. I try to integrate Grice's theory into my own, as presented here, thereby attempting to eliminate Gricean theory's oft-noted weaknesses. My suggestion is to replace the Gricean cooperative principle with the principle of rationality, and to interpret the conversational maxims as a theory of symptomatics. In this way, four things can be illustrated: (a) that every interpretation of what a speaker means with an utterance is of implicative nature—in the cases of the literally meant as well as in those of the nonliterally meant; (b) that the maxims are inherently related to the principle of rationality; (c) that the decision of the speaker to choose the nonliteral path belongs to theory's explanatory realm; and (d) that communication is a special case of rational behavior.

The techniques of sign formation and the processes of sign metamorphosis have a historical dimension. I have demonstrated this with the use of a number of examples. The analyses of historical linguistics can be undertaken from various perspectives. First, they may serve for the reconstruction of past states. This is the classic historical perspective, as

Summary

it were, the view from the present into the past. But this view can also serve the understanding of the present itself. With the reconstruction of past states, we can try to understand the principles of the genesis of the current states, in a sort of forward-looking historical perspective. For the understanding of an invisible-hand phenomenon—as I have noted elsewhere[2]—the understanding of the process of its genesis is necessary. Invisible-hand phenomena are the unintended, cumulative effects of human behavior. Natural languages and linguistic signs are essentially phenomena of this kind. In order to understand their current state, we must understand the principles and aspects of communicative behavior that create them. In this sense, historical linguistics is systematic linguistics.

[2] Keller 1994: 13 ff.

BIBLIOGRAPHY

ADELUNG, JOHANN CH. 1971. *Umständliches Lehrgebäude der deutschen Sprache*. 2 vols. Hildesheim: Georg Olms. (Reprographic copy of the 1782 Leipzig edn.)

ALSTON, WILLIAM P. 1964. *Philosophy of Language*. Englewood Cliffs: Prentice-Hall.

ANDERSEN, HENNING. 1973. "Abductive and deductive change." *Language* 49: 765–93.

ANTTILA, RAIMO. 1989. *Historical and Comparative Linguistics*. 2nd rev. edn. *Amsterdam Studies in the Theory and History of Linguistic Science* 6. Amsterdam: Benjamins.

—— and SHEILA EMBLETON. 1989. "The Iconic Index. From Sound Change to Rhyming Slang." *Diachronica* 6: 155–80.

ARENS, HANS. 1984. *Aristotle's Theory of Language and its Tradition. Texts from 500 to 1750*. Amsterdam: Benjamins.

ARISTOTLE. 1984. *De Interpretatione*. Trans. J. L. Ackrill. *The Complete Works of Aristotle: The Revised Oxford Translation*, vol. 1. Ed. Jonathan Barnes. Bollingen Series 71(2). Princeton, N.J.: Princeton University Press. 25–38.

AX, WOLFRAM. 1992. "Aristoteles." *Sprachphilosophie. Ein internationales Handbuch zeitgenössischer Forschung*. Ed. Marcelo Dascal, Dietfried Gerhardus, Kuno Lorenz, and Georg Meggle. Berlin: Walter de Gruyter. 244–59.

Barnhart Dictionary of Etymology. 1988. Ed. Robert K. Barnhart. New York: H. W. Wilson Company.

BEEH, VOLKER. 1980. "On Linguistic Arbitrariness. Doitsu Bungaku Kenkyu." *Deutsche Kulturwissenschaft* 26. Kyoto University. 1–13.

——. 1993. "Selbstkritik. Sprachgeschichte und Sprachkritik." *Festschrift für Peter von Polenz zum 65. Geburtstag*. Ed. Hans-Jürgen Heringer and Georg Stötzel. Berlin: Walter de Gruyter. 34–45.

BERLIN, BRENT and PAUL KAY. 1969. *Basic Colour Terms: Their Universality and Evolution*. Berkeley: University of California Press.

BICKERTON, DEREK. 1990. *Language and Species*. Chicago: University of Chicago Press.

BIERWISCH, MANFRED. 1979. "Wörtliche Bedeutung—eine pragmatische Gretchenfrage." *Sprechakttheorie und Semantik*. Ed. Günther Grewendorf. Frankfurt-on-Main: Suhrkamp. 119–49.

Bibliography

BRANDON, ROBERT N. and NORBERT HORNSTEIN. 1986. "From Icons to Symbols: Some Speculations on the Origins of Language." *Biology & Philosophy* 1: 169–89.

BRAUNROTH, MANFRED, G. SEYFERT, K. SIEGEL and F. VAHLE. 1975. *Ansätze und Aufgaben der linguistischen Pragmatik.* Frankfurt-on-Main: Athenäum Fischer.

BROWN, ROGER. 1958. "How Shall a Thing Be Called?" *Psychological Review* 65: 14–21.

BRUGMANN, KARL. 1918. "Verschiedenheiten der Satzgestaltung nach Maßgabe der seelischen Grundfunktionen in den indogermanischen Sprachen." *Berichte über die Verhandlungen der Sächsischen Gesellschaft der Wissenschaften zu Leipzig.* Kl.70, H. 6. Leipzig.

CHOMSKY, NOAM. 1972. *Language and Mind.* New York: Harcourt, Brace & World.

——. 1986. *Knowledge of Language. Its Nature, Origin and Use.* New York: Praeger.

——. 1992. "Mental Constructions and Social Reality." *Knowledge and Language: From Orwell's Problem to Plato's Problem.* Ed. Eric Reuland and Werner Abraham. Dordrecht: Kluwer. 29–59.

COSERIU, EUGENIO. 1975. *Die Geschichte der Sprachphilosophie von der Antike bis zur Gegenwart: Eine Übersicht.* Part I. Tübingen: Gunter Narr.

CRUSE, D. A. 1986. *Lexical Semantics.* Cambridge: Cambridge University Press.

DAVIDSON, DONALD. 1978. "What Metaphors Mean." *Critical Inquiry* 5: 31–47.

DERBOLAV, JOSEF. 1972. *Platons Sprachphilosophie im Kratylos und in den späteren Schriften.* Darmstadt: Wissenschaftliche Buchgesellschaft.

Duden Grammatik der Deutschen Gegenwartssprache. 1984. 4th rev. edn. Ed. and rev. Günther Drosdowski with Gerhard Angst. Mannheim: Bibliographisches Institut.

ECO, UMBERTO. 1984. *Semiotics and the Philosophy of Language.* London: Macmillan.

EHRISMANN, OTFRIED. 1986. " 'Die alten Menschen sind größer, reiner und heiliger gewesen als wir.' Die Grimms, Schelling; vom Ursprung der Sprache und ihrem Verfall." *Zeitschrift für Literaturwissenschaft und Linguistik* 16(62): 29–57.

EISENBERG, PETER. 1989. *Grundriß der deutschen Grammatik.* 2nd rev. and enlarged edn. Stuttgart: Metzler.

——. 1993. "Der Kausalsatz ist nicht zu retten." *Praxis Deutsch* 118: 10–11.

ELIAS, NORBERT. 1969. "Wohnstrukturen als Anzeiger gesellschaftlicher Strukturen." *Die höfische Gesellschaft. Untersuchungen zur Soziologie des*

Königtums und der höfischen Aristokratie. Ed. Norbert Elias. Darmstadt: Luchterhand.

ERBEN, JOHANNES. 1993. *Einführung in die deutsche Wortbildungslehre*. 3rd edn. Berlin: Erich Schmidt Verlag.

EROMS, HANS-WERNER. 1980. "Funktionskonstanz und Systemstabilisierung bei den begründenden Konjunktionen im Deutschen." *Sprachwissenschaft* 5: 73–115.

FABIAN, REINHARD. 1975. *Sinn und Bedeutung von Namen und Sätzen. Eine Untersuchung zur Semantik Gottlob Freges*. Vienna: Verband der Wissenschaftlichen Gesellschaft.

FEILKE, HELMUTH. 1994. *Common Sense-Kompetenz—Überlegungen zu einer Theorie "sympathischen" und "natürlichen" Meinens und Verstehens*. Frankfurt-on-Main: Suhrkamp.

——. 1996. "*Weil*-Verknüpfungen in der Schreibentwicklung. Zur Bedeutung 'lernerintensiver' empirischer Struktur-Begriffe." *Schreiben im Umbruch. Schreibforschung und schulisches Schreiben*. Ed. H. Feilke and P. Portmann. Stuttgart: Klett. 40–53.

FLEISCHMAN, SUZANNE. 1982. *The Future in Thought and Language: Diachronic Evidence from Romance*. Cambridge: Cambridge University Press.

FOURQUET, JEAN. 1970. "Zum 'subjektiven' Gebrauch der deutschen Modalverba." *Studien zur Syntax des heutigen Deutsch. Paul Grebe zum 60. Geburtstag*. Ed. Hugo Moser *et al.* Düsseldorf: Schwann. 154–61.

FRANCK, DOROTHEA. 1980. *Grammatik und Konversation*. Königstein im Taunus: Skriptor.

FREGE, GOTTLOB. 1966*a*. "Function and Concept." *Translations from the Philosophical Writings of Gottlob Frege*. Ed. and trans. Peter Geach and Max Black. Oxford: Basil Blackwell. 21–41.

——. 1966*b*. "On Sense and Reference." *Translations from the Philosophical Writings of Gottlob Frege*. Ed. and trans. Peter Geach and Max Black. Oxford: Basil Blackwell. 56–78.

——. 1966*c*. "On Concept and Object." *Translations from the Philosophical Writings of Gottlob Frege*. Ed. and trans. Peter Geach and Max Black. Oxford: Basil Blackwell. 42–55.

——. 1971. *Schriften zur Logik und Sprachphilosophie*. Posthumous writings. Ed. Gottfried Gabriel. Hamburg: Meiner.

——. 1977. "Thoughts." *Logical Investigations*. Trans. P. T. Geach and R. H. Stoothoff. Oxford: Basil Blackwell. 1–30.

——. 1979. *Posthumous Writings*. Ed. Hans Hermes, Friedrich Kambartel, and Friedrich Kaulbach. Trans. Peter Long and Roger White. Oxford: Basil Blackwell.

Bibliography

GADAMER, HANS-GEORG. 1975. *Truth and Method*. Tübingen: J. C. B. Mohr (Paul Siebeck).

GARCÍA, ERICA C. 1985, "Quantity into Quality: Synchronic Indeterminacy and Language Change." *Lingua* 65: 275–306.

——. 1994. "Reversing the Status of Markedness." Manuscript. University of Leiden.

GAUMANN, ULRIKE. 1983. *"Weil die machen jetzt bald zu." Angabe und Junktivsatz in der deutschen Gegenwartssprache.* Göppingen: Kümmerle.

GAUTHIER, DAVID. 1988. "Morality, Rational Choice, and Semantic Representation. A Reply to My Critics." *The New Social Contract. Essays on Gauthier.* Ed. Ellen Frankel Paul, Fred D. Miller Jr., Jeffrey Paul, and John Ahrens. Oxford: Basil Blackwell. 173–221.

GEERAERTS, DIRK. 1988. "Where does Prototypicality Come from?" *Topics in Cognitive Linguistics.* Ed. Brygida Rudzka-Ostyn. Amsterdam: Benjamins. 207–29.

——. 1990. "Editorial Statement." *Cognitive Linguistics* 1(1): 1–3.

GELLNER, ERNEST. 1988. *Plough, Sword and Book*. London: Collins Harvill.

"GEOSKOP: Nachrichten aus der Welt der Wissenschaft." *GEO* Feb. 1993: 144.

GOODMAN, NELSON. 1968. *Languages of Art*. Indianapolis: Bobbs-Merrill.

GOUDGE, THOMAS A. 1965. "Peirce's Index." *Transactions of the Charles Sanders Peirce Society*, vol. 1. 52–70.

GRICE, HERBERT PAUL. 1957. "Meaning." *The Philosophical Review* 66: 377–88.

——. 1968. "Utterer's Meaning, Sentence-Meaning, and Word-Meaning." *Foundations of Language* 4: 1–18.

——. 1969. "Utterer's Meaning and Intentions." *The Philosophical Review* 78: 147–77.

——. 1975. "Logic and Conversation." *Speech Acts. Syntax and Semantics*, vol. 3. Ed. Peter Cole and Jerry L. Morgan. New York: Academic Press. 41–58.

GRIMES, WILLIAM. 1997. "From Merely Loving Sushi to Really Knowing It." *New York Times*, 3 December, natl. edn.: B1, B10.

GÜNTHNER, SUSANNE. 1993. " 'Weil—man kann es ja wissenschaftlich untersuchen.' Diskurspragmatische Aspekte der Wortstellung in WEIL-Sätzen." *Linguistische Berichte* 143: 37–59.

HADORN, WOLFGANG and NEPOMUK ZÖLLNER. 1986. *Vom Symptom zur Diagnose*. 8th edn. Basle: Karger.

HALEY, MICHAEL CABOT. 1988. *The Semeiosis of Poetic Metaphor*. Bloomington: Indiana University Press.

246

Bibliography

HARE, RICHARD M. 1963. *Freedom and Reason*. London: Oxford University Press.

HARRAS, GISELA. 1983. *Handlungssprache und Sprechhandlung. Eine Einführung in die handlungstheoretischen Grundlagen*. Berlin: Walter de Gruyter.

HAYEK, FRIEDRICH AUGUST VON. 1948. *Individualism and Economic Order*. Chicago: University of Chicago Press.

——. 1952. *The Sensory Order—An Inquiry into the Foundations of Theoretical Psychology*. Chicago: University of Chicago Press.

——. 1956. "Über den 'Sinn' sozialer Institutionen." *Schweizer Monatshefte* 36: 512–24.

——. 1960. *The Constitution of Liberty*. Chicago: University of Chicago Press.

——. 1983. "Die Überschätzte Vernunft." *Evolution und Menschenbild*. Ed. Rupert J. Riedl and Franz Kreuzer. Hamburg: Hoffmann and Campe. 164–92.

——. 1988. *The Fatal Conceit. The Errors of Socialism. The Collected Works of Friedrich August Hayek*, vol. 1. Ed. William Warren Bartley. London: Routledge.

HEINE, BERND. 1992. "Agent-Oriented vs. Epistemic Modality—Some Observations on German Modals." Manuscript. University of Cologne, Institut für Afrikanistik.

HERTZ, HEINRICH. 1956. *The Principles of Mechanics, Presented in New Form*. Trans. D. E. Jones and J. T. Walley. New York: Dover Publications.

HESSE, MARY. 1980. *Revolutions and Reconstructions in the Philosophy of Science*. Brighton: Harvester Press.

HJELMSLEV, LOUIS. 1963. *Prolegomena to a Theory of Language*. Trans. Francis. J. Whitfield. Madison: University of Wisconsin Press.

HOCKETT, CHARLES F. 1958. *A Course in Modern Linguistics*. New York: Macmillan.

HURFORD, JAMES R. 1992. "Bedeutung und private Regelbefolgung. Diskussion." *Zeitschrift für Semiotik* 14(4) (ed. Roland Posner): 367–72.

ITKONEN, ESA. 1977. "Grammar and Sociolinguistics." *Forum Linguisticum* 1(3): 238–53.

——. 1983. *Causality in Linguistic Theory*. London: Croom Helm.

——. 1991. *Universal History of Linguistics: India, China, Arabia, Europe*. Amsterdam: Benjamins.

JÄGER, LUDWIG. 1976. "F. de Saussures historisch-hermeneutische Idee der Sprache. Ein Plädoyer für die Rekonstruktion des Saussureschen Denkens in seiner authentischen Gestalt." *Linguistik und Didaktik* 27: 210–44.

JEAN PAUL. 1973. *Horn of Oberon: Jean Paul Richter's School for Aesthetics. Translation of* Vorschule der Aesthetik. Trans. Margaret R. Hale. Detroit: Wayne State University Press.

Bibliography

JIRÁNEK, JAROSLAV. 1992. "Symptom, Index, Konnotation." *Zeitschrift für Semiotik* 14(4): (ed. Roland Posner): 373–5.

JOHNSON, MARK. 1992. "Philosophical Implications of Cognitive Semantics." *Cognitive Linguistics* 3–4: 345–66.

KANACHER, URSULA. 1987. *Wohnstrukturen als Anzeiger gesellschaftlicher Strukturen. Eine Untersuchung der Wohnungsgrundrisse als Ausdruck gesellschaftlichen Wandels von 1850 bis 1975 aus der Sicht der Elias'schen Zivilisationstheorie.* Frankfurt-on-Main: Fischer.

KASHER, ASA. 1976. "Conversational Maxims and Rationality." *Language in Focus.* Ed. Asa Kasher. Dordrecht: D. Reidel Publishing Company. 197–216.

KAY, PAUL and CHAD MCDANIEL. 1978. "The Linguistic Significance of the Meanings of Basic Color Terms." *Language* 54(3): 610–46.

KELLER, RUDI. 1974. *Wahrheit und kollektives Wissen. Zum Begriff der Präsupposition.* Düsseldorf: Schwann.

——. 1975. "Zur Theorie des metaphorischen Sprachgebrauchs. Ein Beitrag zur Semantik von Pragmatik." *Zeitschrift für Germanistische Linguistik* 3.1: 49–62.

——. 1987. "Kooperation und Eigennutz." *Kommunikation und Kooperation.* Ed. Frank Liedtke and Rudi Keller. Tübingen: Max Niemeyer. 3–14.

——. 1992. "Schlußprozesse in der Kommunikation." *Zeitschrift für Semiotik* 14(4): (ed. Roland Posner): 383–90.

——. 1993. "Der Wandel des *weil*. Verfall oder Fortschritt?" *Sprache und Literatur* 71: 2–12.

——. 1994. *On Language Change: The Invisible Hand in Language.* Trans. Brigitte Nerlich. London: Routledge.

——. 1995. "The epistemic *weil.*" *Subjectivity and Subjectivisation: Linguistic Perspectives.* Ed. Dieter Stein and Susan Wright. Cambridge: Cambridge University Press. 16–30.

KELLER-BAUER, FRIEDRICH. 1984. *Metaphorisches Verstehen—Eine linguistische Rekonstruktion metaphorischer Kommunikation.* Tübingen: Niemeyer.

KEMPSON, RUTH M. 1977. *Semantic Theory.* Cambridge: Cambridge University Press.

KLEIN, ERNEST. 1971. *A Comprehensive Etymological Dictionary of the English Language.* Amsterdam: Elsevier Publishing Company.

KÖLLER, WILHELM. 1975. *Semiotik und Metapher—Untersuchungen zur grammatischen Struktur und kommunikativen Funktion von Metaphern.* Stuttgart: Metzler.

KÖNIG, EKKEHARD and S. REQUARDT. 1991. "A Relevance-Theoretic Approach to the Analysis of Modal Particles in German." *Multilingua* 10(1/2): 63–77.

——and ELIZABETH TRAUGOTT. 1988. "Pragmatic Strengthening and Semantic Change: The Conventionalizing of Conversational Implicature." *Understanding the Lexicon*. Ed. Werner Hüllen and Rainer Schulze. Tübingen: Max Niemeyer. 110–25.

KRETZMANN, NORMAN. 1967. *History of Semantics. The Encyclopedia of Philosophy*, vol. 7. Ed. Paul Edwards. New York, London: Macmillan.

KRIPKE, SAUL. 1982. *Wittgenstein on Rules and Private Language*. Oxford: Basil Blackwell.

KÜPER, CHRISTOPH. 1984. "Zum sprechaktbezogenen Gebrauch der Kausalverknüpfer *denn* und *weil*: Grammatisch-pragmatische Interrelationen." *Linguistische Berichte* 92: 15–30.

——. 1991. "Geht die Nebensatzstellung im Deutschen verloren?—Zur pragmatischen Funktion der Wortstellung in Haupt- und Nebensätzen." *Deutsche Sprache* 19: 133–58.

KURZ, GERHARD. 1982. *Metapher, Allegorie, Symbol*. Göttingen: Vandenhoek and Ruprecht.

KUTSCHERA, FRANZ VON. 1975. *Sprachphilosophie*. 2nd rev. and enlarged edn. Auflage. Munich: Wilhelm Fink.

LAKOFF, GEORGE. 1987. *Woman, Fire, and Dangerous Things*. Chicago: University of Chicago Press.

—— and MARK JOHNSON. 1980. *Metaphors We Live By*. Chicago: University of Chicago Press.

LANGACKER, RONALD W. 1990. "Subjectification." *Cognitive Linguistics* 1(1): 5–38.

LAPP, EDGAR. 1992. *Linguistik der Ironie*. Tübingen: Gunter Narr.

LEVIN, JULES. 1994. "Towards a Semeiotic of Change." Manuscript. University of California, Riverside.

LEVINSON, STEPHEN. 1989. "A Review of Relevance." *Journal of Linguistics* 25: 455–72.

LEWIS, CLARENCE IRVING. 1952. "The Modes of Meaning." *Semantics and the Philosophy of Language*. Ed. Leonard Linsky. Urbana: University of Illinois Press. 50–63.

LEWIS, DAVID. 1969. *Convention. A Philosophical Study*. Cambridge, Mass.: Harvard University Press.

LORENZ, KONRAD. 1977. *Behind the Mirror: A Search for a Natural History of Human Knowledge*. Trans. Ronald Taylor. New York: Harcourt Brace Jovanovich.

LYONS, JOHN. 1977. *Semantics*, vols 1 and 2. Cambridge: Cambridge University Press.

MEGGLE, GEORG. 1977. *Handlungsbeschreibung. Grundbegriffe der rationalen Handlungstheorie. Analytische Handlungstheorie*, vol. 1. Ed. Georg Meggle. Frankfurt-on-Main: Suhrkamp. 415–48.

MITSCHERLICH, ALEXANDER. 1969. *Die Unwirtlichkeit unserer Städte. Anstiftung zum Unfrieden*. Frankfurt-on-Main: Suhrkamp.

MÜNCHGESANG, ROBERT. 1948. *Ein kurzweiliges Lesen vom Till Eulenspiegel und was er für seltsame Possen getrieben hat*. The text of 1519, as told by Robert Münchgesang. Reutlingen: Enßlin und Laiblin.

NAGEL, LUDWIG. 1992. *Charles Sanders Peirce*. Frankfurt: Campus.

NERLICH, BRIGITTE and DAVID CLARKE. 1988. "A Dynamic Model of Semantic Change." *Journal of Literary Semantics* 17(2): 73–90.

NIERAAD, JÜRGEN. 1977. *Bildgesegnet und bildverflucht. Forschungen zur sprachlichen Metaphorik*. Darmstadt: Wissenschaftliche Buchgesellschaft.

NOOTEBOOM, CEES. 1993. *Mokusei! Eine Liebesgeschichte*. Trans. Helga van Benningen. Frankfurt-on-Main: Suhrkamp.

NOZICK, ROBERT. 1993. *The Nature of Rationality*. Princeton: Princeton University Press.

NYMAN, MARTTI. 1994. "All You Need Is What the System Needs?" *Suomen kielitieteellinen yhdistys vuosikirja* [*Yearbook of the Linguistic Association of Finland*]. 157–80.

Oxford Dictionary of English Etymology. 1966. Ed. C. T. Onions with G. W. S. Friedrichsen and R. W. Burchfield. Oxford: Clarendon Press.

Oxford English Dictionary. 1989. 2nd edn. Vol 3. Prepared by J. A. Simpson and E. S. C. Weiner. Oxford: Clarendon Press.

PALMER, FRANK R. 1981. *Semantics*. 2nd edn. Cambridge: Cambridge University Press.

PEIRCE, CHARLES SANDERS. 1955. *Philosophical Writings of C. Sanders Peirce*. Selected, ed. and with an introduction by Justus Buchler. New York: Dover.

——. 1965. *Elements of Logic. Collected Papers of Charles Sanders Peirce*, vol. 2 (CP). Ed. Charles Hartstone and Paul Weiss. Cambridge, Mass.: Belknap Press of Harvard University Press.

——. 1977. *Semiotic and Significs: The Correspondence between Charles S. Peirce and Victoria Lady Welby* (PW). Ed. Charles Hardwick. Bloomington: Indiana University Press.

PETERS, ROBERT. 1985. "Mythische Sprachphilosophie: eine Studie zum Verhältnis mythologischer Sprachtheorie und Wilhelm von Humboldts Sprachtheorie am Beispiel ausgewählter Positionen." Dissertation. University of Düsseldorf.

PLATO. 1953. *Cratylus. The Dialogues of Plato*. Trans. B. Jowett, vol. 3 of 4. Revised 4th edn. London: Clarendon Press. 41–106.

Bibliography

PINKAL, MANFRED. 1985. "Kontextabhängigkeit, Vagheit, Mehrdeutigkeit." *Handbuch der Lexikologie*. Ed. Christoph Schwarze and Dieter Wunderlich. Königstein im Taunus: Athenäum. 27–63.

PITCHER, GEORGE. 1964. *The Philosophy of Wittgenstein*. Englewood Cliffs, N.J.: Prentice-Hall.

POSNER, MICHAEL. 1986. "Empirical Studies of Prototypes." *Noun Classes and Categorization*. Ed. Colette Craig. Amsterdam: Benjamins. 53–61.

POSNER, ROLAND. 1991. "Research in Pragmatics after Morris." *Dedalus: Revista Portuguesa de Literatura Comparada* 1: 115–56.

——. 1992. "Believing, Causing, Intending: The Basis for a Hierarchy of Sign Concepts in the Reconstruction of Communication." *Sign, Search, and Communication: Semiotic Aspects of Artificial Intelligence*. Ed. René J. Jorna, Barend van Heusden, and Roland Posner. Berlin: Walter de Gruyter. 215–70.

PRECHTL, PETER. 1991. "Gerechtigkeit und Individualität—gegensätzliche Komponenten einer politischen Ethik? Eine Kritik utilitaristischer Elemente in Vertragskonzeptionen." *Diskursethik und Gerechtigkeitstheorie—Die politische Dimension neuerer Ethikkonzeptionen*. Ed. Walter Reese-Schäfer and Karl Theodor Schuon. Marburg: Schüren. 171–82.

PUTNAM, HILARY. 1978. "Meaning, Reference and Stereotypes." *Meaning and Translation*. Ed. Franz Guenthner and M. Guenthner-Reutter. London: Duckworth. 61–81.

RADTKE, PETRA. 1988. *Die Kategorien des deutschen Verbs: Zur Semantik grammatischer Kategorien*. Tübinger Beiträge zur Linguistik 438. Tübingen: Gunter Narr.

REDDY, MICHAEL. 1979. "The Conduit Metaphor—A Case of Frame Conflict in our Language about Language." *Metaphor and Thought*. Ed. Andrew Ortony. Cambridge: Cambridge University Press. 284–324.

REINBOT VON DURNE. 1907. *Der heilige Georg*. Ed. Carl von Kraus. Heidelberg: Winter.

RICHARDS, IVOR ARMSTRONG. 1938. *Interpretation in Teaching*. London: Harcourt Brace.

RIEDL, RUPERT J. and FRANZ KREUZER, eds. 1983. "Diskussion zwischen Rudolf Haller, Friedrich A. von Hayek, Niklas Luhmann, Erhard Oeser." *Evolution und Menschenbild*. Hamburg: Hoffmann und Campe: 225–41.

RORTY, RICHARD. 1989. *Contingency, Irony, and Solidarity*. Cambridge: Cambridge University Press.

ROSCH, ELEANOR H. 1973. "On the Internal Structure of Perceptual and Semantic Categories." *Cognitive Development and the Acquisition of Language*. Ed. Timothy E. Moore. New York: Academic Press. 111–44.

Bibliography

ROSCH, ELEANOR H. 1976. "Classification of Real-World Objects." *La mémoire Semantique. Bulletin de psychologie.* Ed. Stéphane Ehrlich and Endel Tulving. 242–50.

——. 1979. "Human Categorization." *Studies in Cross-cultural Psychology*, vol. I. Ed. Neil Warren. New York: Academic Press.

RUMELHART, DAVID E. 1979. "Some Problems with the Notion of Literal Meanings." *Metaphor and Thought.* Ed. Andrew Ortony. Cambridge: Cambridge University Press. 78–90.

——. 1980. "Schemata: The Building Blocks of Cognition." *Theoretical Issues in Reading Comprehension.* Ed. B. Spiro, B. C. Bruce, and W. F. Brewer. Hillsdale, N.J.: Erlbaum. 37–61.

SANDERS, WILLY. 1965. *Glück.* Cologne: Böhlau.

SAUSSURE, FERDINAND DE. 1960. *Course in General Linguistics.* Trans. Wade Baskin. Ed. Charles Bally and Albert Sechehaye in collaboration with Albert Reidlinger. London: Peter Owen Limited.

SCHLEPPEGRELL, MARY J. 1991. "Paratactic Because." *Journal of Pragmatics* 16: 323–37.

SCHWARZ, MONIKA and JEANNETTE CHUR. 1993. *Semantik. Ein Arbeitsbuch.* Tübingen: Gunter Narr.

SEARLE, JOHN R. 1969. *Speech Acts: An Essay in the Philosophy of Language.* Cambridge: Cambridge University Press.

——. 1979. "Metaphor." *Metaphor and Thought.* Ed. Andrew Ortony. Cambridge: Cambridge University Press. 92–123.

SHAPIRO, MICHAEL. 1991. *The Sense of Change: Language as History.* Bloomington: Indiana University Press.

SHORT, THOMAS L. 1988. "The Growth of Symbols." *Cruzeiro semiotico* 8: 81–7.

SILBERMANN, ALPHONS. 1966. *Vom Wohnen der Deutschen. Eine soziologische Studie über das Wohnerlebnis.* Frankfurt-on-Main: Fischer.

SOMMER, VOLKER. 1989. "Lügen haben lange Beine." *GEO Wissen* 2 ("Kommunikation"): 149–52.

SPERBER, DAN and DEIRDRE WILSON. 1986a. *Relevance. Communication and Cognition.* Oxford: Basil Blackwell.

——. 1986b. "On Defining Relevance." *Philosophical Grounds of Rationality. Intentions, Categories, Ends.* Ed. Richard E. Grandy and Richard Warner. Oxford: Clarendon. 243–58.

STEINTHAL, HEYMANN. 1971. *Geschichte der Sprachwissenschaft bei den Griechen und Römern.* 2nd edn. Hildesheim: Olms.

SÜßMILCH, JOHANN PETER. 1766. *Versuch eines Beweises, daß die erste Sprache ihren Ursprung nicht vom Menschen, sondern allein vom Schöpfer erhalten habe.* Berlin: Buchladen der Realschule.

Bibliography

SWEETSER, EVE. 1990. *From Etymology to Pragmatics. Metaphorical and Cultural Aspects of Semantic Structure.* Cambridge: Cambridge University Press.

TRÄNKLE, MARGRET. 1972. *Wohnkultur und Wohnweisen.* Tübingen: Tübinger Vereinigung für Volkskunde.

TRAUGOTT, ELIZABETH CLOSS. 1985. "'Conventional' and 'Dead' Metaphors Revisited." *The Ubiquity of Metaphor: Metaphor in Language and Thought.* Ed. Wolf Paprotté and René Dirven. Amsterdam: John Benjamins. 17–56.

——. 1989. "On the Rise of Epistemic Meanings in English: An Example of Subjectification in Semantic Change." *Language* 65(1): 31–55.

——. 1993. "Subjectification in Grammaticalisation." *Subjectivity and Subjectivisation.* Ed. Dieter Stein and Susan Wright. Cambridge: Cambridge University Press. 31–54.

TUGENDHAT, ERNST. 1982. *Traditional and Analytical Philosophy: Lectures on the Philosophy of Language.* Trans. P. A. Gorner. Cambridge, Mass.: Cambridge University Press.

ULVESTAD, BJARNE. 1984. "Die epistemischen Modalverben *werden* und *müssen* in pragmalinguistischer Sicht." *Pragmatik in der Grammatik. Jahrbuch 1983 des Instituts für deutsche Sprache.* Ed. Gerhard Stickel. Düsseldorf: Schwann: 262–94.

VANBERG, VIKTOR. 1994. "Cultural Evolution, Collective Learning and Constitutional Design." *Economic Thought and Political Theory.* Ed. David Reisman. Boston: Kluwer Academic Publishers. 171–204.

VENSKE, HENNING. 1993. "Schultüte für Berni." *Die Zeit,* 20 August 1993: 58.

WATZLAWICK, PAUL, JANET HELMICK BEAVIN and DON D. JACKSON. 1967. *Pragmatics of Human Communication. A Study of Interactional Patterns, Pathologies, and Paradoxes.* New York: Norton.

——JOHN H. WEAKLAND and RICHARD FISCH. 1974. *Change. Principles of Problem Formation and Problem Resolution.* New York: Norton.

WEGENER, HEIDE. 1993. "*Weil*—das hat schon seinen Grund. Zur Verbstellung in Kausalsätzen mit *weil* im gegenwärtigen Deutsch." *Deutsche Sprache* 4: 289–305.

WEGENER, PHILIPP. 1885. *Untersuchungen über die Grundfragen des Sprachlebens.* Halle: Benjamins.

WIERZBICKA, ANNA. 1990. "'Prototypes Save': On the Uses and Abuses of the Notion of 'Prototype' in Linguistics and Related Fields." *Meanings and Prototypes: Studies in Linguistic Catagorization.* Ed. Savas L. Tsokatzidis. London: Routledge.

WIESE, RICHARD. 1987. "Versprecher als Fenster zur Sprachstruktur." *Studium Linguistik* 21: 45–55.

WILLEMS, KLAAS. 1994. "Weil es hat mit Bedeutung nicht viel zu tun . . . Zum Sprachwandel einer Konjunktion." Manuscript. Seminarie Duitse Taalkunde, University of Ghent.

WILSON, EDWARD O. 1975. *Sociobiology: the New Synthesis.* Cambridge, Mass.: Harvard University Press.

WITTGENSTEIN, LUDWIG. 1968. *Philosophical Investigations* (PI). Trans. G. E. M. Anscombe. 3rd. edn. Oxford: Basil Blackwell.

——. 1969. *Philosophische Grammatik*, vol. 4 (PG). Frankfurt-on-Main: Suhrkamp.

——. 1972. *The Blue and Brown Books: Preliminary Studies for the "Philosophical Investigations"* (BB). Oxford: Basil Blackwell.

WRIGHT, EDMOND L. 1976. "Arbitrariness and Motivation: A New Theory." *Foundations of Language* 14: 505–23.

WRIGHT, GEORG HENRIK VON. 1963. "Practical Inference." *Philosophical Review* 72: 159–79.

——. 1972. "On So-Called Practical Inference." *Acta Sociologica* 15: 39–53.

WUNDERLI, PETER. 1981. "Der Schachspielvergleich in der analytischen Sprachphilosophie." *Cahiers Ferdinand de Saussure* 35: 87–130.

——. 1992. "Glanz und Elend des Poststrukturalismus." *Romanistische Zeitschrift für Literaturgeschichte/Cahiers d'Histoire des Littératures Romanes* 3(4): 251–87.

NAME INDEX

Adelung, Johann 138
Alston, William 61
Andersen, Henning 122
Anttila, Raimo ix, xi, 2, 54, 88, 122,
   146 nn. 4, 5, 159, 160 n. 5, 109 n. 7
Arens, Hans 25 n. 4, 29–30
Aristotle 16–7, 24–30, 39, 47, 59, 61,
   238
Ax, Wolfram 29 n. 8

Beavin, Janet H. 1
Beeh, Volker 16, 134
Berlin, Brent 62
Bickerton, Derek vii, 27, 29, 50, 63, 78 n. 7,
   83, 127–8
Bierwisch, Manfred 50 n. 2, 170–5, 180
Brandon, Robert 143–5, 152
Braunroth, Manfred 185
Brown, Roger 62 n. 2
Brugmann, Karl 219 n. 13

Chomsky, Noam viii, ix, x, 117–18, 117 n. 2
Chur, Jeannette 69
Clarke, David 159, 206
Coseriu, Eugenio 12 n. 3, 25 n. 3, 26 n. 6
Cruse, D. 81, 81 n. 11

Davidson, Donald 169 n. 1
Derbolav, Josef 12 n. 3

Eco, Umberto 122
Ehrismann, Otfried 11
Embleton, Sheila ix, xi, 88, 109 n. 7
Eisenberg, Peter 215, 221 n. 1, 222, 225 n. 5,
   232
Elias, Norbert 3
Erben, Johannes 11–2
Eroms, Hans-Werner 225 n. 5

Fabian, Reinhard 31 n. 1
Feilke, Helmuth 64, 70, 170 n. 4, 233,
   233 n. 17, 225 n. 5
Fisch, Richard 192 n. 12
Fleischman, Suzanne 213 n. 4
Fourquet, Jean 219 n. 13
Franck, Dorothea 178

Frege, Gottlob x, 24 n. 1, 30, 30 n. 9, 31–43,
   47–8, 52–3, 59–60, 68, 74, 79, 82–3,
   85–6, 93, 162, 238

Gadamer, Hans-Georg 12 n. 3, 14 n. 5,
   182 n. 1
García, Erica x n. 5, 88
Gaumann, Ulrike 225 nn. 5, 6, 230 n. 14
Gauthier, David 127, 162
Geeraerts, Dirk 71, 77
Gellner, Ernest 126 n. 13, 151
Goodman, Nelson 108–9, 175
Goudge, Thomas 106 n. 4
Grice, Herbert Paul ix n. 4, 89, 103,
   108, 125 n. 9, 176, 183–97, 240
Günthner, Susanne 225 n. 5, 230 n. 13, 233

Hadorn, Wolfgang 107 n. 6
Haley, Michael 160, 160 n. 4
Hare, Richard 75 n. 3, 82
Harras, Gisela 50
Hayek, Friedrich August von 19 n. 7, 20, 63–5
Heine, Bernd 215 n. 7, 216 n. 9
Hertz, Heinrich 16
Hesse, Mary 207
Hjelmslev, Louis 92 n. 7, 93
Hockett, Charles 131
Hornstein, Robert 143–5, 152
Hurford, James 117–22

Itkonen, Esa 12 n. 3, 25 n. 3, 26 n. 6, 29,
   120 n. 6, 126 n. 11

Jackson, Don 1
Jäger, Ludwig 132 n. 3, 134 n. 5
Jean Paul 205
Jiránek, Jaroslav 104, 108
Johnson, Mark 70–1, 71 n. 12, 204

Kanacher, Ursula 3–4, 3 n. 1
Kasher, Asa 157 n. 1, 188–90
Kay, Paul 62
Keller, Rudi viii, 88, 91, 117 n. 2, 118, 119
   n. 5, 120 n. 7, 126 n. 13, 127, 135, 137,
   145 n. 2, 181, 187 n. 6, 188, 195, 203,
   225 n. 5, 226 n. 10, 232, 241 n. 2

Keller-Bauer, Friedrich 169, 177 n. 9
Kempson, Ruth 69
Klein, Ernst 21
Köller, Wilhelm 181, 207 nn. 4, 5
König, Ekkehard 209 n. 7, 220 nn. 15, 16
Kretzmann, Norbert 26
Kripke, Saul 117
Küper, Christoph 225 n. 5
Kurz, Gerhard 209 n. 6
Kutschera, Franz von 52

Lakoff, George 71, 71 n. 12, 62 nn. 1, 2,
    77–8, 77 n. 5, 76 n. 4, 204
Langacker, Ronald 69–70, 213 n. 3
Lapp, Edgar 147 n. 6, 158
Levin, Jules 21, 155 n. 7
Levinson, Stephen 191
Lewis, C. I. 73 n. 1
Lewis, David 28, 94 n. 9, 119–20, 135–8,
    145 n. 1
Lorenz, Konrad 64
Lyons, John 33, 100 n. 2, 101–2, 128, 131,
    214 n. 6

McDaniel, Chad 62
Meggle, George 126 n. 12
Mitscherlich, Alexander 3
Münchgesang, Robert v, viii

Nagel, Ludwig 100 n. 2
Nerlich, Brigitte 159, 206
Nieraad, Jürgen 175 n. 6
Nooteboom, Cees 217
Nozick, Robert 126 n. 10, n. 11, 178,
    189 n. 10
Nyman, Martti vii–viii

Palmer, Frank 70
Peirce, Charles Sanders 11, 100, 105–6,
    111–13, 160 n. 4
Peters, Robert 12
Plato vii-viii, x, 7, 11–23, 24–9, 43, 47,
    59, 61, 111, 130–1, 133–4, 210, 239
Pinkal, Manfred 37, 67, 74, 74 n. 2, 80
Pitcher, George 49
Posner, Michael 78 n. 6
Posner, Roland 89, 93 n. 8
Prechtl, Peter 189 n. 10
Putnam, Hilary 53, 95

Radtke, Petra xi, 81 n. 11, 82 n. 12, 238 n. 1
Reddy, Michael 90 n. 5
Reinbot von Durne 161
Requardt, S. 220 n. 16
Richards, I. A. 164 n. 8

Rorty, Richard 116
Rosch, Eleanor 76–7
Rumelhart, David 165, 180 n. 13, 182 n. 2

Sanders, Willy 161 n. 7
Saussure, Ferdinand de 15, 92–3, 92 n. 7,
    131–5, 139–40, 163, 208
Schleppegrell, Mary 225 n. 5
Schwarz, Monika 69
Searle, John 36 n. 5, 168
Seyfert, G. 185
Shapiro, Michael 88 n. 1
Short, Thomas 112
Silbermann, Alphons 3
Sommer, Volker 103
Sperber, Dan ix, 90, 90 n. 5, 99 n. 1, 115 n. 8,
    119 n. 5, 120, 120 n. 7, 129 n. 14, 146 n. 3,
    176, 178, 184, 188 nn. 7, 8, 9, 190–4
Steinthal, Heymann 12 n. 3
Süßmilch, Johann 130
Sweetser, Eve 214 n. 6, 215, 215 n. 7,
    225 nn. 5, 7

Tränkle, Margret 3–5
Traugott, Elizabeth 164 n. 9, 209 n. 7, 213,
    213 nn. 3, 4, 214 n. 6, 220 n. 15
Tugendhat, Ernst 28 n. 7, 43 n. 6, 44

Ulvestad, Bjarne 219 n. 13

Vanberg, Viktor 63–4
Venske, Henning 221–2

Watzlawick, Paul 1, 192 n. 12
Weakland, John 192 n. 12
Wegener, Heide 222, 222 n. 2, 225 n. 5,
    227 n. 11, 228 n. 12, 230 n. 13, 234
    n. 21, 235 n. 22
Wegener, Philipp 90
Wierzbicka, Anna 76–8, 78 n. 6
Wiese, Richard 223
Willems, Klaas 225 n. 5
Wilson, Deirdre ix, 90, 90 n. 5, 99 n. 1,
    115 n. 8, 119 n. 5, 120, 120 n. 7,
    129 n. 14, 146 n. 3, 176, 178, 184,
    188 nn. 7, 8, 9, 190–4
Wilson, Edward O. 153
Wittgenstein, Ludwig viii, x, 30, 37, 43,
    44–55, 59–60, 75–6, 79, 102, 117,
    121–2, 239
Wright, Edmond 129, 139–40
Wright, Georg Henrik von 123
Wunderli, Peter 114, 132 n. 3

Zöllner, Nepomuk 107 n. 6

SUBJECT INDEX

abduction 123–4, 182
act, communicative 17, 88–91, 91 n. 6, 122,
    139, 149, 174, 190–1, 202
action:
    choice or alternative of 124–8, 136–7, 162,
      185, 189, 232
    interpretation of 144, 179, 181
    irrational 136, 181, 189, 192, 237
    rational 126–8, 136, 178, 189–92, 240; see
      also behavior, rational; rationality
    speech as an 23, 189
    theory 173
adaptability, adaptation of language 63–4
aesthetic 151–2, 195–6
affections of the soul, Aristotelian 25–7, 29, 39
    see also correlates, cognitive; cognitive
      likenesses; idea
agreement:
    and convention 13, 27–8; see also conven-
      tion; custom; habit
    and rules 170
ambiguity 169, 175, 226
    obligation or need to dispel 67, 80, 176,
      180, 184
analogy:
    descriptive, chess as 114, 116
    of words with instruments 60
    used to speak of inner or abstract
      events 204
arbitrariness:
    vs. motivatedness 130 ff.
    of symbols 102, 112
    of words or signs, theory of 12 n. 4, 12–17,
      19, 22–3, 27, 60
artificiality of signs 11
aspect marker 213–14
association:
    and icons 101, 109 n. 7, 109–12, 139–40,
      151, 180
    and metaphor 164–9, 174, 202, 204, 209
    see also inference, associative
associative goal 151, 166
associative impulse 110, 151
associative inference see inference, associative

basic-level category see category, basic-level

Bedeutung 31, 32 n. 2, 33, 47
    see also meaning
behavior:
    collective 133; see also convention; custom
    conventional 135–7
    rational 157, 189, 189 n. 9, 193, 240;
      see also action, rational; rationality
    ritualized 152–3
behavioral regularity 28, 54–5, 119–20, 137
    see also convention; custom
behavorioral sequence 144
bleaching see semantic bleaching

category, categories:
    basic-level 62–3
    cognitive 69, 77–8
    conceptual 14, 27, 61 ff., 76 ff., 239
    creation of 14, 27, 62–8
    and prototype structure 76–9
    and rule of use 79
    wild 66, 66 n. 7
    see also concept; classification
causal inference see inference, causal
change in language see language change
chess, analogy of communication to 51–3,
    114, 116
cite 162
    see also mention
classification:
    ad hoc 76
    as function of language 18, 23, 27, 61,
      64–5, 79, 128
    uncertainty in 66
    see also category; concept
cliché 209
cognitive costs, efforts 190, 195, 237
cognitive likenesses 27
    see also affections of the soul; correlates,
      cognitive; idea
cognitive semantics 69–72, 215
cognitive value 32
cognitive worlds, creation of 238
cognizance 89, 207
    see also understanding
collective knowledge 55, 119 n. 5, 119–20
collective learning 63

257

collective phenomena 117
communicant 91 n. 6
communication:
  animal 143–5
  asymmetry between interpretation and 91
  conceptualization of, metaphors for ix, 90, 90 n. 5
  as coordination problem 137
  definition of 89–90
  everyday 37, 68, 20
  as function of language 18, 23, 61
  as guessing game x, 29, 113, 115, 122, 124, 150, 173
  as mutual influence 129, 202
  instrumentally based notions of 11 ff., 30, 44 ff., 59–60, 239
  non-verbal 128
  representationally based notions of 24 ff., 31 ff., 59–60, 238–9
communicative ability x, 99, 144, 147, 156, 238
communicative attempts, endeavors 88, 127, 139–40, 145, 150, 163, 232
communicative impetus, recognition of 146–7
communicative purpose 91, 202
  see also goals, communicative; intent, communicative
competence:
  individual 135, 165
  language x, 223–4
  semeotic x
compositionality:
  of words 26, 133–4, 208
  principle of 208; *see also* homomorphism, principle of
comprehension *see* concept, comprehension of
concept, concepts 24, 27, 29, 42, 47, 59 ff., 65, 68–70, 73 ff., 85, 92, 100, 158, 239
  acquisition of 71, 77
  boundaries of 37, 68, 73–5, 79, 85–6
  classic idea of 73
  collective 78, 117–21
  comprehension of 73–6, 84
  definition of 73 ff.
  empty 36–7, 118
  essential features of 74
  extension of 33–4, 34 n. 3, 36, 41, 67, 73–4; *see also* subsumption
  formation of 62 ff., 82 ff., 239
  Fregean 35–8, 42, 68, 74, 79, 83, 85–6
  fuzzy 37, 68, 74–5, 74 n. 2, 79 ff., 80, 82–3, 85–6
  intension of 33–4, 34 n. 3, 36, 73–4, 78
  with prototype structure 68, 76, 80, 82–6
  relational 108

and rules of use 69, 73 ff., 79, 82, 117, 119 ff., 239
  with sharp boundaries 37, 68, 74, 85
  structure 62 ff., 68–72
  see also category; classification
conceptual constriction 66
conceptual hierarchy 62, 79, 81 ff.
conceptual models, metaphor as 206–7
conceptual systematicity, systems 71, 205, 211
conceptual vagueness 74, 74 n. 2
conformity 4–5, 86, 120–1, 137, 207
conjunction 45, 125, 162
  epistemization 212–13, 220, 221 ff.
content 12, 31–2, 39, 41–3, 43 n. 6, 60, 90 n. 5, 93, 102, 127, 190, 193, 208
context:
  and icons 111, 114, 151
  utterance 50–2, 85, 94, 114–15, 115 n. 8, 139, 159, 163, 172–3, 176, 190–2, 216 n. 9, 220 n. 16
contextual effect 190 ff.
contextual independence 202, 209
convention, conventionality 6, 12–16, 19, 22–8, 94, 119–20, 119 n. 4, 130–1, 133, 135 ff., 145 n. 1, 163, 169, 177, 179, 196, 203, 205, 207, 210
  see also agreement; custom; habit
conventionalization 12, 139–40, 152, 164 n. 9, 166, 174, 203
  see also lexicalization
cooperative principle 183–97, 240
  see also Humboldt maxim
coordination:
  equilibrium 136–7
  problem of 136–7
correlate:
  cognitive 24, 29, 47, 61, 69; *see also* affections of the soul; cognitive likenesses; idea
  conceptual 24, 28, 64, 69, 106
cultural evolution 20, 63
cultural knowledge 63–5, 71, 110, 146
culture 1–3, 5, 11, 27, 62, 65, 79, 109–110, 159, 178
custom 3 , 22, 51, 65, 174
  see also agreement; convention; habit

decay of language *see* language decay
deduction 123
default assumption 178
definition:
  ostensive 49, 51
  scientific, terms of 11, 87
  words learned by 83, 138

demotivation 152, 208
denotation (denote) 12, 21–2, 32–3 n. 2, 36, 47, 68, 95, 211
  see also designation; indication; signification
denotatum 100–2, 108–9, 111
depiction 16, 108, 159
  see also likeness; imitation; representation; reproduction
derivation, derivational 20–1, 133–4, 173
desemanticization 209 n. 7
designation (designate) 31–43, 84–5, 130–1, 147–8, 152, 160–1, 164–5, 169, 172, 201–2, 211
  see also denotation; indication; signification
determinative chain 171–3
determinative structure 173–4

epistemic argument 125, 228–37
epistemic meaning 20, 212–20, 221 ff.
epistemization 212, 214, 219–20, 221 ff., 232 ff.
epistemological level 24, 27, 32, 47, 77–8, 93
epistemological model, metaphor as 206–7, 209
etymological, etymology 13, 20–2, 26, 155, 160–1, 160 n. 5, 160 n. 6, 203–4, 211, 215
evolution, evolutionary 20, 63–5, 88, 143, 145, 152, 201, 207
explanative, explanativity 183, 207, 209, 224 n. 4
extension *see* concept, extension of

factual argument 125, 225–37
fallacy 16
  instrumentalist 19, 134
  rationalist 19–20
family resemblance 68, 75–6, 82, 85–6
features:
  of objects and word meaning 74–8, 83–4, 172–3
  semantic 53, 55, 172–3
fixation of reference 14, 34, 113, 176, 180
Fregean concept *see* concept, Fregean
frequency of use 53, 66, 85, 110, 153, 155–7, 164–7, 170, 201, 208, 210
function, functions:
  communicative 60, 149
  concepts as 35–8, 85–6
  of language or signs 18, 23, 51–2, 60–1, 92, 102, 149, 151, 238–9
  truth-value 41, 43, 60, 70, 85–6

game:
  communication as x, 46, 51–3, 60, 91, 102, 114–16, 122, 124, 173, 187
  as family-resemblance concept 49, 76, 84–6; *see also* Spiel
  metaphorical technique as 206, 208–9
genesis, of language and signs viii, 7, 54, 87ff., 91, 139, 157, 173, 240
  see also growth of signs
goals:
  common or mutual 188, 193
  communicative viii, x, 89–90, 113, 124, 126, 126 n. 13, 138, 151, 166, 188–9, 192ff., 203, 209, 239–40; *see also* intent, communicative
  interpretive 113
Gricean maxims 183 ff.
growth of signs 11
  see also genesis

habit 14, 110
  see also agreement; convention; custom
holonym 82
homomorphism, principle of 16–17, 108, 134
Humboldt maxim 137
  see also cooperative principle

icon 25, 100, 102–4, 108ff., 109 n. 7, 112, 114, 140, 143ff., 150ff., 157–8, 159–62, 163, 239
  symbolification of 150–55
  symbolization of 159–62
iconification 143 ff.
iconic method or technique 25, 100, 102–3, 109, 145–7, 153, 156–8, 159, 163, 167, 168, 204, 239–40
iconicity 131, 204
idea 24 n. 2, 27–9, 30 n. 9, 40, 44ff., 51, 53, 55, 59–60, 90, 95, 101, 132, 168
  see also affections of the soul; correlate, cognitive; cognitive likenesses
ideational theory 44–7, 53, 65
image 111, 164, 204
  accoustique 92
  schemas 71
  systematicity 204–5, 211; *see also* image schemas
  social 195–96
imagery:
  of metaphor 164
  richness of 206; *see also* metaphor
imitation 21, 59–60, 63, 130, 133, 144, 159
  see also depiction, likeness, simulation, staging

implicative inference *see* inference, implicative
implicative interpretation 181, 187, 190, 197, 240
implicature 125, 176, 182 ff., 218, 240
index, Peircean 100, 105–6, 106 n. 4, 111
indication (indicate) 22–3, 55, 83, 110, 139, 144, 157–8
  see also denotation; designation; signification
indicative form 217
indicator 220
individual competence *see* competence, individual
individualism, methodological 117–19
induction 122–3
inference 90–2, 95
  associative 99–100, 103, 109–10, 140, 146, 150–2, 156–67, 168–9, 174, 177
  causal 99–100, 103 ff., 105–8, 107 n. 5, 110, 112, 145–6, 148, 156–7, 164, 166, 239
  implicative 186, 188
  rule based 99–100, 103, 134–40, 150–1, 157, 164–6, 174–8, 194, 201–2, 205, 209–10, 239
instrumental theory of signs 11 ff., 30, 44 ff., 59–60, 239
instrumentalist fallacy *see* fallacy, instrumentalist
intension *see* concept, intension of
intent, communicative 126, 139, 149, 151, 173, 232
interactive knowledge *see* knowledge, interactive
interpretability 1, 47, 92–3, 99 n. 1, 105, 112, 179, 211
interpretation 1, 6, 31, 47, 90–2, 122, 144–51, 157–9, 169, 179–81, 185–6, 190ff., 205, 218ff., 238–40
  basic techniques of 99–115
  charitable 14, 51
invisible-hand phenomenon 239, 241
irony 114, 147, 158

knowledge:
  contextual 114–15
  interactive 171
  situational 114–15, 171; *see also* knowledge, contextual

language change vii–viii, xi, 88, 122, 128, 162, 232
language decay 11, 221

language, natural 35, 37, 41, 43, 65, 74, 80, 88, 128, 140, 241
langue 49–50, 139, 164
lexicalization 150, 164ff., 174–5, 201, 201 n.1, 205, 208–10, 239–40
  see also semanticization
liège 92
likeness 23, 25–7, 29–30, 111
  see also depiction, imitation, reproduction

mapping 35
maxim:
  Gricean *see* Gricean maxims
  Humboldt *see* Humboldt maxim
meaning:
  conceptualist theory of 70
  epistemic *see* epistemic meaning
  factual 215–20, 225–37
  ideational theory of 44–6
mention 128, 162–3
  see also cite
meronym, meronomy 81–2
metaicon 163
metaphor xi, 19, 70–2, 146, 155, 156ff., 168ff., 201ff., 211ff.
  conventionalization, lexicalization of 164–67, 164 n. 9, 174, 203–10
  metonymical *see* metonymical metaphor
metaphorical metonymy 160
metaphorical technique *see* technique, metaphorical
metaphoricity of knowledge 70
metaphorization 146, 156ff., 220, 240
metasymbol 162
metasymptom 159, 163, 166
  see also metonymy
methodologial individualism 117–18
metonymy xi, 70, 146, 156, 158–9, 160–4, 166–7, 169–70, 197, 202, 239
  metaphorical *see* metaphorical metonymy
metonymical metaphor 160
metonymical technique *see* technique, metonymical
metonymization 146, 156ff.
means-to-end relation 178–9, 182, 190–1, 193–4, 197
motivatedness 21, 54, 130–40, 151, 153–4, 155 n. 7, 163–4
mode of presentation 32–3, 35–6, 38

naming, act of 13–15, 17–18, 20, 72, 152
negation test 226–7

objectivist, objectivism 14, 27, 69–70

Subject Index

onomatopoeia, onomatopoetic 21–2, 59, 130–1, 147, 151–2, 154
organismic metaphor 11
  see also genesis, growth
ostensive definition 49, 51

perspectivity 70
persuasion, maxim of 195–6
phenomenon of the third kind 88
picture theory 21–2
premise:
  signs as ix, 101
  of inference 107, 122–3, 126, 157
preposition 212
presupposition 53, 225–8, 230, 234–5
presentation, mode of *see* mode of presentation
predicate 33–9, 42, 165, 181, 235
predicative structure of metaphor 206–7
private language 117, 121
prototype structure 68, 76 ff., 82–5
prototype theory 76 ff.
psychologistic theory of meaning 29–30, 39–40

rationalist fallacy *see* fallacy, rationalist
rationality 123, 126–8, 136, 157, 162–3, 178–81, 182–97, 232, 237, 240
reference, fixation of *see* fixation of reference
regularity, behavioral *see* behavioral regularity
relevance, principle of 178, 178 n. 10, 190 ff.
representation viii, 21–3, 25–9, 42–3, 44, 46–7, 59–61, 63–4, 94, 102, 109, 127–8. 146, 151, 156
  as function of language 18, 23, 29, 43, 61, 63–4, 128
  self- 3–7, 195–6
  semantic 127
  see also depiction; imitation; likeness; mapping; reproduction
reproduce, reproduction 16, 61
  see also depiction; imitation; likeness; mapping; representation
resemblance 22, 108–9, 131
  family *see* family resemblance
  see also similarity
ritualization 143–5
rule of use 51–4, 60, 68–9, 83–5, 112–13, 115, 140, 149, 151, 155, 157–62, 170, 172–4, 177, 204, 207
rule-based inference *see* inference, rule-based

salience 94, 145
seeing-as, aspect of 206, 209

semantic:
  bleaching 152, 166, 205, 240
  features 53, 55, 172–3
  transparency 133, 139–40, 143, 158, 163, 202
semantics x, 39, 41, 57, 69–72, 112
  cognitive *see* cognitive semantics
semanticization 201, 219
  see also desemanticization; lexicalization
semiotic knowledge x, 232
semiosis 92
sentence x, 24–6, 29, 31–43, 51–2, 85, 102, 113, 116, 170, 173, 176–8, 180–1, 226
sense 31–43, 60, 102, 113–15, 116, 122, 163–6, 183, 186, 197, 239
  metaphorical 163–6, 168 ff., 201 ff.
  see also Sinn
signifiant 92, 132–3
signifié 92, 132–3
significance 54, 60, 91, 111–12
signification (signify) 17, 22, 25–6, 31, 92, 102, 111, 131, 153
similarity 22–3, 25, 28, 75, 85, 99, 102, 108–12, 131, 145, 150, 152, 210
  see also resemblance
simulation 131, 144–50, 156–9
  see also imitation, staging
Sinn 30, 31–3
  see also sense
situational knowledge *see* knowledge, situational
specification:
  prohibition of 74
  requirement 67, 80
speech act 26, 186 n. 5, 196, 233
Spiel 76
  see also game
staging 148–50, 158–9
  see also simulation
stereotype 77–8, 86
  see also prototype
strategy 6, 64, 136, 204
  symbolic 182; *see also* technique, symbolic
  symptomic 144, 182; *see also* technique, symptomic
subjectification 69, 212–14
subjectivist theory of meaning 70
subjectivity 70
subsume, subsumption 36, 83, 107 n. 6, 165
  see also concept, extension of
syllogism:
  practical 123–4, 126
  theory of 25

symbol, symbols 1–7, 11, 25–6, 28, 54–5,
    100, 102–3, 110, 112–14, 143, 148 ff.,
    153–5, 157 ff., 167, 170, 201, 206,
    208–9, 239
  symbolization of 162–4
symbolic character 1 ff., 4, 26
symbolic technique *see* technique, symbolic
symbolification 143 ff.
  of icons *see* icons, symbolification of
  of symptoms *see* symptoms,
    symbolification of
symbolization 2, 7, 27–9, 46, 59
  of icons *see* icons, symbolization of
  of symbols *see* symbols, symbolization of
  of symptoms *see* symptoms, symbolization
    of
symptom, symptoms 26, 100, 102–8, 110,
    143–50, 153–5, 156–9, 162–4, 176–81,
    182, 186, 194, 239
  iconification of 143–8
  symbolification of 148–50
  symbolization of 158–9
symptomatics, theory of 186
synonym, synonymy 46, 225, 228

taxonomy 78, 81–2
technique:

interpretive 99–115, 145–7, 153–4,
    156–67, 168, 173, 178, 180–1, 197,
    239–40
  symbolic 100, 150, 180, 202, 239
  symptomic 100, 107 n. 5, 158–9, 163–4,
    167, 177–81, 182, 194, 239
  metaphorical 160, 166, 177, 201 ff., 211 ff.,
    221, 225, 232
  metonymical 159–61, 166, 202
thought, thoughts viii, 17, 22, 24–6, 29,
    38–43, 55, 59, 64–5, 68–70, 82, 90, 95
tools, words as 51, 63, 65, 134–5
transference 152
  metaphorical, metonymical 160–1, 168,
    175, 219–20
transfer function 175
transparency, semantic *see* semantic transpar-
    ency
truth value 16, 24, 35–8, 40–2, 47, 74, 85–6,
    219

understanding 45–6, 50, 70, 90, 95, 114, 117,
    137, 146, 182
  see also cognizance
use:
  rule of *see* rule of use
  theory of meaning as 30, 47–8, 87, 89